1977

This book may be kept

FOUR

MEANING IN CHILD LANGUAGE

Issues in the Study of
Early Semantic Development

MEANING IN CHILD LANGUAGE
Issues in the Study of Early Semantic Development

by

LAURENCE B. LEONARD

Department of Audiology and Speech Pathology
Memphis State University

GRUNE & STRATTON
A Subsidiary of Harcourt Brace Jovanovich, Publishers
NEW YORK   SAN FRANCISCO   LONDON

Library of Congress Cataloging in Publication Data

Leonard, Laurence B
    Meaning in child language.

    Bibliography: P.
    Includes index.
    1. Children—Language. 2. Semantics. 3. Child psychology.
4. Grammar, comparative and general.
I. Title.
P118.L4   401'.9   76-45665
ISBN 0-8089-0977-0

Grune & Stratton, Inc.
111 Fifth Avenue
New York, New York 10003

Distributed in the United Kingdom by
Academic Press, Inc. (London) Ltd.
24/28 Oval Road, London NW1

Library of Congress Catalog Number 76-45665
International Standard Book Number 0-8089-0977-0
Printed in the United States of America

CONTENTS

ACKNOWLEDGEMENTS

The author gratefully acknowledges permission by the publishers and authors to quote from the following works: "Cognition and Componential Analysis: God's Truth or Hocus-Pocus?" by R. Burling, reproduced by permission of the American Anthropological Association from the *American Anthropologist* 66: 27, 1964; "The Acquisition of Language in Infant and Child" by M. Braine, reproduced by permission of the National Council of Teachers of English from *The Learning of Language*, Appleton-Century-Crofts, 1971; *A First Language: The Early Stages* by R. Brown, reproduced by permission of Harvard University Press, © 1973 by Harvard University Press; *One Word at a Time* by L. Bloom, reproduced by permission of Mouton & Co., Publishers, 1973; "Learning to Code Experience through Language" by G. Wells, reproduced by permission of Cambridge University Press from the *Journal of Child Language* 1: 243, 1974; "Suggested Universals in the Ontogenesis of Grammar" by D. Slobin, reproduced by permission of D. Slobin; "Structure and Variation in Child Language" by L. Bloom, P. Lightbown, and L. Hood, reproduced by permission of the Society for Research in Child Development and L. Bloom from *Monographs of the Society for Research in Child Development* 40: 30–32, 1975, "Relational Concepts Underlying Language" by I. Schlesinger, reproduced by permission of University Park Press, Baltimore, © 1974 by University Park Press, and I. Schlesinger from *Language Perspectives: Acquisition, Retardation, and Intervention*; "Syntactic Styles and Universal Aspects of Language Emergence" by A. Ramer, reproduced by permission of A. Ramer; *Early Syntactic Development: A Cross-Linguistic Study with Special Reference to Finnish* by M. Bowerman, reproduced by permission of Cambridge University Press; "Sensory-Motor Intelligence and Semantic Relations in Early Child Grammar" by D. Edwards, reproduced by permission of Mouton & Co., Publishers, The Hague, from *Cognition* 2: 395–434, 1973; *Infant Speech: A Study of the Beginnings of Language* by M. Lewis, reproduced by permission of Routledge & Kegan Paul and Humanities Press; *Symbol Formation* by H. Werner and B. Kaplan, reproduced by permission of John Wiley & Sons, Inc., © 1963 by John Wiley & Sons, Inc.; "Length Constraints, Reduction Rules, and Holophrastic Processes in Children's Word Combinations" by M. Braine, reproduced by permission of Academic Press and M. Braine from the *Journal of Verbal Learning and Verbal Behavior* 13: 448–456, 1974; "The Relationship of Single Words to Two-Word Sentences" by S. Starr, reproduced by permission of the Society for Research in Child Development and S. Starr from *Child Development* 46: 701–708, 1975; "Concepts and Words in the 18-Month-Old: Acquiring Concept Names Under Controlled Conditions" by K. Nelson and J. Bonvillian, reproduced by permission of Mouton & Co., Publishers, The Hague, from *Cognition* 2: 435–450, 1973; "The Capacity for the Ontogenesis of Grammar" by D. McNeill, reproduced by permission of Academic Press and D. McNeill from *The Ontogenesis of Grammar*; "Production of Utterances and Language Acquisition" by I. Schlesinger, reproduced by permission of Academic Press and I. Schlesinger from *The Ontogenesis of Grammar*; "Learning the Structure of Causative Verbs: A Study in the Relationship of Cognitive, Semantic, and Syntactic Development" by M. Bowerman, reproduced by permission of Stanford University and M. Bowerman from *Papers and Reports on Child Language Development* 8: 142, 1973; "What is Behind Child Utterances?" by D. Parisi, reproduced by permission of Cambridge University Press from the *Journal of Child Language* 1: 97–106, 1974.

PREFACE

The aspect of meaning which receives the major emphasis in this volume is that which deals with the semantic relationships (or "semantic notions") reflected in the child's utterances. This aspect of meaning is often defined in terms of that which is represented in the proposition of an utterance. Such relational meaning is derived from the child's affirming or asserting something of or about the topic of his utterance.

Referential meaning, that aspect of meaning tied more closely to the meanings of individual words, will receive only limited treatment. It is becoming evident that referential meaning is quite related to relational meaning (Bruner, 1974). However, the complexity of this topic warrants more treatment than I could provide in this volume. A number of papers have appeared that deal with this related aspect more fully. Among these are the papers of Clark (1973; 1975) and Nelson (1973).

Pragmatics is another aspect of meaning highly related to relational meaning. This aspect of meaning pertains to the use of language in its social context. Pragmatics will be presented in this volume in part because this aspect is so important to the child's early acquisition of language, and in part because it is so difficult to separate from relational meaning. Nevertheless, the intended emphasis will be on the semantic notions reflected in the child's utterances, with pragmatic considerations discussed when they seem pertinent to a particular issue at hand. Dore (1974), Bruner (1975), and Bates (1976) are among those who provide more direct treatment of pragmatics in child language.

It is often difficult to separate semantic notions from the syntactic constructions used to code them in the child's speech. In fact, this volume includes a look at how underlying semantic notions interact with the linguistic code. Again, however, the matter of emphasis arises; the coding process itself is not a major focus in this volume. This process has received more careful treatment in papers by Bloom, Lightbown, and Hood (1975) and Braine (1976), among others.

Lest the reader think that there is very little of interest that is left to be covered if these related aspects of meaning receive only peripheral treatment, I should point out the difficulty involved in keeping pace with the literature directly pertaining to children's development of relational meaning. I could scarcely finish a rough draft of a single chapter before still another pertinent piece of research on the topic emerged. Even with the aid of manuscripts in press and working papers, keeping up was next to impossible. It seemed that the most appropriate way of handling a topic receiving much investigative attention was to focus on certain questions that seemed to represent important issues within the broader topic. This is the course that I have taken.

Something should be mentioned regarding my use of certain terms throughout this volume. I use the terms "transformational grammar" and "generative semantics" with full awareness that each approach is represented by proponents whose own specific accounts of grammar may differ. I have used "transformational grammar" to refer to Chomsky's (1965) approach and trust that since this approach has been the transformational grammar approach applied most widely by developmental psycholinguists, I won't offend too many transformational grammarians whose treatment of certain linguistic features differs from this approach. My use of "generative semantics" is quite broad. Since the focus of this volume is on Stage I speech, the distinctions between many of the accounts within the realm of generative semantics are not essential here. However, readers who view child language findings in terms of their possible contribution to linguistic theory may wish to keep these points in mind.

A number of people were kind enough to read various sections of earlier drafts and to give me suggestions. Among these were Jill deVilliers, Bruce Fraser, David Ingram, and Donald Morehead. Particularly detailed comments were provided by Melissa Bowerman, Audrey Holland, Richard Schwartz, and Carol Waryas. Their aid is most appreciated. Thanks go to Lorraine Cooper, Donna Douglas, Shirley Rias, and Kathy Simpson for their help in typing the manuscript. Finally, I would like to thank the parents of the children with whom I visited. Without their genuine interest in the issues of this volume, the whole project could not have gotten off the ground.

Introduction

SEMANTIC NOTIONS

For a number of years, investigators of early language development have been aware that the young child beginning his linguistic career is not simply expressing the names of things in his environment. Much of his early language also deals with the expression of relevant relationships in his environment, expressed in order to serve various functions for the child. Such relational meanings serve as the focus of this volume.

Relational meanings are not the easiest of entities to study. They are not themselves observable and they can only be hypothesized on the basis of what the child says, the context in which he says it, and the interpretation of what he says by others. No doubt the meanings are functional for the child, but since his own perceptions of the world are still in a state of flux, it would be quite faulty to assume the child's meanings and ours are one and the same. The view that meaning is sufficiently stable to be sorted into neat components, a controversial enough view of the adult system of meaning (Leech, 1974), is clearly inappropriate for the study of meaning in child language.

Despite the difficulties in capturing the precise meanings that the child intends to convey, we do have an idea about their general nature. Interestingly, it is clear that relational meaning cannot be conveyed by word meanings per se. For example, the meaning of a child's utterance such as *dog walk* is not totally contained in the meaning of the words "dog" and "walk," since these provide no means of specifying that the dog is

1

instigating the walking rather than, say, being led by its owner as in *walk dog*.

These relational meanings are often expressed via specific syntactic constructions, but they are not syntactic themselves. The same relation can be expressed by a number of syntactic constructions. For example, the notion that some animate instigated some action is reflected in both the utterance *the mayor threw the ball onto the field* and *the ball was thrown onto the field by the mayor*. In fact, by relying too heavily on syntactic considerations for semantic interpretation, certain relational meanings can be obscured. The distinction between a process affecting an animate and an action voluntarily performed by an animate, for example, would be lost if the two utterances *the man died* and *the man lied* were interpreted solely on the basis of their syntactic structure. It is the expression of relational meanings, termed "semantic notions" in this volume, coupled with the acts that the child's utterances can perform, that motivate the child in his early language usage. These dimensions of meaning are the focus of this volume.

Another reason exists for examining these kinds of meanings in child language. These meanings are not merely features of specific languages, but rather of languages in general. Fillmore (1968), for example, has suggested that semantic notions may reflect certain innate judgments which humans are capable of making about events going on around them. Schlesinger (1971a) has noted that such notions appear to represent those cognitively based relations which make a difference linguistically. An examination of the semantic notions underlying children's developing language, then, could provide information about which aspects of cognitive structure children in general find significant for communication and how these in turn are developed and organized.

THE CATEGORIZATION OF SEMANTIC NOTIONS

When interacting with a young child, it quickly becomes evident that the precise semantic notions operative for the child and the way in which these notions are organized are not identical with those of the adult system. How then are they to be analyzed? Two directions could be taken: (1) impose the preexisting adult semantic categorizations on the child's language, or (2) determine the semantic categorizations of the child based on the organization of his own language (Tyler, 1969). The latter would clearly be preferable. However, it is questionable whether we ever achieve this goal. Even when using a descriptive system of analysis, there is little assurance that the data will be portrayed in a manner consistent with the manner in which the child actually operates. This problem is not peculiar to developmental psycholinguistics.

> When a linguist makes his investigation and writes his grammar, is he discovering something about the language which is "out there" waiting to be described and recorded or is he simply formulating a set of rules which somehow work? Similarly, when an anthropologist undertakes a semantic analysis, is he discovering some "psychological reality" which speakers are presumed to have or is he simply working out a set of rules which somehow take account of the observed phenomena? . . . It certainly sounds more exciting to say we are "discovering the cognitive system of the people" than to admit that we are just fiddling with a set of rules which allow us to use terms the way others do. (Burling, 1964, p. 27).

Although we attempt to describe the semantic notions underlying the child's language, the notions we eventually arrive at are clearly influenced by our own perceptions of language (Bowerman, 1974a). A number of the underlying semantic notions attributed to children's early language can be seen in Table 1. From the accompanying examplary utterances reflecting these notions, the similarity between these relational meanings and those of the adult system is striking.

Fortunately, the young child, through development, is gradually approximating the linguistic system possessed by the investigators whose own perceptions of language are being imposed on that of the child. This fact makes the biasing factors of adult categorizations less damaging. Some investigators, in fact, can see the value in this state of affairs.

> Since the purpose of the analysis is to discover the child's own generative rules, the analyst clearly must treat the idiolect contained in his corpus of texts as a linguistic system sui generis. However, this requirement does not mean that the investigator sets aside his knowledge of the adult system. Knowledge of the adult system is used in several ways. First, it serves as a set of hypotheses as to the rules that may be present in the texts: children's texts usually reflect partial knowledge of the adult system . . . . Second, owing to the finite nature of the corpus, there are many words that cannot be assigned to classes purely on the basis of the contexts in which they occur . . . . Here the investigator first establishes what part-of-speech distinctions the child does make on the basis of the corpus alone. These distinctions will usually be found to correspond to some broad distinctions made in the adult system. (Braine, 1971, p 19)

From the above discussion, it should be clear that investigators must create circumstances which allow the *child* to provide the evidence of how

Table 1
Some Frequently Cited Semantic Notions Underlying
Children's Early Language

Nomination	The naming of an inanimate or animate *That's a shoe*
Agent	The recognition that an animate initiated an activity *The boy threw the stone*
Possession	The recognition that an object belongs to or is in the frequent presence of someone or something *My shirt is stained*
Object	The recognition that an inanimate was receiving the force of an action *The grass was cut*
Location	The recognition of a spatial relationship between two objects *The socks are on the radiator*
Experiencer	The recognition that an animate was affected by an event *Sandra fell ill*
Attribution	The recognition of properties not inherently part of the class to which the object belongs *The room was chilly*
Denial	The rejection of a proposition *Toads do not cause warts*
Nonexistence	The recognition of the absence of an object that was once present *The ring was missing*
Rejection	The prevention or cessation of the occurrence of an activity or the appearance of an object *Stop the singing*
Instrument	The awareness that an inanimate was causally involved in an activity *He was scratched by the pin*
Recurrence	The awareness of the potential for marking the reappearance of an object or reenactment of an event *I'd like some more grits please*
Notice	The recognition that some object has appeared or some event has occurred *Hi, Pedro*

4

semantic notions are partitioned in his linguistic system. Only by obtaining data that we feel reflect the semantic notions and organization operative for the child and not merely the investigator, can we make strides toward developing an explanatory theory of children's development of relational meanings.

THE USE OF SPONTANEOUS UTTERANCES

The present trend in developmental psycholinguistics of sampling the child's spontaneous utterances produced in a natural setting lends itself well to the goal of obtaining data based on the child's system of relational meanings. The use of observational evidence actually has its origins in much earlier work. Tiedemann (1787) was one of the first on record to observe and record the linguistic development of a child. Subsequent work of this nature was performed by Darwin (1877) and Taine (1877). The most extensive observational account in the early literature was provided by Preyer (1888), who made careful daily notations of his child's development during the first three years. Subsequently, classic observational studies were performed by Stern and Stern (1907) and Leopold (1949). The various values of observational evidence were apparent to early investigators. For example, as Sully (1895) noted

> Are we to regard all our ideas as woven by the mind out of its experiences, as Locke thought, or have we certain "innate ideas" from the first. Locke thought he could settle this by observing children. Today when the philosophic interest is laid not on the date of the appearance of the innate intuition, but on its originality and spontaneity, this method of interrogating the child's mind may seem less promising. Yet if of less philosophical importance than was once supposed, it is of great psychological importance. (pp 7, 8)

By utilizing observational data, the investigator can come close to what semantic notions and organizations are employed by the child himself. What the child says and how he says it can more safely be attributed to the child's own linguistic system under such circumstances since his language would not be bound by the questions, directions, and experimental arrangements of investigators with their own views of language.

For example, assume that a child uses utterances such as *kitty eat* and *Mommy wash* in contexts, respectively, of the family cat eating and the mother washing her face. An investigator may be quite predisposed toward categorizing as actor the semantic notion reflected in such utterances, or some other term roughly similar to the syntactic classification, subject.

Such a categorization appears reasonable since the cat and the mother are participating in some act. But is this a correct portrayal of the relationship the child is intending to express? Let us assume that during the same period the child produces *sweep broom* and *cut knife* in contexts where someone was sweeping the floor with a broom and cutting meat with a knife, respectively. The broom and the knife are participating in acts in these circumstances. Yet they are treated differently from the participants in the previous two utterances. Such evidence might suggest reserving the semantic notion actor only to utterances of the first type and ascribing instrument or some such term to the second type of utterances.

Utilizing differences in the way a child linguistically codes different semantic relationships is one way of categorizing semantic notions. The sampling of the child's language over time permits another means of categorization. Assume, for example, that all of the utterances reflecting actor involved the participants in acts which they themselves instigated; none described acts which affected the participant. If utterances expressing the latter type of relationship appear only later (e.g., *Mommy hear*, *I need it*), evidence would be provided that the two types of relationships should be categorized as different semantic notions. The former type, for example, could probably have been termed agent, the latter could be termed experiencer. The means by which these notions could be distinguished, treating two otherwise similar relationships differently linguistically and expressing one relationship prior to another otherwise similar relationship, arise from the child himself.

The investigator can further reduce the confounding effects of his own biases by capitalizing on a recently revitalized method by which children's utterances are sampled. The method is that of "rich interpretation," in which the function of an utterance is determined by utilizing both the structural characteristics of the child's utterances as well as the nonlinguistic context in which they occur (Bloom, 1970). The usefulness of employing contextual information when interpreting children's utterances can be seen in the following example. Utterances such as *that ball*, *that truck*, *there car*, and *there shoe* are often interpreted as if they are used by the child to indicate the name of some object in his surroundings (Starr, 1975). This interpretation would suggest that a semantic notion such as nomination might be appropriate in these circumstances. If, however, close inspection of the accompanying nonlinguistic contexts of the utterances containing "that" revealed that the child routinely pointed to or touched the referent object, while he seemed to unexpectedly come upon the referent objects represented in his utterances containing "there," these two types of utterances could be categorized differently. Semantic notions such as nomination and notice might be appropriate for the two types, respectively. Without the use of the accompanying nonlinguistic context, this distinction would not be possible.

The approach of portraying contextual information used in this volume is adapted from Bloom (1970; 1973). To the left of each of the child's utterances, in parentheses, is a description of the nonlinguistic context in which it occurs, along with relevant utterances produced by those individuals interacting with the child. Utterance boundaries are indicated by "/." Phonetic notions are marked by "/ /." Events are listed in succession. When an activity changes in the sample, the first event of that activity is numbered. Some examples are

1. (Cory turns and sees the toy camel and approaches it)   moo cow/cow moo/
   (Cory picks up the camel)   cow/
   (Cory holds the camel up to Larry)   cow/cow/
2. (Cory points to a picture of a cat in a picture book)   /da/
   Kelly: "Maybe she's trying to say /da/ . . . or maybe /dæ/" Daddy/
   Kelly: "Daddy"   Harvey/

For instance, from the second example it can be seen that Cory produced /da/ while pointing to a picture of a cat. Kelly (Cory's babysitter) then attempted to decipher what Cory had said. Upon hearing Kelly's production of /dæ/, Cory said *Daddy*. Kelly then repeated Cory's use of this word, which was followed by Cory's production of *Harvey* (which, interestingly, is the name of Cory's father).

THE REPRESENTATION OF THE DATA

The use of spontaneous utterances with accompanying contextual information as data seems to lend itself to the discovery of which semantic notions are significant to the child. But how is the organization of these notions to be portrayed? One method is by representing the organization through the use of branching-tree diagrams. The previous examples regarding the distinctions among the notions agent, instrument, and experiencer can be represented hierarchically by the tree diagram

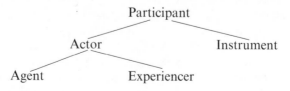

Such an organization should be justified by the data, of course, and in our examples this requirement was met. Initially, the child showed evidence of distinguishing instrument from agent on the basis of differences in linguistic coding, that is, on the basis of whether the name of the participant preceded or followed the name of the act. This relationship can be represented as

Subsequently, utterances were noted which described acts affecting participants. Since this relationship clearly emerged at a point in time after agent, there is a basis for considering it a separate semantic notion. The manner in which this new notion is represented in the tree diagram is an important issue. The representation

would indicate that experiencer functions in the child's linguistic system as a notion that shares no particular relationship with one as opposed to the other notion subsumed under participant. The preferred hierarchy of organization, however, is the one presented in the first branching-tree diagram.

Admittedly, the evidence supporting the organization seen in the first tree diagram is not overwhelming. However, the utterances reflecting experiencer in our examples (e.g., *Mommy hear*) were linguistically coded in the same manner as those reflecting agent (e.g., *Mommy wash*), with the name of the participant preceding the name of the act. These are healthy examples to present, I think, because they also reveal that, despite precautions to prevent it, room often remains for the investigator to impose his knowledge of language onto the data. No doubt my inclination to attach agent and experiencer to the same higher order label (node), actor, was dictated in part by my view of the organization of language. At the present time, our methodology seems to rest somewhere between discovering the organization of relational meanings that are operative for the child, and imposing our own organization on him.

Another method of characterizing the organization of the semantic notions underlying the child's utterances is through the use of rewrite rules. The rewrite rules discussed in this volume are those rules used to enumerate (or generate) those semantic notions postulated as relevant to the child within the organization permissable in his linguistic system. The term "rewrite" refers to the actual function of these rules, to break down a higher order node into its components.

The specific organization revealed by rewrite rules can vary considerably, and specific notations are used to express these differences. Using our examples of agent, instrument, and experiencer, some of the more common types of rewrite rules will be discussed. The rule

$$\text{Participant} \rightarrow \begin{Bmatrix} \text{Agent} \\ \text{Instrument} \end{Bmatrix}$$

states that the higher order node participant can be rewritten as agent or instrument. Such a rule is appropriate for a set of utterances such as

Mommy go
cut knife
kitty walk

The rule

$$\text{Participant} \rightarrow \text{Agent} + \text{Instrument}$$

requires that the utterances used reflect both agent and instrument, as in the following utterances.

Mommy cut knife
Daddy sweep broom
Randy hit hammer

In these utterances, it is assumed that the adult equivalent would be "Mommy is cutting with a knife" and so on, where the knife, broom, and hammer are being used as tools, rather than receiving the action. The rule

$$\text{Participant} \rightarrow \text{Agent (Instrument)}$$

states that instrument is an optional notion. Agent, of course, remains obligatory.

Patty eat spoon
kitty eat
Daddy open

Some rules require the use of both braces and parentheses. For example, the rule

$$\text{Participant} \rightarrow \text{Agent} \begin{Bmatrix} \text{Instrument} \\ \text{Experiencer} \end{Bmatrix}$$

accounts for utterances such as

> *Daddy hit hammer*
> *Mommy hurt me*

If the child was observed to say, in addition, the utterances

> *Daddy eat*
> *kitty sit*

the rule would need modification in order to make instrument and experiencer optional.

$$\text{Participant} \rightarrow \text{Agent} \left(\begin{Bmatrix} \text{Instrument} \\ \text{Experiencer} \end{Bmatrix} \right)$$

Another important rule is characterized by overlapping parentheses.

$$\text{Participant} \rightarrow (\text{Agent})(\text{Experiencer})$$

This rule states that the child's utterances reflect agent, experiencer, or agent + experiencer. Though both agent and experiencer are optional, at least one must be reflected.

> *Mommy hear*
> *kitty eat*
> *kitty hurt baby*

It is important to note that the specification of rewrite rules represents more than a method of categorizing and organizing observed data. For example, the rule

$$\text{Participant} \rightarrow \text{Agent (Instrument)}$$

not only accounts for the particular utterances reflecting participant that the child was observed to produce, but it represents a statement about the nature of other utterances reflecting participant that the child *might* produce. This rule states that the utterance *Daddy cut scissors*, though not observed in the child's speech, is a permissable one in his present system of relational meanings. Thus, although the rules are constructed on the basis of what the child says, they actually transcend the child's utterances. Such rules, then, can estimate linguistic capacity.

The rules put to use in this volume, representing what the child is capable of expressing through language, should be put in proper perspective. Such rules should in particular be examined in light of the distinction between linguistic competence and performance (Chomsky, 1965; Fodor and Garrett, 1966). Linguistic performance represents that which is actually expressed through language. Competence, however, has been used in two different senses. Chomsky (1965) chose the stronger sense, defining competence as the knowledge of the language that provides the basis for actual use of language by an ideal speaker. But Chomsky states that this should not represent a model for the use of language, since such a model would reflect little more than performance. A performance model would also have to deal with such extraneous factors occurring in speech as distractions, hesitations, repetitions, and the like. Some linguists do not view the distinction between performance and competence to be quite as great as Chomsky makes it out to be. As Fromkin (1968) points out, much of linguistic performance is lawful and predictable. A case can also be made that what is termed competence can only be defined by linguistic performance. Linguistic structure or function is not built up out of utterances but is something that receives realization as part of the process of speech production and comprehension (Derwing, 1973). Any linguistic unit exists as a unit only because the language user treats it as a unit.

Linguistic capacity as it is used in this volume represents a weaker sense of competence than that intended by Chomsky. In this sense of competence, it is not expected that the child's performance will give a precise portrayal of the semantic notions and organization of notions that represent his knowledge of relational meaning. However, the position is taken that this knowledge can at least be estimated from the child's performance. Following the importance that Campbell and Wales (1970) placed on context when discussing competence, it can be added that in this volume linguistic capacity represents the child's knowledge of relational meaning that is estimated from the child's utterances produced in particular nonlinguistic contexts.

While the contexts in which utterances are used are most helpful in determining the relational meanings operative for the child, it might also be said that they are part of the child's relational meanings. Children do not only learn a set of relational meanings, but also the contexts in which these meanings are expressed and the uses to which the expression of these meanings may be put (Bates, 1976). A child does not learn that "ball" refers to a given round referent without having been exposed to "ball" in a number of contexts (e.g., someone throwing, rolling, or pointing to a ball). Similarly, a semantic notion such as agent is not acquired independently of the child's exposure to this relationship in a number of contexts, such as the mother opening a window, a boy pushing a toy truck and so on.

This view stems from the positions of philosophers such as Quine (1960) and Austin (1962), and suggests the importance of "pragmatics" (the rules governing the use of language in context) to the child's relational meanings. Although the main focus of this volume is the nature of the child's set of relational meanings and not the uses to which these meanings can be put, it should be remembered that this is only a matter of emphasis. One cannot entirely divorce pragmatic from semantic considerations of language.

In short, the use of branching-tree diagrams and rewrite rules permit a portrayal of the child's knowledge of (context-dependent) relational meanings, in terms of underlying semantic notions and the organization of such notions. Further information can be gained by examining how this organization changes with increasing linguistic development. It seems quite useful to discover the relationship between the child's organization of relational meanings and the organization of relational meanings seen in the linguistic system he is approximating. In order to examine the changes in organization that take place with increasing linguistic development, a suitable measure of linguistic development must be utilized.

Because children acquire language at widely varying rates, chronological age is not a suitable gauge of general linguistic development. A much more suitable measure is mean length of utterance. Brown (1973) notes

> The mean length of utterance (MLU) is an excellent simple index of grammatical development because almost every new kind of knowledge increases length: the number of semantic roles expressed in a sentence, the addition of obligatory morphemes, coding modulations of meaning, the addition of negative forms and auxiliaries used in interrogative and negative modalities, and, of course, embedding and coordinating. All alike have the common effect on the surface form of the sentence of increasing length (especially if measured in morphemes, which includes bound forms like inflections rather than words). (pp 53, 54)

Some of Brown's rules for calculating mean utterance length are paraphrased in Table 2.

Brown has also been influential in establishing levels of mean utterance length which are frequently used by investigators to mark specific stages of linguistic development. The principal stage of development of interest in this volume corresponds to what Brown (1973) termed "Stage I." In the original work by Brown and his colleagues, Stage I referred to the period of a child's linguistic development when his mean utterance length was between 1.75 and 2.25 morphemes (Brown, Cazden, and Bellugi, 1969). Since this time, however, Stage I has been lowered to include the period when the child first begins producing two-word utter-

Table 2

Some of Brown's (1973) Rules for Calculating Mean
Utterance Length

Utterances containing portions of doubtful transcription or blanks (*Mommy, here* _____) are excluded.

For repeated efforts at a word (*kit . . . kitty*) the word is counted once, in its most complete form.

Exclude fillers such as "oh" but include those representing words such as "hi" and "yeah."

Compound words ("baseball"), proper names ("Santa Claus"), and ritualized re-duplications ("night-night") are counted as single morphemes.

Irregular past tense verbs ("saw") are counted as one morpheme.

Auxiliaries ("is," "have," "will," "can") and catenatives ("gonna," "wanna") are counted as single morphemes.

Inflections such as plural "-s," possessive "'s," third person singular "-s," regular past "-d," and progressive "-ing" are counted as separate morphemes.

---

ances, that is, when utterance length rises above 1.00 (Brown, 1973). For convenience, in this volume, Stage I refers to the entire period of linguistic development up to a mean utterance length of 2.25 morphemes. It is interesting to note, though, that the use of mean utterance length as an index of linguistic development is not the only possibility. Crystal (1976) for example, questioned why this measure is preferable over measures such as tone groups within an intonation contour, phrase or clause types used in an utterance, and so on.

In summary, the meanings in child language serving as the main focus of this volume are relational semantic notions. The semantic notions operative for the child as well as his organization of these notions seem best captured through the use of sampling the child's spontaneous utterances in a natural setting, taking into account the nonlinguistic contexts in which the utterances are produced. The child's organization of semantic notions can be represented through the use of branching-tree diagrams and rewrite rules. How this organization gradually approximates that of the adult system can be traced by plotting changes in the organization relative to the child's increasing mean length of utterance.

1

The Nature of Semantic Notions

SEMANTIC NOTIONS UNDERLYING EARLY LANGUAGE AND PRIOR COGNITIVE ATTAINMENTS

It seems fair to say that with the increasingly recognized need for rich interpretation in studies of children's emerging language, the centrality of meaning in the child's early language usage became highlighted (Bloom, 1970; Bowerman, 1973a). With the recognition of semantic factors playing such a key role in this early acquisition came the search for what underlies these factors. The logical step from linguistic to nonlinguistic meaning was a short one, and soon investigators of early language development were assessing the adequacy of various models of cognitive development as explanatory theories of language acquisition (Olson, 1970; Macnamara, 1972).

The cognitive view most widely used as a model for the underlying basis for language development was that of Piaget (1952). Certain aspects of the Piagetian position made it quite appealing as a framework within which to study children's early meanings. In the Introduction it was noted that the child's early meanings are as much something he does as something he has. That is, these meanings might best be characterized as types of (linguistic) actions carried out in context, rather than static entities. This interpretation fits quite nicely into the Piagetian way of thinking; the child's early meanings may be sensorimotor in nature, representing a set of action schemata rather than a set of deep structures (Bates, 1976).

At first, the relationship between cognitive and language development was put in quite general terms, often by simply noting the importance of the child's attainment of cognitive skills during the sensorimotor period since such skills might prefigure the emergence of language (Bloom, 1970). The concept of object permanence was the general cognitive attainment most frequently cited in this regard. Before the child could acquire language it was assumed that he must be able to abstract an object from its movements and locations vis-à-vis other objects as well as from its responses to the child's actions upon it (Edwards, 1973). Having acquired a concept of objects that is independent of action on the object, the child may be equipped to acquire semantic notions such as object and action at a subsequent point in time.

The importance of various sensorimotor attainments to language development was stressed in subsequent papers, with more details of their relationship to language provided (Leonard, 1974; Morehead and Morehead, 1974; Moerk, 1975). In one effort, Sinclair (1971) devoted an entire paper to the importance of sensorimotor action patterns as a necessary condition for the acquisition of syntax. Her conclusion was that the young child's developing ability to use a whole category of objects for the same action, or apply a whole category of action schemata to one object (an attainment of the fifth stage of sensorimotor development) may represent the motor equivalent for grammatical relations seen during the sixth stage of sensorimotor development. Such cognitive skills have, in fact, been viewed as necessary attainments for the development of language. For example, according to Bloom (1973), "children learn a language as a linguistic coding of developmentally prior conceptual representations of experience" (p 16).

As more was learned about the meanings expressed in children's early language usage, investigators added more detail to the nature of the cognitive–linguistic development relationship. That is, the notions expressed in early language were taken to be verbal, although imprecise approximations of the child's underlying cognitive structures. Sinclair-deZwart (1973) noted that the child's initial utterances accompany an action done by the child or interesting to him, or a desire for an action to be performed either by him or by someone else. She further suggested that early utterances are related to the child's initial grasp of the first permanent properties of entities in his surroundings, namely, their very existence. Such utterances are only subsequently supplemented by descriptions of past events or properties of objects or persons.

Brown (1973) presented a far more specific account of the relationship between sensorimotor and language development. His intent was to examine the possible sensorimotor origins of certain notions expressed in child language. Three of these semantic notions are nomination, recurrence, and nonexistence. Brown noted that the first two seem to presume the ability to anticipate objects and actions in given circumstances and to notice when such anticipations are not confirmed. These abilities, "recognition, anticipation based on signs, the concept of the enduring object, awareness of a single space that contains the self as well as other objects, are all developed in the period of sensorimotor intelligence" (p 199). He provided more detail by noting that Piaget describes two processes during the third stage of sensorimotor intelligence (approximate age, four to eight months) which seem like primitive forms of nomination and recurrence. When the child sees a familiar object, he may perform in abbreviated fashion the action schema most habitually associated with it. Such "motor recognition," according to Brown, is something like nomination, a form of recognition represented through an action of articulation.

During this same sensorimotor stage, the child also develops a means of preserving events in his surroundings. This attainment, according to Brown, bears a resemblance to the notion of recurrence.

> The third-stage child develops an interest in external effects and, when he accidentally produces an interesting one, he repeats the movement in an effort to cause the effect to recur. This procedure is tried even for spectacles at a distance over which the child's movements have no direct causal control. The recurrence construction, used to request rather than to comment, is a kind of generalized and socially efficacious "procedure for making interesting sights last." (p 199)

Not long after this point, the sensorimotor origins of semantic notions of an ergative nature can be identified. These represent semantic notions such as agent, object, and experiencer where the referents may play one role on one occasion (e.g., agent) and another role on another occasion (e.g., experiencer). Such notions seem to presuppose the knowledge that the child and others are potential sources of causality and recipients of actions, where the child conceives of his own body as being subject to the actions of things as well as a source of actions that operate on them (Piaget, 1954). The child does not generally achieve this sense of causality until approximately the fifth stage of sensorimotor intelligence, when the child is between the ages of 12 and 18 months.

In his account of the cognitive underpinnings of early child language, Wells (1974) seemed to take a holistic view of the child's sensorimotor achievements in relating such factors to the notions observed in the speech of young children.

> Piaget's first "group structure" of schemata concerning spatial displacement depends on a growing understanding through action of

the schemata of object permanency, spatial location, and causation, in which each schema is intimately related to the others and none can be seen to take precedence. All these schemata receive linguistic realization in the very early stage of structured speech. (p 263)

Sinclair (1970) noted, in a longitudinal study of children from ages 12 through 26 months, that her subjects progressed through 3 stages which serve as bases for language usage. In the first (12–16 months), the children engaged in activities concerned with acquiring knowledge of the objects themselves; in the second stage (16–19 months), the children's activities introduced some organization into the objects; and in the third stage (19–26 months) the children acted on objects as if they were other objects. Sinclair interpreted the appearance of nominative utterances (e.g., *that car*) as reflecting an object-knowledge level of thinking, whereas topic-comment utterances (e.g., *Mummy cup*) may have reflected the organizing activity of the child. Similarly, Morehead and Morehead (1974) suggested that such utterances might derive from physical knowledge and logical-mathematical knowledge, respectively.

Considering that Piaget is known more for his emphasis on the development of intelligence in general than of language in particular, it is interesting that so many useful insights regarding the relationship between cognition and language acquisition have been derived from his model. Nelson (1974) has identified certain difficulties in applying the Piagetian model to explain the relation between cognition and language acquisition. The model she proposed as a substitute borrows characteristics from not only Piagetian theory, but also concept formation theory and semantic feature theory. According to Nelson, the dynamic functional relations of objects play a key role in the child's early acquisition of meaning, since these are translated by the child into conceptual core meanings to which identifying features of concepts are attached. Nelson noted

the child must detach the functional object concept from the totality of its relationships so that the functional core retains only the object-specific functions plus abstract markers for other relations into which it can enter. (p 280)

The course of this development seems to have considerable parallel in language development. The abstract specifications (noting other, non-core relations into which any object concept can enter)

are also shared with other object concepts where they serve similar functions. When the differentiation of the functional core from other relational specifications has taken place the child becomes able both to name the concept independently of its involvement in a defining relationship (for example, as represented in a picture or in a new location) and to express the concept and the relations independently, thereby making it possible to form relational statements, that is, two-word (or longer) utterances. (Nelson, 1974, p 280)

The integral relationship of linguistic with cognitive development proposed by these and other writers seemed to revitalize investigations into universal features of language, an outcome in part due to the more readily accepted universality of cognitive development. Such proposals as Slobin's (1970a), that "the rate and order of development of semantic notions expressed by language are fairly constant across languages, regardless of the formal means of expression employed" (p 1), seemed to reflect this general acceptance. The distinction was made, however, between cognitive structure and the semantic notions underlying the child's utterances. The latter seem to be those aspects of cognitive structure having some form of linguistic realization. There is no reason to assume that the child needs the ability to express (or even comprehend) the linguistic equivalents of the relations he understands in his nonlinguistic environment (Bloom, 1973). But as we shall see, there appears to be some similarity between the order of development of concepts and the order in which semantic notions serving as linguistically expressable counterparts to these concepts are developed. This similarity is a particularly interesting one, since it does not follow from the fact that semantic notions may be dependent on certain cognitive attainments, that the order in which semantic notions emerge must necessarily be the same as the order of the child's acquisition of concepts serving as their foundation (Fodor, Bever, and Garrett, 1974).

Another important point deals with the types of similarities that may be thought to exist, given any observed parallel between a child's general cognitive development and the order in which the semantic notions underlying his speech emerge. A child's conceptual knowledge that he or others are capable of initiating actions that have effects on other objects, that objects can be located in space, or that people have territorial rights over certain objects does not necessarily mean that the semantic notions underlying his utterances can be neatly parceled into categories such as agent, location, or possession. The fact that a child may have acquired certain concepts does not require his semantic categories to be specified according to particular types (Slobin, 1966). For example, the cognitive attainment of causality may enable the child to partition the relationships that he expresses into notions such as agent or action, but there is no reason why he should form such categories instead of more narrow ones (Bowerman,

1976). For instance, the child might view activities expressed in utterances such as *put box*, *throw ball*, or *give cookie* differently from those expressed in utterances such as *break it*, *open box*, or *cut pie* since the former involve a change in location while the latter involve a change in state. He may, in fact, mark such distinctions by using different syntactic rules to express each of them. Similarly, relationships expressed in utterances such as *Daddy face* and *Daddy bed* might not be viewed as the same (possession) but rather as different, since one involves an animate and his body part and the other an animate and an object to which he has privileged access. It should be kept in mind that the categories used by investigators in their study of the order in which semantic notions emerge are not necessarily isomorphic with specific cognitive structures.

COGNITION AND EARLY COMMUNICATION

It is clear that expression through language appears after the concepts themselves are acquired. While the semantic notions underlying the child's first words may be related to some stage in cognitive development, the very emergence of communicative functions, which is quite apparent in children prior to their first words, also suggests certain cognitive attainments (Carter, 1975a).

In a study with three children, Bates, Camaioni, and Volterra (1975) traced the development of certain communicative functions. They proposed the following course of development. Upon learning that his own actions are not the source of all world events, the child soon attains the ability to analyze means-end relations in which he does not participate. This attainment, during the fifth stage of sensorimotor development, allows the child to make greater use of the external world (people and objects) in the service of his own goals. During this same period, the child demonstrates a fifth-stage capacity in social sequences. That is, the child communicates signals with an illocutionary force as a means to use adults to obtain objects (the proto-imperative) and to use objects to gain adults' attention (the proto-declarative). Bates, Camaioni, and Volterra summarize this development

> three kinds of tools develop during cognitive stage 5: the use of objects to operate on objects, the use of human agents to obtain or operate on objects, and the use of the object itself to operate on human attention. In Piagetian terms, then, we suggest that stage 5 causal developments are the prerequisites for what we have called the illocutionary stage in communication. (p 219)

The cognitive requirements for gestural communication have also been outlined by Dore (1973) and Moerk (1975). Unfortunately, their conclusions varied. Moerk suggested that the child uses gestures for communication during the third stage of sensorimotor development when the process of recognitory assimilation becomes established, as seen by the child's abbreviated acts of motor recognition. Dore described the development of gestures as a fourth-stage attainment when the child learns means-end sequences with himself as agent. However, both Moerk and Dore arrived at their conclusions by examining the age at which children acquired gestural communication and comparing this information with age norms for sensorimotor development; they did not examine whether the children involved were in fact operating at these sensorimotor stages at the time that gestures were acquired.

Another factor seems to contribute to this inconsistency. Investigators have differed in their interpretation of the dividing lines of Piaget's sensorimotor stages. For example, Morehead and Morehead (1974) noted that the child's realization that other objects and persons can also be the source for action occurs during the fourth stage; an attainment which Bates, Camaioni, and Volterra seemed to ascribe to the fifth stage of sensorimotor development. A close inspection, in fact, reveals that Morehead and Morehead, and Bates, Camaioni, and Volterra agree on the general chronological ages at which this attainment is reached; apparently their differences result in Morehead and Morehead's tendency to attribute the beginnings of this attainment to the earlier stage (or, conversely the tendency of Bates, Camaioni, and Volterra to attribute these beginnings to the later stage). This is not particularly surprising, since a child may frequently be observed succeeding on certain individual fifth stage tasks, for example, before it is clear that his overall developmental abilities can be attributed to the fifth stage of sensorimeter intelligence (Ingram, 1975).

THE SEQUENCE OF EMERGENCE OF
SEMANTIC NOTIONS: EVIDENCE FROM
SINGLE-WORD UTTERANCES

While most studies of children's language acquisition have been concerned with the two-word stage and beyond, a growing number of investigations of children's single-word usage are appearing. The interpretation of semantic notions underlying single-word utterances is a risky endeavor, since few structural cues are available from the utterances themselves. With considerable notations of the nonlinguistic contexts of such utterances, however, some investigators apparently feel that this problem is reduced (Bloom, 1973; Greenfield, Smith, and Laufer, 1972). These studies will be discussed here, reserving judgment for now as to whether the underlying notions of single-word utterances can properly be thought to reflect the same semantic specificity attributed to multi-word utterances.

Some general confirmation of Sinclair-deZwart's (1973) character-ization of children's early judgments dealing with an action the child wants to perform or have performed immediately by someone else was provided by Greenfield, Smith, and Laufer (1972). Appearing in Table 1-1 is Schlesinger's (1974) presentation of the longitudinal stages observed by Greenfield, Smith, and Laufer. The possible roles of each word are pre-sented within Schlesinger's framework of agent + action + object; the italicized role was that role played by the word actually spoken by the child.

Table 1-1
The Longitudinal Stages of
Greenfield, Smith, and Laufer
(1972) Presented within
Schlesinger's (1974) Framework

Agent	Action	Object
I	demand	*animate*
I	demand	*inanimate*
animate	*acts*	
animate	acts	*inanimate*
inanimate	*acts*	
animate	acts	*animate*
animate	acts	

It appears from the stages in Table 1-1, then, that a general shift occurred from utterances related to the child's own desires, to descriptions of events the child is not necessarily involved in. As will be shown later, Greenfield, Smith, and Laufer's own account provides more detail when taken out of the agent + action + object mold. In a general sense, Nelson's (1973) study also supports the idea that early language at the single-word stage initially reflects those aspects dealing with the child himself; initial words often represented objects the child himself could act upon. The Nelson study was concerned with lexical development at the single-word stage, however, and her method of categorizing words for lexical analysis was not always useful for interpreting the relational roles which these single-word utterances may have been serving. One of her categories, for example, was termed "nominals" and represented things that could be used in labeling, demanding, or relations involving agents or objects.

Ingram (1971) provided an account based on the single-word utterances used by Hildegard Leopold (Leopold, 1949) which seems also to provide support for the proposition that the order of early usage mirrors the order of acquisition of what the child knows of his world. According to this account, the child initially notes the existence of objects in his environment, which Ingram referred to as "intransitivity." This development seemingly relates to utterances marking nomination and other semantic notions dealing with inherent characteristics of objects. Subsequently, the child develops transitivity; that is, the child notes that objects can operate upon other objects, that activities can have agents, etc. Intransitive notions seem to have cognitive counterparts in the third stage of sensorimotor intelligence, according to the Brown (1973) account discussed previously. Transitivity, on the other hand, seems to have counterparts in the fifth stage, that is, when the child develops concepts related to causality.

Thus far, then, some support exists that semantic notions such as nomination (existence) and recurrence appear very early in usage, while those fitting within an ergative framework such as action, agent, and object appear later. But when do the notions reflecting states (e.g., possession, attribution, location) appear relative to these notions? McNeill (1970) provided some indication in his interpretation of data acquired by Greenfield (1967). The child under study in this investigation first used single-word utterances marking nomination, followed by utterances indicating properties (e.g., attribution). The final stage consisted of utterances reflecting notions such as agent. This seems generally consistent with the observations made by Stern and Stern (1907) that the child first uses nouns (presumably inanimate), then verbs, with adjectives appearing later. This apparent sequence seems to hold up against the findings of Ramer (1975). In her study of two children's development of single-word utterances, Ramer noted that the semantic notions that emerged during this period were existence (nomination), nonexistence, recurrence, action, and prohibition (rejection). Apparently, evidence for agent or attribution was not found.

How consistent are the Greenfield, Smith, and Laufer (1972) data with this sequence? With some qualifications, they are quite consistent. Presented in Table 1–2 is the sequence of acquisition for the cases employed by Greenfield, Smith, and Laufer in their analysis of the single-word (and beyond) usage of Nicky and Matthew, the two children studied.

While it appears that properties and other states may precede agent in acquisition, the states were acquired after the other semantic notions

Table 1-2

Order of Acquisition of Greenfield, Smith, and Laufer
(1972) Cases

Case	Example	Context
Pure performative	*pat*	Said while Matthew was clapping
Naming	*ball*	Said while Nicky pointed to a ball
Vocative	*Kelly*	Said while Nicky wanted Kelly to come
Object of demand	*milk*	Said while Nicky was reaching for some milk
Negative or affirmative	*no*	Said after Nicky rode his toy car as far as his mother (who was blocking his path)
Action of agent	*up*	Said while Nicky goes up a step
Inanimate object of direct action	*fan*	Said after Nicky has just turned the fan off
State or action of an inanimate object	*hot*	Said while Nicky was blowing on some cooked food
Possession and habitual location	*shoe*	Said as Nicky pointed to Laufer's bare feet
Endpoint location	*chair*	Said immediately prior to Nicky's placing of an object on the chair
Experiencer	*Mommy*	Said as Nicky gives a book to his mother
Agent of action	*Daddy*	Said by Nicky after his father goes out the door
Direction, time, or manner of event	*wait*	Said as Nicky, with hand on the toilet flush, waits to pull it

serving an ergative function, action of agent, and object of action. This order of acquisition seems predictable from a cognitive standpoint; objects are not initially coded in terms of perceptual characteristics (e.g., attribute, location) alone, but rather are derived from shared properties found in known actions and familiar contexts (Bruner, 1971). The sequence, then, seems consistent with the findings of other investigators. Action of agent utterances, it should be pointed out, were initially in the form of descriptions of the child's own actions (and, more specifically, in the form of words serving as adverbs of location and direction such as *up* and *down*). The order of this case in the sequence, then, seems in keeping with Sinclair-deZwart's (1973) proposals.

The sequence observed thus far appears to parallel the order in which words are thought to be acquired in Macnamara's (1972) cognitively based approach. This order of acquisition is (1) names for entities, (2) names for their variable states and actions, and (3) names for more permanent attributes.

The evidence from the single-word stage of language development seems to be consistent with Slobin's (1970a) hypothesis concerning a regular order of appearance of underlying semantic notions. This order also shows considerable similarity to the general course of cognitive development during the sensorimotor period.

THE SEQUENCE OF EMERGENCE OF SEMANTIC NOTIONS: EVIDENCE FROM TWO-WORD UTTERANCES

Considerably more data are available at the two-word stage of language development, due to the obvious influence of transformational grammar on developmental psycholinguistics in the early 1960s. Some two-word data elude examination regarding underlying semantic notions because of early transcription methods that excluded nonlinguistic, contextual information. But there are substantially more data for this period than for the single-word stage.

It might be assumed that two-word utterances provide more information regarding the semantic notions they reflect than single-word utterances. In fact, however, investigators' attempts to categorize the semantic notions reflected in two-word utterances have been met with some criticism. Howe (1976) has pointed out a number of weaknesses in such attempts. First, investigators have not agreed on the relevant categories to be used in classifying the meaning of two-word utterances. While one investigator may have proposed a general category such as x + locative (Schlesinger, 1971a), another may have proposed two categories entailing the same meanings, such as action + locative and entity + locative (Brown, 1973). Further, an utterance typically viewed as reflecting possession (Slobin, 1970b), such as *my baby*, might have been categorized by other investigators as attribution (Bloom, 1973).

Another difficulty pointed out by Howe has been that a number of presumably different semantic notions (e.g., location, agent + object, possession) have been coded by the same syntactic rule (e.g., noun + noun). Thus the semantic notions reflected in two-word utterances have often not been obvious from surface structure alone. This fact has prompted investigators to adopt two additional analytical techniques. The first has involved an inspection of the accompanying nonlinguistic context, that is, an observation of the relation between the referents of each utterance. While this technique has clear value, it relies on certain assumptions which may not be true. For example, it relies on the assumption that the child consistently is attempting to communicate the nonlinguistic relationship as he sees it. No provision seems to be made for the possibility of prevarication or fantasizing.

The second of these techniques has involved the use of the nonlinguistic context in concert with the use of the word order of the utterance used by the child in that context. Thus, an utterance such as *Daddy hat*, produced in the context of the child's father wearing a hat, might be interpreted as "Daddy is wearing a hat" or "Daddy has a hat." The assumption that the child's word order adequately represents his intended message, however, may not always be justified. For example, such a child may have been attempting to communicate that the hat is on the father. Finally, Howe reinforced the often-noted suspicion that many of the semantic notions ascribed to the child may actually be operative only for the adult linguistic system.

Howe's criticisms are most useful since they serve to identify methodological weaknesses in the manner in which semantic notions reflected in children's early utterances have been analyzed. These weaknesses should be kept in mind in the following sections that deal with the sequence in which semantic notions have been reported to emerge in the language of young children.

What is the order of appearance of the semantic notions reflected in utterances at the two-word stage? The evidence suggests that the order somewhat extends that observed at the single-word stage, with the addition of a few new semantic notions. Allison Bloom's initial two-word utterances reflected such notions as nomination, nonexistence, disappearance, cessation, "upness," and recurrence (Bloom, 1973). Subsequently, utterances reflecting relations among persons, objects, and events were noted, such as possession, location, action, and attribution. However, it should be pointed out that this sequence was based on data that included single-word utterances as well as two-word utterances. Bloom's (1970) more advanced subjects in another study showed early expression of the notions attribution, genitive (possession), and recurrence, while conjunctive and locative notions followed.

In a longitudinal study of seven children, Ramer (1974) noted that of the 12 semantic notions examined, possession, attribution, location, quantity (indication of number as in *two spoon*), and recurrence emerged first. Time, manner (indication of the way something occurred, as in *other way*), conjunction, and explicit deixis (specific indication of one rather than another, as in *that one*) appeared somewhat later. Dative (indirect object as in *give Daddy*), instrument, and disjunction (either-or relationship as in *bunny either*) appeared last, if at all. This finding seems consistent with Slobin's (1970a; 1973) hypotheses that location emerges earlier than time and that conjunction emerges before disjunction.

Analysis of the notions reflected in children's negative utterances was also possible at the two-word stage. The child studied by McNeill (1968)

79385

first expressed negative utterances reflecting denial, followed by those reflecting rejection. Unfortunately, the reverse was true for all of Bloom's (1970) subjects who, in fact, produced negative utterances reflecting non-existence before the others. Ramer (1974) found great discrepancies in the order of these notions expressed by negatives among her seven subjects.

Since it is at the two-word stage that the basic grammatical relations of subject + verb, subject + object, and verb + object occur (Bloom, 1970), it would be of interest to determine if, based on their underlying semantic notions, they can be ordered developmentally. The longitudinal studies of Bloom (1970) and Ramer (1974) found, for some subjects, almost simultaneous use of all three grammatical relations. The remaining subjects in both studies, however, expressed the verb + object relation first (and, in fact, continued using it frequently).

Similar findings have been reported in papers whose primary emphasis was on syntactic rather than semantic structure. Menyuk (1969) explained the emergence of predicate before subject on the basis that the early two-word utterance period constitutes expressions of overt acts rather than representing a referential system where the child reports observations of acts by others. Gruber (1967a; 1973) proposed that all children pass through two basic phases during the two-word utterance period. Initially, these utterances consist of predicate constructions that function as performatives. The performatives are used to demand or indicate but do not attribute a topic to the sentence. During the second phase, utterances take the form of reportatives with topics provided. Only in this phase are subject + predicate constructions seen. Since the Menyuk and Gruber accounts are based on a syntactic model, it can be assumed that their use of predicate is probably more general than one such as action + object.

Sinclair (1973; 1975) also shed light on the possible earlier appearance of action + object before agent + action or agent + object, in her case, within a cognitive framework. According to her account, the early syntactic period consists of utterances expressing some action the child performs or is about to perform, the results of an action, or some combination of the action and result (usually object). In all these instances agent is implicit since this role is played by the child himself. The distinction between self and others as agent is acquired later. Such predetermined stages are attributed to universal cognitive activity.

A study by Braine (1976) seems to call into question the presumed earlier appearance of action and object relative to agent. Braine noted evidence of agent + action (in his terms, actor + action) in two-word constructions that were more consistently productive in several children's language than constructions reflecting action + object. In addition, Braine pointed out that when the latter occurred they seemed to reflect meanings that were more narrow than previously described in the literature.

These two points will be discussed in reverse order. First, the previous descriptions to which Braine was referring were in fact those which dealt in terms such as verb + object. Such descriptions, of course, do not permit a differentiation of utterances such as *hurt Andrew* or *have ball* from those such as *bite block*. After an analysis of the types of meanings reflected in verb + object utterances, Braine suggested that a more restricted type of category, such as action + object-moved-or-manipulated-during-the-act, would be more appropriate. Such a suggestion seems appropriate enough; certainly only those categories that are justified by the data should be proposed. But does this mean that action + object, even with a more narrow definition, is not as early an acquisition as agent + action?

An examination of the data at Braine's disposal suggests that a distinction must be made between underlying semantic notions and the syntactic constructions used to code them. Braine's basis for viewing actor + action as an earlier acquisition than action + object seemed based on the latter. That is, certain syntactic constructions (or, in Braine's terms, positional formulae) that reflected actor + action became productive in children's speech before those reflecting action + object. In fact, an examination of these data for the first appearance of utterances reflecting action + object, shows that such utterances are seen as early as those reflecting agent + action.

Some of the data utilized by Braine were cross-sectional in nature, coming from other sources such as Braine's (1963) earlier work, and that of Bowerman (1973a) and Kernan (1969). For some other children, longitudinal data were utilized. These came from Bowerman (1973a), Lange and Larsson (1973), and some previously acquired samples from Braine's own files. I examined the samples used by Braine for the first appearance of utterances reflecting agent + action and action + object. My observations are summarized in the form of examples in Table 1–3.

From this table it can be seen that in each sample in which an utterance reflecting agent + action was observed, an utterance reflecting action + object was also observed. In a few other cases, evidence of action + object was seen when none was noted for agent + action. My observations do not affect Braine's conclusions, provided that the latter are interpreted to mean that for the children studied, positional formulae for agent + action were productive before those for action + object. It would be quite another thing to conclude that the semantic notion agent emerges before object. This does not seem to be the case. Any argument that agent

Table 1–3
Examples of Utterances Reflecting
Agent + Action and Action + Object in the
Samples Studied by Braine (1976)

Sample	Example of Agent + Action	Example of Action + Object
Andrew		
Kendall I	*Kendall sit*	*carry it*
Kendall II	*Kimmy spit*	*bite finger*
Seppo[a]	*Mother opens*	*sets-up car*
Sipili[a]		*bring Tasi*
Tofi[a]	*baby sleeps*	*bring candy*
Jonathan I		*eat banana*
Jonathan II	*Andrew walk*	*bite block*
Odi[a]	*Odi hello*	*put comb*
David I		*drink milk*
David II	*Daddy sit*	*hold it*
Embla I[a, b]	*Embla build*	*pick flower*
Embla II[a, c]	*Mother wipe*	*eat berry*

[a] English gloss of child's utterance.

[b] This sample was the product of Braine's collapsing of the second, third, and fourth sampling sessions of Embla.

[c] This sample was the product of Braine's collapsing of the fifth, sixth, and seventh sampling sessions of Embla.

emerges before object would be based on the mistaken assumption that an underlying semantic notion is given its status on the basis of its expression in a productive syntactic construction.

It probably should be concluded that agent + action and action + object emerge at approximately the same point in development, although if one emerges first it is probably action + object. It is interesting to point out that while this conclusion is based on the results of several investigations, it is generally consistent with one of the first observations made regarding this matter. Stern and Stern (1907), discussing their observations in syntactic terms, noted that one of their children acquired verb + object constructions before subject + verb constructions, while their other child acquired both at approximately the same point in development.

Brown (1973) performed a cross-sectional analysis of semantic notions reflected in children's speech at different levels of linguistic development, as measured by mean utterance length. The raw data were obtained from the studies of Adam, Eve, and Sarah by Brown, Cazden, and Bellugi (1969) and the studies by Bowerman (1973a), Kernan (1969),

Rydin (1971), and Tolbert (1971). Since the speech samples from which Brown obtained his data ranged from a mean utterance length of 1.10 to 2.06 morphemes, much information about the semantic notions underlying the children's two-word utterances was available. Brown's method of categorizing semantic notions was unfortunate in some cases. Notions such as nomination and nonexistence were generally grouped and categorized under "other constructions." Apparently this was done because Brown did not view them as relational in the sense that agent + action or action + object might be viewed. Another early semantic notion, recurrence, was grouped into Brown's entity + attributive category.

Nevertheless, it was the cross-sectional nature of Brown's data that made it the most difficult to interpret for purposes of examining the sequence in which semantic notions might emerge. Brown's intent was simply to present the major semantic notions of Stage I, not their sequence of emergence. As it turned out, the child with the lowest mean utterance length, Kendall at 1.10 morphemes, showed evidence of all of the major notions. Since all of the remaining samples analyzed represented mean utterance length levels of at least 1.42 morphemes, it was not surprising to find all of the major Stage I semantic notions reflected in the utterances contained in them. Thus, no sequence could be ascertained.

Thus far, it has been noted that when underlying semantic notions evidenced at the single-word stage are observed at the two-word stage, they appear in the same developmental order seen earlier. Yet a close inspection seems to suggest differences between them. With the onset of syntax at the two-word stage, the child must have (1) internalized coordinated action schemes permitting relational aspects of the referent to be represented in the absence of the referent, and (2) the knowledge that objects or events can function in different, though related manners (Morehead and Morehead, 1974). This capacity for internal representation is a product of the sixth stage of sensorimotor intelligence. Thus, while some of the notions underlying single-word utterances seem to resemble those seen in two-word utterances, the former may not yet be truly relational.

This explanation is similar to the one offered by Bloom (1973) to explain the difference between the single- and two-word stage. The child, at the latter stage, may be able to represent mentally a complete action scheme, rather than being able to represent only one successive movement of the scheme at a time. To be sure, the utterances during the single-word stage (e.g., *no*, *more*, *up*) suggest semantic notions such as nonexistence, recurrence, and action. At this period, during the fifth stage of sensorimotor intelligence, however, the concepts underlying such utterances are still action-based (Morehead and Morehead, 1974).

Nelson and Bonvillian (1973) have suggested that at an early stage of language, spoken words may serve as actions themselves. In their investigation it was noted that object classes (e.g., canteens, sifters) that children showed evidence of discriminating on the basis of the actions they performed on each, were those that generally were named with low frequency. Those object-classes not clearly differentiated on the basis of action were frequently named instead. The position that early utterances may serve as alternatives to action has also been taken by Sinclair (1971) and Werner and Kaplan (1963). It should be mentioned, however, that toward the end of the six-month period during which Nelson and Bonvillian's subjects were studied, they were of the age at which a number of children start producing two-word utterances. Nelson and Bonvillian did not specify the language level at which their subjects were operating, however.

Ingram (in press) has shed further light on the cognitive distinctions between the single- and two-word periods. Ingram rearranged the observations made in Piaget's writings in chronological order for each child described. The observations dealt with linguistic as well as behavioral attainments of the children. When organized in this fashion, Ingram noted that single-word utterances were associated with the fifth stage of sensorimotor intelligence. Multi-word utterances were reported at a time when the children were operating at the sixth stage.

Ingram, Ingram, and Neufeld (forthcoming) performed a longitudinal investigation of 4 children aged 7 to 19 months. Data took the form of observations and performance on Piagetian tasks. Preliminary findings indicated that the speech of 3 out of the 4 children was limited to single-word utterances during the fifth stage of sensorimotor intelligence with more rapid linguistic development, including the acquisition of multi-word utterances, taking place during the sixth stage. The remaining child, however, began producing multi-word utterances during the fifth stage. Ingram suggested that this unexpected finding may have pertained to the child's advanced imitative abilities.

In a longitudinal study by Bates, Benigni, Bretherton, Camaioni, and Volterra (1976), the fifth and sixth stages of sensorimotor intelligence were also associated with two different periods of linguistic development. These periods were not defined in terms of number of words per utterance (e.g., single-word versus two-word), but rather in terms of whether the child's speech was nonreferential (speech in the service of performative functions such as requesting) or referential (speech which stands for objects or relations). The latter did not appear until accompanying behaviors consistent with the sixth stage of sensorimotor intelligence were evidenced.

An alternative explanation of the similarities in the semantic notions underlying single-word and two-word utterances seems plausible. Interestingly, this explanation also stems from a Piagetian framework. Upon reaching a new stage of development, linguistic in this case, the set of principles operative for the child at a prior stage is again set in motion (Sinclair-deZwart, 1973). Such an explanation would suggest that the semantic notions underlying utterances at the more advanced, two-word stage are the result of the child reapplying old information.

Toward the end of the two-word stage, semantic notions not seen during the single-word stage (e.g., instrument) begin to emerge. The fact that they were not seen at all during the single-word stage suggests that they, too, fit within the developmental continuum of emerging semantic notions. Although the order of development of these notions seems to be generally of the same sequence as that seen in the development of the nonlinguistic concepts that resemble them, the parallel is not perfect.

Utterances reflecting agent are generally used earlier than those reflecting instrument. This difference in acquisition seems difficult to justify from a conceptual standpoint. Instrument and agent may arise from the child's development of physical and psychological causality, respectively (Edwards, 1973). Physical causality refers to the causal action that one object exerts on another through direct physical contact, while psychological causality refers to causality involving intentions along with the capability of causal action. Though both types are subsumed under Piaget's concept of causality in the fifth stage of sensorimotor intelligence, physical causality does not appear to be a more complex attainment than psychological causality. An inspection of Piaget's (1954) observations reveals examples of physical causality (e.g., daughter Jacqueline's use of a stick to bring an object closer to her, at 13 months) at approximately the same period as those of psychological causality (e.g., Jacqueline, at 12 months, placed herself in position for her father to blow on her hair). The later appearance of instrument relative to agent, then, could possibly be due to other than conceptual factors. Nevertheless, there is a question as to how to reliably ascertain that the child, thought to have attained the concept of psychological causality, is actually displacing the capability of action an another. For example, Jacqueline's placing herself in a position for her hair to be blown could be interpreted as an action *she* performs in order to produce an interesting result. When one notes that the blowing activity was initiated by the father a moment before, this interpretation seems feasible.

At this point, it is appropriate to discuss the work of Braine (1976) which was mentioned earlier in connection with the emergence of agent + action and action + object. After examining his mixture of cross-sectional and longitudinal Stage I data, Braine concluded that there was a great deal of similarity among the children in the semantic notions reflected in their utterances, but much variability in the order in which these notions emerged.

As can be recalled, Braine's examination of semantic notions was quite dependent upon the appearance of productive syntactic constructions used to express them. Another qualification is that what Braine termed variability in order of emergence was often simply variability in some of the notions reflected in the utterances of different children. This seems to be a different issue and one that is discussed in Chapter 2. The most suitable means of assessing whether there is much variability in the order in which semantic notions emerge is to examine Braine's longitudinal data.

I examined the semantic notions reflected in the utterances produced by the four children from whom Braine had acquired longitudinal data. I identified evidence for the following semantic notions in the utterances produced by Kendall in the first sample.

Nomination (*that book*)
Recurrence (*more lights*)
Action (*Kendall walk*)
Agent (*Kendall walk*)
Object (*carry it*)
Possessor (*Daddy book*)
Location (*pig water*)
Attribution (*refrigerator on*)
Experience (*Kendall hurt*)
Experiencer (*Kendall hurt*)
Conjunction (*Kimmy Pam*)
Classificatory (*Kimmy girl*)

I am somewhat unsure about attribution, experience, and experiencer. I presume that if my analysis of *Kendall hurt* was improper, it would be taken to reflect attribution. It can be seen, then, that a number of the notions reflected in Kendall's first sample were those generally seen early in Stage I by other investigators.

What differences were there between the notions reflected in the first sample and the second sample? I saw evidence in the second sample of all of the notions seen in the first, with the probable exception of experiencer. Kendall's utterance, *bite finger*, comes the closest but it would probably be more reasonable to view "finger" as object. Given that the utterance reflecting experiencer in the previous sample may just as easily have been categorized as attribution, this does not seem to be a difference of much importance. Interestingly, all of the notions evidenced in the second sample were also noted in the first sample.

The following notions were noted in the first sample from Jonathan.

Nonexistence (*all gone stick*)
Recurrence (*more book*)
Action (*eat grape*)
Object (*eat grape*)
Possessor (*Daddy pipe*)
Attribution (*little key*)
Experience (*hurt toe*)

In the second sample, several new notions emerged.

Agent (*Andrew walk*)
Experiencer (*hurt Andrew*)
Instrument (*eat fork*)
Classificatory (*Mommy girl*)
Comitative (*walk Daddy*)
Conjunction (*sock shoe*)

The only notion that one would expect to appear in the first sample is agent. However, this finding is not surprising considering the earlier discussion regarding possible reasons for the later appearance of agent relative to that of object and action. The remaining notions noted in the second but not in the first sample are generally observed to be later developments according to other investigators as well. It should be pointed out that I am somewhat unsure of my analysis of *sock shoe* as conjunction, since contextual information accompanying this utterance was not provided. Finally, all of the notions observed in the first sample were noted in the second sample as well.

In the first sample from David, I observed evidence of the following semantic notions.

Nomination (*this one here*)
Notice (*here milk*)
Recurrence (*more balloon*)
Action (*fix it*)
Object (*fix it*)

Several new notions emerged in David's second sample.

Agent (*Daddy sit*)
Attribution (*good boy*)
Possessor (*baby toy*)

Experience (*like it*)
Experiencer (*baby cry*)
Completion (*all finish that*)

Admittedly, it is not clear that David's *baby cry* reflected an awareness on his part that the baby was undergoing an experience as opposed to performing an action. Nevertheless, the longitudinal data from David's speech seemed to mirror the results from the longitudinal studies of other investigators.

Braine (1976) combined the utterances from the second, third, and fourth sampling sessions of Embla, which I will refer to as the first sample. Braine also combined the utterances from Embla's fifth, sixth, and seventh sessions; these will represent what I refer to as the second sample. The semantic notions evidenced in the first sample were

Nomination (*den bilen*; *it car*)
Action (*plocka blomma*; *pick flower*)
Object (*plocka blomma*; *pick flower*)
Agent (*barn simma*; *child swim*)
Attribution (*stor pippi*; *big bird*)
Possessor (*katten ora*; *cat ear*)
Location (*där tarta*; *there cake*)

In addition, Embla used an utterance (*nej kossa*; *no moo cow*), with negation, but without accompanying nonlinguistic information it is difficult to determine whether such an utterance reflects nonexistence, denial, or rejection. Embla's use of *katten ora* was different from the privileged access form of possession usually noted. This utterance, referring to a cat's ear, seemed to be one of inalienable possession instead.

All of the notions evidenced in the first sample were noted as well in the second. In the latter, however, two new notions were evidenced.

Recurrence (*mer vatten*; *more water*)
Conjunction (*hästar och kosso*; *horses and cows*)

In addition, Embla produced a number of utterances with negation, but without their nonlinguistic contexts they could not be taken to reflect any specific semantic notion. Although conjunction has been viewed as a characteristically later acquisition than the more common Stage I notions, the relatively late evidence for recurrence seemed counter to that noted by other investigators.

In summary, it appears that when the longitudinal data used by Braine are examined for the first evidence of a semantic notion reflected in children's utterances, the order in which these notions emerge is consistent with that of other studies. Out of the 14 instances in which a notion that was not noted in the first sample was evidenced in the second sample, 12 or possibly 13 (depending on one's interpretation of the existing findings regarding agent) represented notions which, according to other investigations, were later to emerge than those of the first sample. In addition, in only one instance was a notion that was noted in the first not evidenced in the second sample. It should be pointed out that if this exception, *Kendall hurt*, was categorized as attribution, not only would every notion noted in the second sample have been evidenced in the first sample, but another instance of a supposedly later-emerging notion (experience) would have been noted in the second but not in the first sample. Quite clearly, then, that when analyzed in this manner, there is a fairly orderly sequence in which semantic notions emerge.

Perhaps Braine's most important contribution to the study of the emergence of notions was his observation that a notion reflected in one child's utterances may not be reflected in the utterances of another child. An example of this occurrence can be seen in the samples of Embla and Jonathan where, unlike the speech of Embla, Jonathan's speech showed no evidence of the common notion, nomination. Such a finding is interpreted by Braine as evidence that semantic notions can be acquired independently of one another. I tend to agree with Braine on this point. Since semantic notions may represent aspects of cognitive structure that have the potential to be communicated linguistically, I see no reason why a child must produce utterances reflecting one notion before another. It would be quite another matter to suggest that the concepts necessary for the acquisition of semantic notions are independent of one another, but I do not think that Braine is suggesting this. The interesting topic of why children may show differences in the semantic notions reflected in their speech will be discussed in the next chapter.

THE SEQUENCE OF EMERGENCE OF SEMANTIC NOTIONS: EVIDENCE FROM BROAD RANGE LONGITUDINAL STUDIES

Several investigations have been performed with the intent of examining children's acquisition of underlying semantic notions over a broad range of language development. One of these was performed by Wells (1974). In this study, children's language usage was observed from shortly after the appearance of single words to a point when utterances were three morphemes or more in length. The first structured utterances noted seemed to indicate interpersonal functions, composed of a morpheme specifying an object or situation desired by the child plus a morpheme from the class of nominals. Such utterances as *more record* and *that pussy* were representative of these utterances. According to Wells, the functional morpheme in these utterances can be thought of as an operator signaling the interpersonal purpose of the speaker with respect to the object or situation that is referred to by the nominal morpheme. Such operators seem to serve functions reminiscent of nomination, recurrence, and the like.

Subsequently, utterances began to emerge that were concerned with the physical attributes and functions of people and objects, with evaluation of objects, and with their location and possession. Later, utterances appeared that served as experiential clauses. These were concerned with experiences of feeling, both physical and emotional, and of perception. From the standpoint of cognitive development, it would follow that these utterances would emerge after those dealing with functions of people and objects. While utterances such as *like candy* are not superficially different from those such as *eat candy*, the latter deal with overt actions and their meaning is therefore assimilable by the cognitive structure of sensorimotor intelligence (Edwards, 1973). This sequence, commencing with utterances reflecting semantic notions such as nomination and recurrence, progressing through utterances reflecting state and action, and terminating with those reflecting experience, seems highly consistent with the sequence observed in the previous studies reported.

There are some difficulties in discussing any sequence of acquisition when dealing with as wide a range of linguistic development as did Wells. The categories utilized to capture underlying semantic notions have been designed primarily as analytical tools for Stage I speech (Brown, 1973), and Wells was still applying his methods of analysis to child utterances with a few children whose mean utterance length exceeded 3.50 (Stage IV). Considering that we have been trying to relate the emergence of semantic notions underlying children's utterances to attainments during the period of sensorimotor intelligence, one can see why the enterprise of applying the same type of analysis to Stage IV utterances is questionable. Fortunately, when only those utterances used by Wells's subjects during Stage I are viewed in terms of the semantic notions reflected in Stage I speech, we continue to see a correspondence with other studies. For example, if we divide Wells's Stage I data into utterances marked as operator + nominal (reflecting notions such as nomination, recurrence, and nonexistence) and those reflecting such notions as state, experience, and action, we can see a greater proportion of the former in the earlier rather than later samples. This can be seen in Table 1–4.

Table 1–4

Wells's (1974) Data Analyzed According to Semantic Notions
Evidenced During Stage I Speech

Sample	Mean Utterance Length	Operator + Nominal	State, Action, Experience
Polly II	1.22	.17	.18
Polly III	1.64	.16	.39
Wayne II	1.44	.28	.20
Wayne III	1.78	.16	.39
Benjamin II	1.17	.39	.16
Benjamin III	2.16	.15	.62
Dawn I	1.17	.46	.17
Dawn II	1.71	.19	.44
Lara I	2.08	.24	.39
Lara II	1.31	.48	.16
Lara III	2.23	.15	.55
Jacqueline I	1.41	.57	.22
Jacqueline II	1.54	.35	.41

Some of Wells's subjects (Adam and Paul) could not be included since their data did not include two samples at Stage I. Samples with mean utterance length equaling 1.00 were also not included, of course, since single-word utterances could not be analyzed as operator + nominal in Wells's system of analysis. The data are fairly consistent in suggesting that over time during Stage I (for each child), operator + nominal utterances decreased, while those utterances reflecting state, action, and experience increased in proportion. There is one exception, however. Operator + nominal utterances increased (with those reflecting state, action, and experience decreasing) from Lara's first sample to her second sample. It can also be noted that mean utterance length also decreased, which was probably due to some sampling error such as a transitory shift in mood. Nevertheless, the fact that the proportion of these classifications varied with mean utterance length rather than with maturation over time opens up the possibility that underlying semantic notions might be integrally related to utterance length, even when utterance length represents something other than general linguistic development, as in Lara's second sample. Few would suggest that Lara's general linguistic development regressed from the first to the second sample.

Another investigation covering a broad range of early language development was performed by Bloom, Lightbown, and Hood (1975). These investigators reanalyzed Bloom's (1970) data for Eric, Gia, and Kathryn, and collected and analyzed data from a fourth child, Peter.

Table 1–5
The Major Relations Examined by Bloom, Lightbown, and
Hood (1975)

Category	Example	Context
Existence	*this book*	Said while Kathryn was picking up a book
Negation	*no 'chine*	Said while Eric was pointing to a tape recorder which he was told earlier he could not play with
Recurrence	*more rabbit*	Said while Gia was looking through a book for a picture of a rabbit, after seeing one
Attribution	*party hat*	Said while Kathryn was picking up a party hat
Possession	*Mommy sock*	Said while Kathryn was pointing to her mother's socks
Action	*open drawer*	Said while Kathryn was opening a drawer
Locative action	*tape on there*	Said while Peter was putting masking tape on a toy car
Locative state	*light ə hall*	Said while Peter was pointing to an overhead light in the hallway
Notice	*look at that*	Said while Peter was looking in a mirror box
State	*I want pretzel*	Said while Peter was standing next to a cabinet where pretzels were kept
Intention	*I want ə blow nose*	Said while Gia was reaching to get a tissue from Lois

The data were analyzed according to semantic-syntactic relations between two or more constituents and some of these relations represented modifications of the manner in which underlying semantic notions had been analyzed previously. Appearing in Table 1–5 are the Bloom, Lightbown, and Hood relations that occurred most frequently.

Existence (nomination), negation (nonexistence, denial, rejection), and recurrence were the first relations observed in the speech of their subjects—a finding consistent with other studies. The order of appearance of the remaining relations was a bit more variable, however. The sequences of acquisition for the different children are presented in Table 1–6.

Though variability existed, action and locative action generally appeared before locative state, state, and notice. Intention was generally last to appear. These general findings seem consistent with the sequence usually reported. While children's early utterances often reflect actions related to themselves, the Bloom, Lightbown, and Hood categories of action and locative action are sufficiently broad to include actions performed by other persons, and thus it cannot be determined for certain

Table 1–6

Sequences of Acquisition of the Relations Examined by
Bloom, Lightbown, and Hood (1975)

Eric	Gia	Kathryn	Peter
Action, Notice	Action,	Action	Action
State	Locative action	Attribution	Attribution
Locative action,	State, Possession	Locative action,	Locative action
Locative state,	Attribution	Possession	Possession
Attribution	Notice	State	Locative state,
Possession	Locative state,	Locative state,	Notice
Intention	Intention	Intention	State
		Notice	Intention

whether the early appearance of two-word utterances reflecting these semantic notions are consistent with the sequence of notions usually seen. However, one gets the impression that action was initially expressed as it related to the child.

> Thus, in the present study, encoding relations between objects and persons or between objects appeared to depend upon ongoing or intended action by the child or by another at the child's direction. Only after a child learned to encode person–object relations with the support of relevant action was he able to encode static relations among objects in which neither he himself nor his actions were necessarily relevant to the state of affairs represented in his message. (Bloom, Lightbown, and Hood, 1975, p 32)

The relatively late appearance of notice is seemingly due to the requirement by Bloom, Lightbown, and Hood that a verb must be included. Thus vocatives such as *juice, Mommy* were not included.

It is unclear whether utterances used to indicate objects desired or about to be picked up or retrieved (e.g., *want ball*) would be included in the state category; the latter represents internal experiences, where verbs such as "like," "need," or "want" may be used. Utterances with "want" have been observed early in the use of some children (Wells, 1974), generally as requests, and therefore their inclusion in a category with utterances containing verbs such as "like" or "need" may be clouding the findings somewhat (Gruber, 1967b; Edwards, 1973). Finally, the late appearance of intention is quite expected since its definition required the use of a form expressing causality or intention coupled with one of the other relations. It is unlikely that such an utterance could be accomplished by a child until he had the capacity for utterances longer than two words in length.

Bloom, Lightbown, and Hood see that their data, in a general way, reflect a trend of increasing semantic (and, we might imply, cognitive) development. But on the other hand, they feel that this is only part of the story: "Although relative cognitive complexity is a factor in explaining linguistic development, it appears to function to determine linguistic development only in complex interaction with the linguistic code that the child is learning" (pp 30, 31). The nature of this interaction is explored in the next chapter.

2
The Coding of Semantic Notions

Chapter 1 mentioned that a distinction is made between the child's cognitive structures and the semantic notions underlying his utterances. These, in turn, should be distinguished from the ways that semantic notions might be coded for communication purposes. While concepts and perhaps even semantic notions may be related to fairly fixed, universal developmental processes, it seems that their linguistic coding shows more variability.

STRATEGIES IN ACQUIRING LANGUAGE

Bloom (1970; 1973) was one of the first investigators to propose that at any given stage of early language development, generally defined by utterance length, children may use utterances reflecting different semantic notions. Examining her data from the two-word stage, Bloom (1973) identified two different kinds of semantic relationships between words. In one kind, there were structural meanings that occurred with different words and derived from a transitive relationship between the words, such as agent + action or action + goal. In the second kind, the relational meaning between the words seemed dependent upon the meaning of one of the words. This kind of relationship was seen when certain words, such as "more" and "no" combined with many different words to express a consistent semantic function. Usually the resulting utterances coded such notions as recurrence and nonexistence. Bloom suggested that the first types of meaning were coded by "basic grammatical relations" (e.g., verb + object) while the second types were coded by the "functional relations" between words.

In a longitudinal study of language usage by children from the single-word stage to a period when three-word utterances were used, Ramer (1974) also observed that children differed in noticeable ways. Ramer referred to these differences as differences in "style," a term which she felt did not smack of the intentionality implicit in a term such as "strategy." The three boys in her study developed new syntactic classes slowly, while the four girls progressed more rapidly. The rapid syntactic developers proceeded from single-word utterances to Ramer's criterion for completion in less than four and one-half months. The slow developers required at least six and one-half months to reach criterion.

Acquisition rate was not the only variable that distinguished the two groups, however. The slow developers made extensive use of different types of presyntactic forms: dummy forms (e.g., the production of a vowel such as /ə/ preceding a word), reduplication (one word produced twice as a "two-word" utterance), and empty forms (the use of a "word" that has no identifiable referent, such as /ɪdi/, preceding a word). These presyntactic forms emerged at the onset of syntax and were employed throughout the period observed. The rapid developers, on the other hand, used presyntactic forms less extensively, and such usage, when it occurred, was limited to a short span of the observation period.

The two groups also differed in their use of indeterminate forms, with such usage being more frequent by the rapid developers. Ramer proposed that the relatively heavy dependence upon indeterminate constructions by the rapid developers in contrast to the slow developers may have signaled a difference in risk-taking behavior related to speech. Finally, the rapid developers specified the three grammatical relations of subject + verb, subject + complement, and verb + complement at the onset of syntax. The slow developers began by specifying only the verb + complement, of the three.

The linguistic features that seem to reflect different styles have been observed in other studies as well. For example, Bloom's (1973) functional relations seem to be responsible for what has been termed the "pivot look." Brown (1973) suggested that the pivot look results from two factors.

1) The child's understanding of an elementary closed semantic set comprising: referent existence (nomination), referent recurrence, and referent nonexistence; 2) existence, recurrence, and nonexistence may be predicated of just about any person, place, action, or quality,

and so have a very broad combinatorial potential quite unlike that of such semantically limited terms as "swim," "eat," "hot," "pencil." (p 144)

Brown termed such notions "operations of reference" and noted that these operations of reference are quite accessible to the child of 18 months since they are among the attainments of sensorimotor intelligence.

Discussing Bloom's (1970) findings, Brown pointed out that the nearer the child is to the beginning of syntax, the more striking is the pivot look. This interpretation seems due to the observation that of the Stage I data to which Brown had access, the sample showing the pivot look (the second from a child named Eric) also showed the lowest utterance length, 1.10 (the first sample from Eric had too few multi-word utterances to make analysis possible).

Werner and Kaplan (1963) identified two types of early word combinations, one where the expression of the word combination could be likened to a single-word expression, since the individual elements overlap too extensively to form a true grammatical relationship, perhaps resembling functional relations, and the other representing word combinations where the two elements of the utterance emphasize different features of the presented event and approach a sentential relationship. Such word combinations seem to resemble what Bloom (1973) termed grammatical relations. Consistent with the observations of Brown (1973), Werner and Kaplan pointed out that the former types of utterances seem to appear before the latter.

What factors account for the seemingly different styles noted by Bloom and Ramer? Bloom (1975), using the term "strategy" rather than "style," remarked that these strategies represent inductions that children make about grammar. She went on to note that the particular strategy adopted by the child is presumably determined by his cognitive development. Elsewhere, she explained that

> there are different kinds of experience, and it appears to follow that their mental representations differ. It should not be surprising, therefore, that such representations are coded differently by the language as well. (1973, pp 122, 123)

It is unclear to what degree Bloom's account assumes that the child's concepts are integrally tied to particular linguistic codings. The actual distinction between concepts and their linguistic coding seems to have been made quite early in the study of children's language development. Stern and Stern (1907), for example, noted that the young child's speech seems to represent a linguistic mapping, using data derived from external sources, onto his "internal systems." However, the question of whether or not the concepts themselves can lead to different styles of linguistic coding has not been dealt with in any depth.

An alternative account is that functional relations (those frequently showing the pivot look) represent earlier points on a developmental continuum than grammatical relations. It was pointed out in Chapter 1 that those cognitive attainments resembling semantic notions typically coded by functional relations (e.g., nomination, recurrence) are seen, conceptually, by the third stage of sensorimotor intelligence, while those resembling semantic notions underlying grammatical relations (e.g., agent, experiencer) are not seen until the fifth stage (Brown, 1973).

Other accounts of cognitive development, although not designed to explore the cognitive distinctions between functional and grammatical relations, may support this position as well. Nelson (1974) noted that in acquiring knowledge about some object, the young child must initially detach the functional object concept from the totality of its relationships so that only the object-specific functions plus abstract markers (for other relations into which the object can enter) are retained in the functional core. It seems reasonable to expect that the earliest non-core relations to be marked would resemble semantic notions representing frequent functions such as disappearing (nonexistence), recurrence, and the like. For example, following Nelson's format, the concept BALL might be represented as

$$
\begin{bmatrix}
\text{1.} & \text{Functional core relationships: rolls, bounces . . .} \\
\text{2.} & \text{General non-core relationships: can be named, can disappear,} \\
& \text{can recur . . .} \\
\text{3.} & \text{Specific non-core relationships: set of locations, set of actions,} \\
& \text{set of agents . . .}
\end{bmatrix}
$$

In fact, it might be suggested that general relations resembling such notions as nomination and nonexistence give the child the occasion to express the linguistic equivalents of the core relationships themselves. Nelson suggested that

> core relationships will be expressed only if the function is apparently missing, for example, the child may protest the lack of Mommy's putting him to bed, or request that the ball be rolled to him. (p 282)

Such events seem to suggest such general relations as nonexistence (of an expected event) and the like. Thus, general non-core relationships expressed in language seem like Bloom's (1973) functional relations, while specific non-core relationships might be expressed via grammatical relations. If one accepts my added specifications to Nelson's account, it would seem that the general non-core relationships would appear earlier in speech than specific non-core relationships, given the greater number of

Table 2–1

Summary of Analysis of Group 1 and Group 2
Utterance Types in Ramer's (1974) Data

Child	Number of Samples with at Least Five Two-Word Utterance Types	Number of Sample Comparisons	Number of Comparisons	
			Showing Decrease of Group 1 Types from Preceding Sample	Showing Increase of Group 2 Types from Preceding Sample
Lisa	3	2	2	2
Marjorie	5	4	4	4
Emily	8	7	4	5
Danielle	3	2	2	1
Greg	6	5	4	4
David S	6	5	4	2
David N	8	7	4	4
Total	39	32	24	22

circumstances in which they may enter. Like functional relations, general non-core relationships seem suited for expression through word combinations with a pivot look.

If the two strategies represented in children's early word combinations during Stage I (functional relations and grammatical relations) relate to two points on a developmental continuum, should not the former be seen in greater proportion than the latter in early Stage I samples, with the proportion of the latter increasing over time? In order to test this hypothesis, I reexamined longitudinal data from children in the Ramer (1974) study. As a means of controlling for confounding variables, I examined only the spontaneous two-word utterances in each sample. Ramer provided a description of the linguistic and nonlinguistic context surrounding each utterance. These descriptions were sufficient to analyze the data according to those semantic notions typically reflected in functional relations such as nomination, nonexistence, recurrence, and notice (Group 1 utterances) and those usually reflected by grammatical relations such as agent + action, action + object, and agent + object (Group 2 utterances). To the latter I added possession, attribution, and location since the meaning of such semantic notions cannot be derived from the meanings of only one of the words of the combination. Presented in Table 2–1 is the summary of this analysis, in terms of the comparison among successive samples of the proportion of Group 1 and Group 2 utterance types.

Some of the samples contained only a small number of utterances, and thus a considerable amount of sampling error may be reflected in

Table 2–2
Summary of Analysis of Group 1 and Group 2 Utterance
Types in Braine's (1976) Data

Child	Proportion of Group 1 Utterance Types		Proportion of Group 2 Utterance Types	
	First Sample	Second Sample	First Sample	Second Sample
Kendall	.08	.06	.92	.94
Jonathan	.19	.05	.81	.95
David	.23	.18	.77	.82
Embla	.00	.09	1.00	.91

this table. If we allowed any proportional change in Group 1 or Group 2 utterance types away from the predicted direction that was no greater than 5 percent to simply represent random error, 28 out of 32 sample comparisons for both Group 1 and Group 2 utterance types would be in the predicted direction.

Thus, it would seem that two-word utterances over time might show a general trend toward those utterances reflecting semantic notions usually coded by grammatical relations and away from those reflecting semantic notions usually coded by functional relations. A still more rigorous test, however, would make use of the longitudinal data analyzed by Braine (1976). Not only did Braine conclude from his data that semantic notions did not appear in any particular order (a point questioned in Chapter 1), but the particular children examined by Braine produced utterances reflecting a number of later emerging semantic notions typically coded by grammatical relations. In fact, in the first samples obtained from the children examined by Braine, no less than 80 percent of each child's utterances reflected notions usually coded by grammatical relations.

Appearing in Table 2–2 are the proportions of utterances reflecting semantic notions typically coded by functional relations (Group 1 utterance types) and grammatical relations (Group 2 utterance types) for the first and second samples of the children examined by Braine.

As can be seen from this table, for three of the four children the proportion of Group 1 utterance types decreased from the first to the second sample with a corresponding increase in the proportion of Group 2 utterance types. With so few comparisons it is difficult to interpret this finding as strongly supporting the hypothesis that the two types represent two points on a developmental continuum. But the results were generally in this direction.

Ramer identified differences among children at the same general level of linguistic development during Stage I speech that related to speed of acquisition as well as the types of utterances used. Thus, it is important to discover if these particular differences can also be placed on a developmental continuum. We have already noted the possibility that verb + complement utterances may typically be acquired before subject + verb or subject + complement utterances. Ramer's slow developers began their syntactic careers expressing only the first of the three, while the rapid developers expressed all three constructions at the onset of syntax. A question logically follows: If verb + complement utterances in fact reflect an earlier notion, why are some children presumably at the same level of linguistic development showing evidence of more advanced semantic notions? Other findings from Ramer's work prompt the same question. The rapid developers, all of whom were several months younger than the slow developers at the final stages of observation (which was determined by linguistic development) produced utterances reflecting fewer types of semantic notions. Ramer explained this finding by suggesting that although the level of structural syntactic sophistication was consistent for all of the children by the final stage of observation, the younger age of the rapid developers may have provided them with less opportunity to acquire some of the semantic notions evidenced in the speech of the slow developers. In addition, Ramer's description of the slow developers' continued use of presyntactic forms suggests that the two styles may not be equated on the basis of underlying semantic development.

> They appear to allow the child to combine elements without having to deal with reference, word order constraints, and relational indicators. The presyntactic forms appear to be a way of easing into syntax. That is, the children were able to practice the combining of elements without having to deal with the substance of these combined elements. (1974, p 120)

Given Ramer's proposal of greater complexity of word order and relational indicators, we can also arrive at an alternate explanation for why greater use of indeterminate constructions was seen by the rapid developers. Such constructions (representing not-clearly-specified relations) may be examples of cases where the child's underlying semantic notions and superficial linguistic skills were not at the same level of development.

The conclusion that semantic notions and superficial features of language may at particular times lie at different points in development is a reasonable one. The child's linguistic system can be thought to be composed of a number of subsystems (e.g., semantic notion system, morphological system). While each subsystem can be expected to develop, the development of one subsystem need not necessarily closely match the development of another (Jones, 1970).

The present position that many of the differences in styles (or strategies) in early language development may be a reflection of two different points on a developmental continuum is not a claim that strategies have no place in linguistic development. Bloom, Lightbown, and Hood (1975), for example, noted that two of their four subjects (Eric and Peter) made much use of pronominal forms, while the other two (Kathryn and Gia) made use of nominal forms. In the use of pronominal forms, when expressing utterances reflecting notions such as action, location, and possession, it appeared that the nature in which the pronominal forms (e.g., "I," "it") combined with the other words resembled the same kind of functional relations noted during the expression of utterances reflecting nomination and recurrence. It is highly plausible that the use of pronominal forms rather than nominal forms represents a linguistic strategy, but one that pertains to more superficial features of language. Obviously, a child must learn to code many semantic notions in some linguistic form. But this is not a strategy related to underlying semantic development. For example, while Eric and Peter employed pronominal forms in functional relations reflecting semantic notions such as action and possession, they did so only after previously using utterances coded by functional relations that reflected earlier notions such as nomination and recurrence.

Nelson (1975) found that the children in her longitudinal study could be divided into two groups based on (among other things) the extent of their use of pronouns. While the two groups were found to differ significantly in the percentage with which they used nouns as well as pronouns at the early mean utterance length levels, they did not differ statistically in the relative proportion of the various semantic notions evidenced in their speech. One notion, agent, was associated with a difference between the groups that approached significance. These findings seem consistent with the view that differences in nominal or pronominal usage may be related to differences in mapping superficial linguistic forms onto underlying semantic notions. It must be pointed out that pronouns, unlike nouns, code certain features that have semantic as well as syntactic relevance (e.g., $\pm$ animate, $\pm$ plural, the case role in the utterance). However, these features do not appear to enter into distinctions among semantic notions that are not seen for nouns.

Bowerman (1976) has pointed out that it is not always possible to divorce semantic notions from lexical items that might be utilized to reflect them. For example, "more" seems to be one of the few available words (along with "another") that English-speaking children may have to reflect recurrence. This state of affairs may lead to a particular semantic notion being associated with a particular type of coding. In this case, recurrence would be associated with a lexically-based rule involving "more" in combination with another word. Since a notion such as action is not associated with one particular word, it may be coded in speech by a more general, categorical rule involving a word belonging to a category of words on the basis of its function in combination with another word.

It should be clear that in such instances it is not the type of combining rule that influences the underlying semantic notion. If anything, the influence is exercised in the other direction. The semantic notion assumes responsibility for what is expressed in the child's utterances. If it so happens that in a particular language a semantic notion is coded by a limited number of lexical items, it may be that the notion is ultimately expressed by a lexically-based combining rule. But, as of yet, I have seen no evidence that a child's tendency to use lexically-based rules (even when such rules are used as general strategies to code a number of different notions) dictates which semantic notions will be reflected in his speech. This would represent a bizarre case where linguistic form would determine content.

Two different strategies or styles can exist at the same general level of linguistic development. Further, closer inspection reveals that the two strategies may reflect differences in underlying semantic development. What, then, is the relationship between utterance length and the semantic notions underlying these utterances?

THE ROLE OF UTTERANCE LENGTH

With the increasing emphasis on the importance of meaning in early language development, it has been easy to slide into the assumption that with increasing development of cognitive structures and underlying semantic notions, linguistic complexity reflected in utterance length also increases. The child may also have to acquire rules for word order and other syntactic features, but this factor has been deemphasized because cognitive abilities have seemed much more important to the process of language development as a whole. Not only may cognitive development serve as the basis for language acquisition in the first place, but it also seems to be responsible for allowing the child to express increasing numbers of relationships observed in his nonlinguistic experience (Schlesinger, 1971a; Sinclair, 1971).

Some correspondence probably exists between utterances reflecting increasing semantic as well as cognitive development and increasing utterance length. For example, my analysis of the Wells (1974) data in

Chapter 1 suggested a general decrease in the proportion of operator + nominal utterances (reflecting, for example, nomination and recurrence) as utterance length increased, with a corresponding increase in the proportion of utterances reflecting notions such as possession, location, and agent. Yet this trend also occurs when utterances of the same length are analyzed over time, judging from my analysis of the Ramer (1974) and Braine (1976) two-word data in this chapter. The implication is that utterance length during Stage I is not as closely related to semantic and perhaps cognitive processes as has previously been assumed. Other investigators seem to be raising this possibility as well. For instance, in explaining how a child might produce an utterance expressing elements that would ordinarily exceed his usual sentence complexity limit, Brown (1973) suggested

> Very possibly sentences of this type represent the child's effort to say what he already knows how to conceive but has not yet learned how to say in a fully grammatical way. They may be evidence of cognitive development in advance of strictly linguistic development. (p 139)

One might also raise the question as to whether the development of surface features of language can proceed in advance of the development of underlying semantic notions, since the relation between the two does not appear to be exact. Certain children's use of empty forms, one of Ramer's (1974) categories of presyntactic forms, may aid in answering this question. Empty form usage was first noted by Bloom (1973) during observation of her daughter Allison's transition from single-words to syntax. At 16 months, Allison was observed to say *Dada widə/* when watching her father read a newspaper. Subsequently, she uttered *Mimi widə/* when watching her babysitter enter an elevator, and other utterances containing "widə" that varied in the situations in which they were used. With no identifiable consistent referent, Bloom concluded that "widə' apparently referred to anything and everything, and thus it 'meant' nothing" (p 34). Since "widə" appeared in a virtually fixed position, after other words in juxtaposition, it appeared that Allison's use of such utterances demonstrated her having learned something about relative position of words in general in sentence usage. This observation suggests not only that the development of surface features of language and under-lying semantic development may be separable, but that certain superficial syntactic processes may precede the expression of meaningful relations.

In a relatively recent paper, I discussed some findings from two children which may shed further light on this matter (Leonard, 1975a). One of these children, Phoebe, produced two-word utterances limited to nomination, such as *that's Fred/*. She was also observed to use sequences of single words such as *Mommy/washing/*, with variable word order. In contexts where Phoebe was describing some event, the empty form "gɔkɪŋ" was observed.

> (Larry showing Phoebe a picture of a man
> finding a penny)
> Larry: "Hey, what do you think is happening
> here?"   him gɔkɪŋ/
> Larry: "What's he doing?"   him gɔkɪŋ/

Such occurrences did not seem due simply to Phoebe's unfamiliarity with a particular word.

1. (Larry showing Phoebe a picture of a
   lighted fireplace)
   Larry: "What is happening in here?"   it gɔkɪŋ/
   Larry: "What is it doing?"   burning/
   Larry: "What's happening?"   it gɔkɪŋ/
2. (Larry displaying a picture of a woman
   washing her feet)
   Larry: "Tell me about this picture."   Mommy/washing/
                                                          her gɔkɪŋ/
   Larry: "What?"   Mommy gɔkɪŋ/

One might conclude that in describing essentially the same event, Phoebe could produce a sequence of related single word utterances (e.g., *Mommy/washing/*), a lexical item plus empty form utterance in a specific order (e.g., *Mommy gɔkɪŋ/*), but not a two-word utterance with specific word order (e.g., *Mommy washing/*). Phoebe did, however, produce other two-word utterances representing different construction types (e.g., *that's Fred/*). Utterances such as *Mommy/washing/* suggest that Phoebe possessed only a general awareness of the relational aspects of the events about which she spoke. Utterances such as *Mommy gɔkɪŋ/* and *that's Fred/* suggest that she could produce two-word utterances with specific word order.

But why weren't utterances such as *Mommy washing/* produced? It seems likely that she could form utterances such as *that's Fred/* because they represented functional relations. Lexical items such as "that" are inherently relational, and a child's development from nominative utterances such as *moon/* to *that a moon/* might represent little more than a purely syntactic phenomenon. The meaning of the relations between the combined words seems dependent simply upon the meaning of the individual words of the utterance. An utterance such as *Mommy washing/* might involve a more refined relation, such as agent + action. Such an utterance (coded by grammatical relations) would involve something more than knowledge of the meaning of each of the lexical items; Phoebe would need to understand the relational meaning that Mommy is the instigator of the washing, rather than, say, the recipient. Such an additional meaning component is not seen in the functional relations expressed by Phoebe.

Thus, Phoebe had reached a stage in her linguistic development where she could produce two-word utterances according to a word order rule. But she apparently had not attained a level of underlying semantic development where she could specify all of the relations codable by the linguistic rule. Therefore, we can conclude that the only features of linguistic development that might appear more advanced than the development of underlying semantic notions are quite superficial in nature.

In the same paper, I pointed out that one of Ramer's (1974) subjects, David S., showed similar usage with the empty form "ıdi." At a mean utterance length of 1.16 morphemes, David used no two-word utterances containing words denoting action, yet he produced *ıdi open/* when giving his mother an apple to be cut open. Even if this utterance was interpreted roughly as David wanting Mommy to open the apple (agent + action) or David wanting the apple to be made open (factitive + state or action + state), no two-word utterances of these types were seen. Other empty form utterances were seen in circumstances (with additional clues provided by the placement of the lexical item) that might be interpreted as action + object, location + object located, and agent + object. Again, nothing spoken by David indicated that he used these two-word utterance types.

A related issue has been pointed out by Nelson (1975). On the basis of the nature of their speech, the children in Nelson's study were divided into two groups, the referential and the expressive. The former used a substantial proportion of nouns, though such usage was seen predominantly in nonsentential contexts. On the other hand, the expressive group made considerable use of pronouns, thus showing less lexical specificity, according to Nelson. Unlike the children in the referential group, who may have been expressing "concept relations" in conjunction with object names, Nelson suggested that the children in the expressive group may have been expressing relations via relational words and general dummy terms that stand for any object or person, before having learned the specific lexical terms for the things that may enter into these relations. Thus, there seems to be some similarities between the utterances produced by the expressive group and empty form usage. Of course, this parallel can be drawn only up to a point. For example, it is doubtful that pronouns are as devoid of meaning as empty forms. Further, as was noted earlier in this chapter, the two groups of children were not different in terms of the semantic notions reflected in their speech. Rather, the speech of the two groups, according to Nelson, may have represented different points along a continuum of greater or lesser "lexical-syntactic" emphasis.

An alternative to the proposal that differences in Stage I utterances reflect different strategies of a semantic nature is the proposal that at any point in early semantic development, meaning may be assigned to the vocal act. The vocal act, as evidenced in the progression from vegetative noises to babbling (and perhaps even extending in a more limited sense to empty form usage) has also been developing, independent of meaning. That is, the child coding functional relations reflecting notions such as nomination may have had meaning assigned to the vocal act when he was at an earlier stage of semantic development, while the child coding primarily grammatical relations that reflect notions such as agent and possessor may have had meaning assigned at a later stage. Thus, while a child must proceed cognitively from, say, an object knowledge stage to an organizational stage, the child need not progress through a parallel sequence in the semantic notions actually reflected in his speech.

It is unclear to what degree the lack of correspondence between utterance length and semantic notions actually represents a lack of correspondence between development of superficial features of language and cognitive development. Clearly, a minimum level of cognitive development must be reached before a child can express meaningful relations through the vocal act. Further, it is unlikely that a child could express new semantic notions in his developing language that were not part of his attainments in cognitive development. The difficulty in answering this question seems to rest in the difficulty in determining the degree to which semantic development can operate independently of cognitive development. For some time we have had evidence of a different sort, that cognition and the vocal act may be, to a degree, separable.

One need look no further than Sinclair's (1969) well-known attempt to teach preoperational children the language of conservation and seriation; the results of which have lent considerable support for the Genevan view that cognition is the primary source of symbolic activity. Actually, the children could, with some difficulty, be taught the expressions ordinarily used to describe such cognitive processes. Since the children's cognitive development was not affected as a result of such exposure, it follows that language is not as capable of affecting cognition (at least early in the developmental process) as is cognition capable of affecting language. But we also know from the children's use of the expressions taught them that the vocal act can be altered independently of cognition.

Probably the major argument against attributing the lack of correspondence between utterance length and semantic notions to cognitive development is the fact that the semantic notions that appear to most resemble certain types of cognitive attainments in fact emerge at a later period than the cognitive attainments themselves. This seems to be true for all children. For example, both the children coding functional relations as well as those coding grammatical relations in Bloom's (1970) study were well beyond the cognitive attainment (of causality, an attainment of the fifth stage of sensorimotor intelligence when the child is between ages 12 and 18 months) that most resembled the most advanced of the semantic notions reflected in the speech of these children. Rather, then, it may be proper at this point to speak only in terms of the lack of correspondence that seems to exist between the child's development of more superficial features of language and his development of underlying semantic notions.

Thus, two children may differ in underlying semantic development but not in utterance length. Earlier in the two-word utterance period one child's utterances might reflect semantic notions such as agent or possessor, while the other child's early two-word utterances might be limited to those reflecting notions such as nomination and recurrence. Such a proposal requires that once a child acquires an earlier notion such as nomination it remains within his potential expressive repertoire, although in time it will be supplemented by more advanced notions. We would therefore expect to see a child producing utterances reflecting notions such as nomination, recurrence, and others frequently coded through functional relations during the same period when he is producing utterances (perhaps, but not necessarily, coded through grammatical relations) reflecting notions such as agent and possessor. This does not run counter to the data interpreted as reflecting different strategies, however. Bloom (1973) pointed out that the alternative strategies she proposed were not mutually exclusive; both seemed to be evident in varying extent in the speech of different children.

The lack of mutual exclusion can be explained by noting that once early semantic notions such as nomination and recurrence are acquired, they are maintained (through adulthood, in fact) because they serve a useful purpose. The same is true once later notions are acquired. At an early point in Stage I speech, notions such as nomination, nonexistence, recurrence, and notice will be evidenced, with notions such as location, attribution, possessor, and agent also possible but not obligatory. The converse during this early period would not seem to be true. As the child advances through Stage I speech, any substantial shift in the proportion of semantic notions reflected will be in the direction of less frequent appearance of notions such as nomination and nonexistence (but probably no complete elimination), with the more advanced notions being evidenced more frequently. A shift in the opposite direction would not be expected.

Dore (1973) has devoted some attention to a similar issue. He proposed that there are two principal lines of development that the child undergoes in acquiring language. One arises from the child's cognitive schemas dealing with the relations between objects and events in his environment. The other line arises from the child's orectic attitudes, that is, his affective attitudes toward people and objects, and conative intentions to obtain what he desires. The first line deals with the child's development of the relational notions underlying language, while the second line is concerned with developing grammatical attitudes such as the expression of some desire.

Dore has suggested that these lines reflect partly independent developmental processes such that a given child at a given time may have progressed considerably along one line of development while developing only a little along the other line. Dore proposed that the involvement of two partly independent processes could result in differences in the way children acquire language. Data obtained from two children seemed to support this proposal; one child seemed to produce utterances suggestive of certain underlying cognitive schemas while the other produced utterances notable in their illocutionary force.

Ramer (1975) has also noted these two lines of development in her longitudinal study of two children. She proposed, consistent with Vygotsky (1962), that prelinguistic development and the child's earliest attempts to communicate may have social-emotional origins, while the child's development of specific semantic notions relevant to language may derive from the emergence of representational abilities. At some point in time quite early in the child's linguistic development, these lines of development merge. In a more recent paper, Dore and Ramer have collaborated and further developed this general thinking (Dore, Franklin, Miller, and Ramer, 1976). One outcome of this effort was the proposal that the young child acquires syntagmas when the two lines of development merge; syntagmas are structural units that correlate sounds and prosodic patterns with meanings in the process of speaking. According to this view, the child's earliest multi-word utterances do not yet constitute evidence of the emergence of semantic (or syntactic) relations. Rather, they seem to represent the organization of conceptual schemas in terms of phonetic strings (McNeill, 1974).

These findings appear generally consistent with the proposal that at some varying point in development meaning may be assigned to the vocal act. However, I think that the work of both Dore and Ramer suggest the need to further specify those dimensions of development involved in this proposal. By "vocal act," I am referring to the child's early communicative functions (expressed in this case by vocal means) in the absence of semantic substance. These communicative functions, of course, may have their own cognitive underpinnings (Bates, Benigni, Bretherton, Camaioni, and Volterra, 1976). "Meaning," as used in this particular proposal, should be restricted to the semantic notions reflected in language independently of their illocutionary force. According to this proposal then, two children may differ in the point of development at which underlying notions (which have their own cognitive parallels) and the communicative function merge. In Chapter 3, I will discuss some characteristics that must be possessed by any Stage I grammar attempting to incorporate both communicative functions and semantic notions.

3
Developing a Grammar of Stage I Speech

In this chapter an approach to grammar writing is introduced that will be put to use in examining the emergence of semantic notions and their interaction with the linguistic code. First, however, some considerations central to the development of this approach need to be presented. These considerations and indeed the proposed approach itself have benefited from other investigators' semantic approaches to analysis. For the interested reader, a number of these approaches are reviewed in Appendix B.

RELATING ORDER OF EMERGENCE TO A GRAMMAR

It would seem useful to devise a means of writing grammars that takes into consideration the order of emerging semantic notions underlying Stage I speech (Jones, 1970). This would have the advantage of being able to justify the manner in which the child's grammar is organized on the basis not only of the relationships between the elements in the grammar, but on the similarities or differences in the origin of these elements as well. From the outset, such a grammar would have to provide for three basic divisions. One would include the earliest semantic notions that appear: nomination, nonexistence, recurrence, notice, rejection, and denial. Such notions are reflected in the first single-word utterances to appear according to the Greenfield, Smith, and Laufer (1972) data, and represent the early stage of intransitivity in Ingram's (1971) approach. The coding of these semantic notions at the two-word stage is generally responsible for the pivot look, and such notions are among those involved in Brown's (1973) operations of reference, Wells's (1974) operator + nominal, and Bloom's (1973) functional relations, all of which are seen early in the two-word stage. Further subdivision of these semantic notions might be possible if the data warranted it; unfortunately, varied methods of analysis and small samples in some cases have yielded only general findings. We are left with grouping semantic notions that, as in the case of nonexistence, rejection, and denial, emerge in no clear order.

A second division would include the semantic notions of action, agent, and object. Single-word utterances of this sort were observed by Greenfield, Smith, and Laufer (1972) to appear after utterances used in naming (nomination), demanding, and negating (nonexistence, denial, rejection). Single-word utterances of this type seem to be transitive in nature (Ingram, 1971). Since the notion of agent was observed later in the single-word stage than notions such as action and object (Greenfield, Smith, and Laufer, 1972), we could probably subdivide further, although parallels could probably not be drawn for cognitive development. This is because it is not clear that a cognitive sequence exists where only actions and objects are recognized but not agents of the actions. Instead, early actions that are verbalized are typically performed by the child and thus the inclusion of the agent in the utterance would be redundant. It would be difficult to imagine that the child at this level of development would be conceptually unaware of his role as an agent. At the two-word stage, the notions agent, action, and object are often coded as grammatical relations (Bloom, 1970). We have some evidence suggesting that object utterances appear before those involving agent (Bloom, 1970; Ramer, 1974) a condition similar to that of the single-word stage.

There is a third group of semantic notions underlying Stage I utterances. These include the notions possessor, attribution, and place. The order of their appearance relative to the notions within the second division is not conclusive. Consistent with this assumption is the finding of Greenfield, Smith, and Laufer (1972) that attribution, possessor, and place appeared before the semantic notion of agent, although after both action and object when the latter were related to the child's own activity. The available evidence from the two-word stage is often discussed in general terms, and in such cases these notions are presented as appearing slightly after notions like action and object. The Bloom, Lightbown, and Hood (1975) data tend to concur with this interpretation.

There may be an explanation for the finding that these semantic notions are the last of the common Stage I notions to emerge. Notions such as nomination, recurrence, and nonexistence can be viewed as relating to general non-core relations in the sense of Nelson's (1974) proposals, since they can involve a very large number of entities in the child's environment. They seem to represent the first relational information the child learns through his actions on objects in his environment; actions on objects that make them disappear and recur (Piaget, 1954). Bloom (1973) noted that the notions of existence (nomination), nonexistence, and recurrence seemed to be action-dependent during the single-word period. Such notions seem to represent examples of Sinclair's (1970) object knowledge stage and Ingram's (1971) period of intransitivity.

Subsequently, the child appears to encode relations between his specific actions and objects. Notions such as action, object, and agent seem to relate to this level of knowledge; the early point when the child discovers and makes use of the functions of objects (organizational stage), where he notes that objects can be acted upon (transitivity), etc. Elsewhere, I attempted to trace the course of this development from the child's initial global actions on objects to his eventual description of specific events around him that need not involve his own actions (Leonard, 1974). Apparently only after the child encodes such notions with the support of relevant action is he able to encode static relations among objects in which neither he himself nor his actions are necessarily relevant to the state represented in his message (Bloom, Lightbown, and Hood, 1975).

As can be recalled from the studies of Ramer (1974) and Bloom, Lightbown, and Hood (1975), other semantic notions have been seen toward the end of Stage I or even later. These include notions such as instrument, experiencer, time, and manner. They appear with low frequencies in Stage I and will not be discussed in detail here. It would appear that these semantic notions might in some cases serve as new additions to the existing categories (instrument, for example, might be a later developing extension of agent), while in others a new stage of semantic development might be represented.

While it appears that any grammar for Stage I speech that provides for an order of emergence is useful, it is important to clearly specify the nature of the elements thought to emerge in this particular order. Some of the elements proposed in other approaches are not clearly defined and one cannot determine in such instances whether the child's developing grammar is thought to represent linguistic or cognitive growth. It is probable, as seen in Chapter 1, that the order in which some of the elements emerge in a child's grammar might be related to his cognitive development. Nevertheless, there is little doubt that the child perceives, comprehends, and constructs many hypotheses about the relations between people, objects, and events in his world that are never reflected in his speech. It appears, then, that the underlying elements of a child's grammar must reflect aspects of cognition pertinent to language development.

REQUIREMENTS OF A STAGE I GRAMMAR

It seems clear that any grammar of Stage I speech must satisfy certain linguistic criteria. Several such criteria, as they pertain to child grammars, have been suggested by van der Geest (1974). First and foremost, a grammar should present a formal description of the rules underlying all utterances. Such rules should specify which utterances are permissable in the grammar and which are not. The rules should be finite in number, yet able to account for an infinte number of specific utterances.

Basic in the grammar should be a way to deal with universal features, features common to all languages. The grammar should also provide the means of accounting for features whose characteristics may vary from language to language, such as word order considerations. Linguistic operations representing alterations of the base structure (such as question inversion in English) should be included in the grammar. Finally, and importantly, the grammar must provide a way for semantic information to be represented.

In addition to linguistic criteria, it would seem that some general requirements of a Stage I grammar can also be suggested by investigators' findings regarding the nature of Stage I speech. One requirement has to do with what is included in the grammar. In Chapter 1, sufficient evidence was reviewed suggesting, in agreement with Bowerman (1973a), that

> children initially are not searching for the means provided by their language for expressing the relations between grammatical concepts like subject and predicate . . . but rather for the way to express the relations between a limited number of semantic concepts. (p 189)

Schaerlaekens (1973) has made two observations consistent with this view: (1) the child, at the two-word utterance period, never uses a combination of words where the only distinguishable relationship between them is syntactic (e.g., *car sing*) and (2) the child himself restricts the type and number of semantic relations between two words that are reflected in his utterances. Thus while utterances such as *throw dolly* may be produced, utterances such as *like dolly* may not be evidenced.

According to Brown's (1973) calculations, these semantic relations (or "semantic notions," the term I have used in this volume) number between 8 and 15. It appears, therefore, that a Stage I grammar should accommodate these notions.

Hierarchical organization in a grammar should be proposed only when the evidence suggests that such organization is in some way functional for the child, not because it is present in the adult grammar that the child will eventually acquire. On the other hand, it is essential that the grammar be capable of extending to more complex speech where justified and not be restricted to the types of relationships expressed during Stage I. Such relations as subject and predicate do have a reality at some point in linguistic development, even though early in Stage I the child may not be seeking the means of expressing such abstract relations, but rather expressing the interaction between such things as agents and actions and objects and their locations. It is true that some investigators have suggested that the salience of the latter notions continues for a longer period than a superficial examination of a child's usage might at first suggest. Schlesinger (1974) raised the possibility that when the child observes *baby see, Daddy need*, and other expressions reflecting experiencer + experience, following the same order rule as the previously learned agent + action constructions (e.g., *Daddy play*), he comes to regard the notion of experience as a kind of action, experiencer as a kind of agent, and so on. That is, one semantic notion is taken as a special instance of another.

It seems fair to say, however, that at some point, through linguistic experience, the child begins to recognize similarities in the way different notions are formally dealt with in his language, and gradually to reorganize his linguistic system according to the more abstract grammatical relationships that are functional in the language he is acquiring (Bowerman, 1973b). No doubt this is an ongoing process throughout the early stages of language development.

> At any point in time, some of the concepts which are functional in the child's competence may be primarily semantic and others primarily syntactic. If this is true, the optimal grammar for child language must be capable of operating with both semantic and syntactic concepts. It must also be flexible enough to represent shifts over time to new levels of abstraction, so that, for example, a sentence constituent which at one time might be represented as an "agent" would at a later time be represented as "sentence subject." (Bowerman, 1973a, p 227)

This view seems consistent with the possibility raised by Brown (1973) that the system of analysis adopted by Schlesinger (1971a) might reflect grammars at an early point in Stage I speech, with early grammars giving way to those more appropriate to Bloom's (1970) approach to grammar writing, based on Chomsky's (1965) transformational grammar.

Yet the means by which this transition can be reflected in a grammar is not readily apparent from previous investigations of child language. The semantic approaches proposed for accounting for the types of underlying semantic notions salient in Stage I speech have not had the formal representational capabilities for handling this task. The transformational grammar approach adopted by Bloom (1970) may have come the closest, although in keeping with the strengths of the semantic approaches constituents should probably be described in terms other than those describing abstract relations such as subject or predicate that are not justified by the child's usage. But this still would not solve other problems with the transformational grammar approach, where structural information such as the order of morphemes is contained in the deep structure, perhaps a debatable feature from the linguistic point of view (Lakoff, 1970), but particularly handicapping when one is trying to find a means of capturing the underlying semantic notions of early language usage independent of the manner in which they are coded syntactically.

Just as troublesome a feature of transformational grammar is the means of arriving at the meaning of an utterance. In transformational grammar, the semantic component operates on the (primarily syntactic) deep structure to produce a semantic interpretation. This process seems a bit backward in sequence, if taken as a model of a causal sequence by which utterances are generated by a young child. It would suggest that the child generates an utterance and then decides what meaning he wants to convey. A way out of these last two difficulties may be to adopt some of the proposals of generative semantics. The most useful features of generative semantics for this purpose are (1) generating an utterance commencing with a semantic interpretation, (2) a nonsyntactic, nonlexicalized deep structure representing universal notions, and (3) transformational rules responsible for both lexicalization and the generation of syntactic structure seen in the surface structure, with no fixed order of rule application. Finally, it appears that a proper Stage I grammar must include some means of representing the functions that the child's utterances serve. The incorporation of some of the applicable features of the speech act approach may help fill this void.

A PROPOSED APPROACH TO GRAMMAR WRITING

The following approach to grammar writing is designed to offer a systematic means of examining the underlying semantic notions of a child's linguistic system during Stage I speech. It attempts to capitalize on the strengths of other semantic approaches, presented in Appendix B, while solving some of the problems inherent in each.

An important point should be made about the nature of the Stage I grammar arising from this approach. Its source of data is the language usage of a number of children operating at a given stage of linguistic development. As such it does not purport to be a theory of the structure or function of language per se, or a description of the ideal speaker's intrinsic competence. Rather, it can best be described as a description of the child's knowledge of relational meaning that can be estimated from his linguistic performance at Stage I. As was mentioned in the Introduction, this description, like any other for child language, may represent a set of categorizations useful for analysis by investigators as much as it represents what is actually operative for the Stage I child. Hopefully, though, it will assist in illustrating some of the considerations facing any grammar of Stage I speech.

The Source of Meaning

In the proposed approach, semantic interpretation begins the sentence generation process, as in generative semantics. Specifically, the sources of meaning are those aspects of cognitive structure that the child might communicate. Quite obviously, this is similar to Schlesinger's (1971a; 1971b; 1974) *I* markers, with some qualifications. The *I* markers discussed by Schlesinger seem to serve as the underlying markers for the generation of individual utterances. The approach I am proposing is one designed to estimate the semantic notions reflected in the entire set of utterances the child might produce. The underlying semantic notions I am proposing should represent that for which there is some evidence in the child's speech. The underlying semantic notions are universal, unlexicalized, unordered, and otherwise nonsyntactic in nature. They represent the underlying semantic notions whose sequence of emergence and interaction with the learning of the linguistic code represent the focus of this volume.

It is important to point out that these notions reflect what the child may know about his world that he is capable of expressing through language. In essence, what is being examined is the child's knowledge of how to match an utterance to a nonlinguistic perception. The emphasis is not upon his knowledge of the internal structure of the words he may use to express this perception. Bowerman (1974c) noted that knowledge reflecting certain aspects of cognitive structure expressable through language should be distinguished from knowledge of semantic structure. Cognitive structure expressed through language is at the heart of this examination. For this reason the proposed underlying notions are unlexicalized and are not equipped with "n-place predicates" and other linguistic mechanisms seen in the underlying structure of generative semantics that seem designed to reflect knowledge of semantic structure per se, independent of the nonlinguistic perceptions made by the child.

As in other recent approaches, these underlying notions can be described in terms such as agent, possessor, and the like. Such terms may only imprecisely portray the child's underlying semantic notions, however. They may well be too broad (or too narrow) to do justice to the child's perceptions. They must be viewed as tentative, for if closer inspection reveals that the child's utterances reflect even finer, or simply different, relationships in his world, further modification will be necessary. I suspect that the notions we ascribe to the child are tainted by our view of language to almost the same degree as abstract relations such as subject and predicate are. None of the frequent semantic notions cited in the child language literature differ markedly from those suitable for the adult system. Fortunately, though, these notions are more specific than those proposed in syntactic terms and thus may lie closer to what the child may perceive in his world (Slobin, 1973).

Nevertheless, certain notions, notably action and experience, are not as specific as seen in some other approaches (Chafe, 1970; Cook, 1972). The reason for not proposing notions such as action-process benefactive, rests in the difficulty of testing the adequacy of such notions as descriptive categories of the child's speech at Stage I. An enormous number of utterances would have to be sampled before examples of such fine categories could be identified, even if they were operative for the child. Thus, I decided that the safest strategy would be to propose initially semantic notions that could subsequently be subdivided if evidence from the child's speech warranted it.

The method by which these notions are reflected in speech is substantially different from that proposed by Schlesinger (1971a). In the proposed approach, the semantic notions are realized in surface structure form through transformational rules of the generative semantics type. The specific rules proposed would have to be based on an analysis of the child's utterances, but for Stage I they must be considerably more simplified than those commonly described by generative semanticists such as Lakoff (1972). Most notable is a scarcity of derivational constraints that in the adult grammar prevent lexicalization until the permitting constituent structure is derived. The transformational rules in the proposed approach bypass any grammatical deep structure. They are responsible, with no fixed order of application, for the functions of lexicalization, the ordering of morphemes, and, where appropriate, the assignment of grammatical categories.

Since all ordering of elements in this approach is considered a function of transformational rules, each syntactic coding in surface structure must be associated with a rule. I will assume that such rules can be represented in a manner similar to the transformational rules used by Bloom (1970) to account for surface structure orders that differed from the order of elements she presumed to exist in the deep structure. It should be recalled that Bloom utilized the transformational grammar approach of Chomsky (1965). Such rules, for example, may be represented in the form

$$X_i + X_j \Rightarrow X_1 + X_2$$

where X_i and X_j are different and unordered elements. Similarly, lexicalization is handled by transformational rules in the proposed approach. For convenience, I will represent such rules in a straightforward manner, as seen in

$$\text{Agent} \Rightarrow boy$$

Such a rule can be viewed as an abbreviated representation of unlexicalized substructures over which lexical entries are superimposed.

In the proposed approach, the child's knowledge of the internal structure of words is also reflected by transformational rules. Though operating on underlying notions with no grammatical structure, the transformational rules in this approach should be viewed as generating the same features of surface structure as the rules of transformational grammar (Lakoff, 1972). As in the generative semantics approach, the transformational rules of the proposed approach perform more functions than those of transformational grammar and perhaps are equally subject to criticisms from linguists such as Jackendoff (1972) who suggest that such a conception of transformations is too unconstrained.

From the perspective of early language acquisition, at least, assigning a greater role to transformational rules may be a healthy thing; such rules seem to be the means by which a child's underlying notions are coded for surface structure realization, and it may be safer at this point in our knowledge to place such rules in a framework that permits one to test the possibility that they are learned. That is, the transformational rules might be viewed as reflecting what the child learns, from the language spoken around him, about the means by which his underlying perceptions can be coded linguistically. In this regard, the transformational rules of the proposed approach have some similarities with Schlesinger's (1971a) proposals. Unlike Schlesinger's position rules, though, the transformational rules responsible for the order of morphemes in this approach would not be based on the relations between morpheme pairs but rather on the relations among all of the underlying notions playing a role in the child's utterance. That is, in the proposed approach, the transformational rules responsible for an utterance such as *no eat cookie* would be based on the relations denial + action + object, not on the relations denial + action, denial + object, and action + object.

The Specifications in the Grammar

The grammar proposed here is designed to permit an examination of development throughout Stage I and, hopefully, will be amenable to further extension to account for later stages. The specifications in the grammar representing early achievements will be presented before those suggestive of later ones. As will be seen, the manner in which the elements of the grammar unfold differs considerably from approaches based on the adult grammar, where underlying structure always seems to be more complex than surface structure. It is certainly true that cognitive structure may be richer than what is revealed from the child's speech; certain concepts may not be expressed because they may not be important for communication, for example. The underlying notions of the proposed grammar represent linguistically significant aspects of cognitive structure, and it is important not to attribute such notions to a child unless there is confirmation from the child's speech. Three different types of evidence are used to categorize the semantic notions presented in the grammar: (1) differences in the point in time at which two otherwise similar semantic relationships are reflected in the child's utterances, (2) differences in the lexical or syntactic coding of utterances reflecting otherwise similar semantic relationships, and/or (3) consistent differences in the non-linguistic behaviors accompanying the use of utterances reflecting otherwise similar semantic relationships.

The first specification is for the utterance as a whole.

This representation is for the child's initial attempts at communication, ranging from the prelinguistic vocalizations associated with pointing, reaching, etc., to the initial single-word utterances usually used by the child. Like Dore (1973), I have adopted illocutionary force as an element of the utterance. The illocutionary force, like the modality proposed by Fillmore (1968) and Ingram (1971), acts on the sentence as a whole;

however, the illocutionary force will include here only such markers as declare and request, the first acquired and most general illocutionary acts (Bates, Camaioni, and Volterra, 1975; Carter, 1975b).

It should be pointed out that markers such as declare and request at this point in development represent performative intentions, to be distinguished from performative conventions. The latter are the conventional means by which these intentions might be communicated in the adult system (Bates, 1976). Even my use of "intentions" implies that the child possesses knowledge of the functions his vocalizations may serve. At the point in the child's development at which it is appropriate to represent his communication system in a grammar, this is reasonable enough. Nevertheless, it should be kept in mind that as early as four months of age, the child's vocalizations may serve various functions (Bruner, 1974).

Shortly, after declare and request, question enters into illocutionary force, although initially only in the form of intonation, Subsequently, question will also have an effect on the representation of other utterance elements, such as the expression of a nominative element through the use of "what," a place element through "where," and so on. The request marker is intended here to represent vocatives as well as the later developing imperatives. As will be seen later, request will be partly responsible for the realization of vocative utterances such as *Mommy!* or *Mommy, up.* Considering that Fillmore's (1968) modality constituent includes tense, mood, aspect, certain adverbs, as well as interrogation, it is not surprising that Brown (1973) finds this constituent unnecessary for Stage I speech. The illocutionary force that I am proposing, however, contains markers seen prior to and throughout Stage I speech.

The element designated simply refers to that which is specified in the child's utterance. Initially, of course, the child's prelinguistic vocalizations (e.g., Hildegard Leopold's *ah*) will be quite unspecific, since the illocutionary force serves the communicative function. This poses no dilemma, of course, because in the proposed account underlying elements are not lexicalized anyway. By single-word acquisition, designated begins to represent that which is named, not present, reappears, requested, noticed, acted upon, located, etc. It usually serves as the named entity toward which the child's activity or attention is directed. Prior to the child's acquisition of two-word utterances, designated can be viewed as the same as Dore's (1975) rudimentary referring expressions, since the relational meaning of the child's utterances are dependent upon the relation between the word and the context, not between words.

When the child initially acquires the use of two-word utterances, designated is subsumed under another element, proposition, which is represented in the following branching tree diagram. For convenience, the elements subsumed under illocutionary force, declare, request, and question, are not listed in this and subsequent representations, as further development centers around that of proposition.

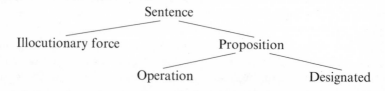

The element operation can generally be viewed as the same as Brown's (1973) operations of reference. It includes the specifications of operations most responsible for the pivot look. Since the available data do not permit a further division based on some clear sequence of acquisition, operation is subject to the rewrite rule

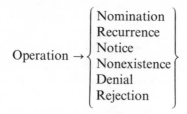

Thus, a two-word utterance such as *no ball*, assuming supporting non-linguistic evidence, could be represented as

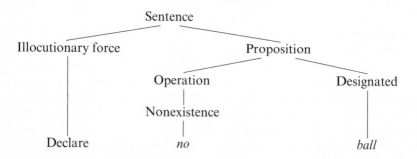

It is important to recall from Chapter 1 that no clear differences were noted in the order in which nonexistence, denial, and rejection emerged. Their treatment as distinct semantic notions, then, rests solely on their expression via different syntactic rules or lexical items. The most common lexical items reflecting nonexistence are "no" and "all gone." The most common items reflecting rejection are "no" and one requesting cessation such as "stop." If "no" was the only lexical item marking these semantic notions in a child's speech and if "no" always appeared in the same word position, these notions would have to be (and for a number of children probably should be) grouped together to reflect the more general notion, negation. This, in fact, was the tactic employed by Bloom, Lightbown, and Hood (1975).

The next types of notions reflected in Stage I speech include agent, action, and object. Though the latter two are usually evidenced first, enough exceptions to this finding have been noted to permit the possibility of introducing them into the grammar together. This is done by proposing a new element, ergative. The term "ergative" is used generally in the same vein as Lyons's (1969) use of the term—that which implies some sort of cause-and-effect relationship. The inclusion of ergative necessitates a higher order element to differentiate the general relations of operation from the specific ones within ergative. The term "function" seemed satisfactory. Thus, we have

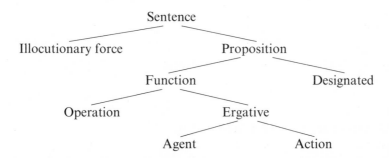

It can be noted that no new element is added to the designated node. An alternative tactic would have been to propose elements such as "specified" and "affected," subsumed under designated, to serve as targets toward which the events in operation or ergative, respectively, are directed. However, this was not proposed because the child during this period shows no differential linguistic treatment between objects specified (e.g., *no ball*, *there cookie*) and objects affected (e.g., *throw ball*, *eat cookie*); both specified and affected objects generally follow the word used to reflect function. The interpretation of "ball" in the utterance *throw ball* being an object affected by the activity rather than merely specified as being related to the activity (as "ball" is related to disappearance in *no ball*) may well be one made by speakers of the adult linguistic system rather than one made by the child. Thus, designated, during this period, is similar to Edwards's (1973) object; it is the "pivotal participant" around whose relation to function the whole system (thus far) operates.

In addition to including overt actions such as "eat" and "throw," action includes some early request forms such as "want" and "see." The lexical characteristics of such requests are suggestive of internal states, reflecting notions such as experience, which are later achievements. A close inspection of the contexts in which utterances like *want ball* and *see Heidi* are produced, however, reveals that they represent requests for some overt action such as giving a ball to the child or looking toward the family dog (Edwards, 1973).

The next semantic notions to emerge are those of place, possessor, and attribution. These notions are incorporated into the grammar by expanding designated.

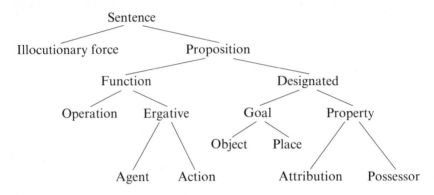

Object represents a notion of little added specificity to designated, still representing the object toward which the function is directed; however, such objects can at this period be differentiated from the location in which the function occurs. Such utterances as *put truck window* and *sweater chair* seem to exemplify this distinction. Since object refers to the object involved in either operation or ergative functions, there is no need to distinguish locative states from locative actions. In addition, it appears that the notions locative state and locative action emerge at approximately the same period and in no clear order (Bloom, Lightbown, and Hood, 1975; Braine, 1976). From a conceptual standpoint, the two seem highly related. Edwards (1973) discussed the cognitive requisites for locative notions, causality in groups of spatial displacements.

> In his solution of the "invisible displacements" problem the child was able to infer the operation and element which would complete a spatial group—that is, to infer that the experimenter must have removed the object while it was out of sight behind screen B or C and left it there. Note that the child is not inferring merely an object— location relation but an agent–action–object–place relation. (p. 422)

The new node, property, is necessary for representing possessor and attribution. The addition of property to designated enables further description of that contained in goal, allowing such utterances as *little car*, *Mommy sock*, *get big truck*, and *sit Adam chair*. As is evident from the representation in the grammar, the relationships among the semantic notions in property with those in goal are static. The two most frequent types of words reflecting attribution, for example, physical properties (e.g., "hot") and evaluations (e.g., "naughty"), are used by children during this period as relatively unchanging states (Edwards, 1973). Thus, the treatment of attributes as processes that effect some state on an object or person (and hence represented as a type of verb), as seen in the work of linguists such as Jacobs and Rosenbaum (1968), would not be justified on the basis of developmental evidence.

The utterances reflecting possessor can also be regarded as relatively permanent states rather than changes of ownership. Two types of possession best exemplifying this state are inalienable possessives (e.g., *Daddy thumb*) and what might be termed "privileged access" possessives such as *Mummy glasses*. Edwards (1973) suggests another type, transitory possession, which would be represented in utterances such as *gimme dolly*. I prefer to view this as I do other early requests (e.g., utterances containing "want") as a type of action, since it is by no means clear that the child at this period perceives his receiving a requested object as a change in ownership.

Thus, with the emergence of place, possessor, and attribution, the relations encoded by the child are no longer dependent upon the support of relevant action. This does not mean, however, that the development of semantic notions reflecting dynamic relations ceases. At the end of Stage I, the semantic notions instrument, experience, and experiencer are beginning to appear, although these notions are not seen this early in all children. These additions require some new higher order elements.

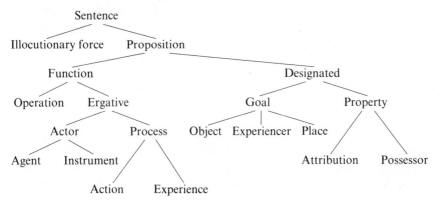

The above representation seems to portray utterances such as *sweep broom* and *Daddy hurt*. It is evident that these later appearing notions are not only acquired later than the notions subsumed under the same higher order elements (agent, action, object), but they make use of a number of lexical items not employed in the expression of their earlier acquired counterparts. In addition, experiencer and instrument are associated with a number of lexical items (e.g., "hurt," "cry," "sweep," "cut") represented in process but not usually associated with object or agent.

The particular order in which the grammar unfolds reflects the sequence in which semantic notions emerge for most Stage I children studied. As was seen in Chapter 2, however, certain children may differ from others in the semantic notions reflected in their speech at the same level of linguistic development as defined by mean utterance length. It can be assumed that the proposed order would be appropriate for all Stage I children if meaning were assigned to the vocal act at the same point in their semantic development.

COMPARISON WITH OTHER
STAGE I GRAMMARS

To show how the proposed approach to grammar writing compares with other approaches in representing Stage I speech, a Stage I grammar based on transformational grammar (Brown, 1973) and case grammar (Bowerman, 1973a) are compared with the proposed grammar, in Table 3–1. All three utilize data from the studies reviewed by Brown (1973).

The proposed grammar accounts for all of the utterances generated by the other two approaches. Not only does the proposed grammar contain and provide an organization for the semantic notions evidenced in children's Stage I speech, but it also possesses the capability of handling the combining of relations that result in utterances longer than two words in length. Brown (1973) has discussed two basic kinds of new combinations: (1) the "stringing together" of two or more two-term relations with deletion of redundant terms, and (2) the expansion of one term (generally a noun phrase term) in what is generally a two- or three-term relation. An example of the first type would be agent + action + object, where this combination seems to have been formed by combining agent + action and action + object with deletion of one of the redundant action terms. An example of the second type is action + possessor + object, where the object term is expanded by the inclusion of possessor. It should be noted that the proposed approach handles such operations without recourse to grammatical categories like noun phrase.

Table 3–1

Stage I Grammar Based on Transformational Grammar,
Case Grammar, and Proposed Grammar

	Transformational Grammar
Sentence	→ Nominal + Verb phrase
Verb phrase	→ $\begin{cases} \text{Predicate} \\ \text{Verb (Noun) (Noun phrase) (Locative)} \end{cases}$
Predicate	→ $\begin{cases} \text{Adjective} \\ \text{Noun phrase} \\ \text{Locative} \end{cases}$
Nominal	→ $\begin{cases} \text{Noun} \\ \text{Demonstrative} \end{cases}$
Locative	→ Noun phrase
Noun phrase	→ (Modifier) Noun
Modifier	→ $\begin{cases} \text{Modifier} \\ \text{Noun} \end{cases}$

	Case Grammar
Sentence	→ Modality + Proposition
Modality	→ $\begin{cases} \emptyset \\ \text{Question} \\ \text{Negation} \end{cases}$
Proposition	→ $\begin{cases} \text{Verb (Agentive) (Objective) (Locative)*} \\ \begin{cases} \text{Locative} \\ \text{Dative} \\ \text{Essive} \end{cases} \text{Objective} \end{cases}$

	Proposed Grammar
Sentence	→ Illocutionary force + Proposition
Illocutionary force	→ $\begin{cases} \text{Declare} \\ \text{Request} \\ \text{Question} \end{cases}$
Proposition	→ (Function Designated)
Function	→ (Operation Ergative)
Designated	→ (Goal Property)
Operation	→ $\begin{cases} \text{Nomination} \\ \text{Recurrence} \\ \text{Notice} \\ \text{Nonexistence} \\ \text{Denial} \\ \text{Rejection} \end{cases}$
Ergative	→ (Agent Action)
Goal	→ (Object Place)
Property	→ $\begin{cases} \text{Possessor} \\ \text{Attribution} \end{cases}$

* Limited to three elements

All three grammars of Table 3–1 are based on rules across a number of children at Stage I. Individual children may not show many of the utterances accounted for in the above grammars. Some examples of these exceptions will be discussed, along with how the proposed grammar would account for them.

Some children would not require a rule such as function → (operation|ergative) but rather one such as function → $\begin{Bmatrix} \text{operation} \\ \text{ergative} \end{Bmatrix}$. Utterances requiring the former involve semantic notions such as nomination with action (e.g., *this cleaning*). Similarly, goal → $\begin{Bmatrix} \text{object} \\ \text{place} \end{Bmatrix}$ might be seen rather than goal → (object|place), since utterances representing the latter (e.g., *put truck window*) are not always evidenced in Stage I speech.

In almost any sample acquired from a child, some utterances are obtained that seem almost designed to test the power of an approach to grammar writing. Some of these will be discussed, along with how the proposed grammar would attempt to account for them. They are presented as a means of providing a closer look at how the proposed approach might differ from other approaches. The representation of each utterance is based on the assumption that it occurred during the latter part of Stage I, in order to ensure some consistency in hierarchical organization.

The appearance of Wh words in a child's speech has been somewhat of a problem for some approaches to grammar writing, particularly case grammar. In some cases, illocutionary force plays an intergral role in the representation of such utterances. For example, in *what that?* the question marker in illocutionary force will in part dictate how designated is lexicalized.

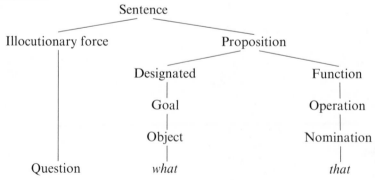

In other instances, though, representation can get quite sticky. For example, the utterance *where can?* can have two somewhat different meanings. If the child intends to learn the location of the can, the utterance would be represented as

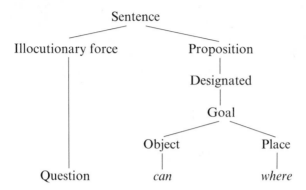

If, on the other hand, the utterance merely reflected the child's awareness that the can was gone, the following would be appropriate.

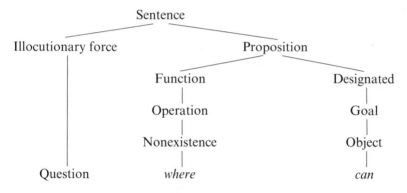

A point should be made about the representation of these Wh words. In utterances such as *what that*, the Wh word or "slot to be filled in" serves the function of object. In turn, "that" serves the function of nomination as in declarative utterances. In utterances such as *what that*, "that" has been taken to represent object by other investigators, perhaps because the child's gesture of pointing coincides in time with his production of "that" in the utterance. Yet an inspection of the child's production of declarative utterances reflecting nomination with object clearly specified (e.g., *that car*) will reveal that the pointing gesture again coincides with, or slightly precedes, "that." This situation does not hold true for utterances such as *where can*, however. Object is specified in such utterances, and Wh words such as "where" serve the function of locating or marking the absence of object.

Another difficulty noted by investigators is how to represent utterances that seem to contain violations of adult (grammatical) category rules. Since the underlying notions of the proposed grammar are not lexicalized, this seems to pose no problem. Two examples should suffice: *anymore pull* (interpreted as "They are not pulling anymore") and *more write* ("I am writing again"). These are represented as

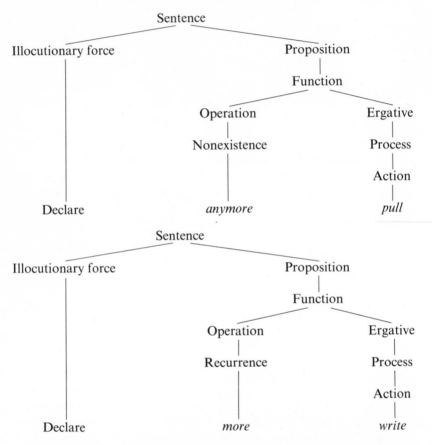

Similarly, the appearance of utterances that violate adult morpheme order is of no serious concern to the representation of underlying semantic notions in the proposed approach. These notions, it can be recalled, are unordered in this approach. Thus, the utterance *balloon throw* would be represented in the same manner as *throw balloon*, given supporting non-linguistic evidence.

This approach, then, permits the representation of underlying semantic notions throughout the two-word period, including the early

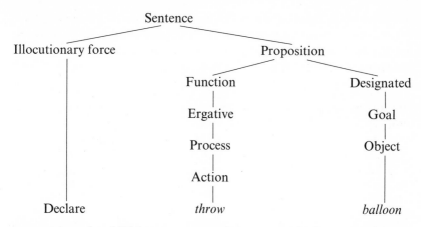

stages when the child has not yet settled on a particular syntactic construction to code a semantic notion (the "groping patterns" of Braine's 1976 account of Stage I speech).

There are some Stage I utterances that are represented somewhat differently by the proposed approach than the manner in which they are handled in other approaches. One type of utterance involves prolocatives such as "here" and "there." Bloom (1970) suggested that utterances such as *there phone* (spoken as the child points to a phone) carry a deictic function, that is, an orientational function. This function seems to be viewed as a type of locative by some investigators, but I think of this function as one that calls attention to (orients one toward) an object or person. In this sense, *there phone* (as well as *phone there* in the same context) could be viewed as reflecting the relationship

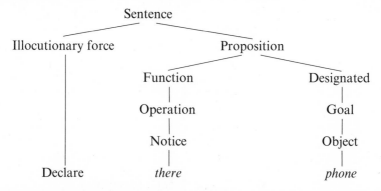

This has been suggested by others as well.

The words "here" and "there" and their equivalents in other languages can function as prolocatives, as forms replacing full locative phrases. In the case under consideration, however, it seems more sensible to think of them as a kind of demonstrative for, it is clear, the adult question *Where's X?* is not a true locative question at all. (Brown, 1973, p 189)

One of the sources for the way the proposed grammar would differ from others in the way it represents certain utterances no doubt stems from its nonsyntactic underlying structure. For instance, in transformational grammar the utterance *girl dress* would be represented quite differently depending upon whether it was interpreted as "girl's dress" or "girl has dress." The proposed grammar accounts for both interpretations in the same way.

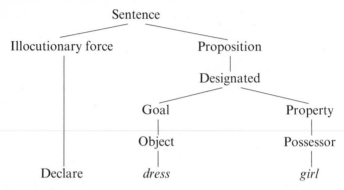

Another example may serve to illustrate this point. From the perspective of transformational grammar, *give Rina* might require the inclusion of indirect object into the grammar. In the proposed approach, it can be viewed as a type of goal.

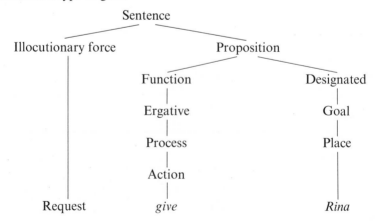

Such a representation is consistent with the proposals of Lyons (1967). The appropriateness of this representation, however, rests with whether or not animate recipients and inanimate locations appear in the child's language at different points in time or are expressed via different lexical items or syntactic structures that in the adult system distinguish semantic notions. If, in fact, the child does make a distinction himself, utterances such as *give Rina* would require the postulation of a semantic notion such as Edwards's (1973) beneficiary. Similarly, place would need to be subdivided if the child's usage showed a distinction between static and dynamic locatives with action, such as *put box* and *eat outside*, respectively.

Several types of utterances that have been slighted in other systems are represented in the proposed grammar. One of these can be exemplified by *hi shadow*. Sometimes such utterances are excluded from analysis because they serve as greetings and thus may be stereotypical, and at other times they are described through a pivot rule. This utterance is represented in the proposed grammar by treating "hi" as a type of notice.

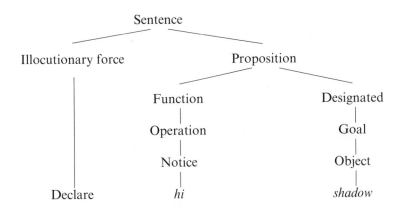

Another type of utterance previously treated lightly is represented in the proposed grammar—the class of utterances with vocative function. Vocatives represent instances in which an element representing an individual whose attention is being gained (frequently to serve some function for the child) appears in lexical form in surface structure. The appearance of the lexical item, in the form of a name, stems from an optional rule for notice operative only when the marker for illocutionary force is request. Thus, an utterance such as *Mother, look* would have the following representation.

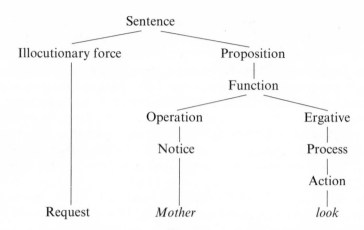

Unfortunately, there are some Stage I utterances reported in the literature that seem too complex to be accounted for in the proposed grammar. They are few in number and are not accounted for in other grammars either. Some reflect underlying notions of greater complexity than presented here (e.g., time, as in *leaves soon*), while others would seem to arise from a double-base source (e.g., conjunction, as in *umbrella boot*). Some of the latter can occasionally be interpreted differently and therefore accounted for, but this would be taking the risk of introducing inoperative features into a child's grammar.

In summary, the proposed approach to grammar writing accounts for the vast majority of utterance types seen in Stage I speech. It accounts for those handled adequately in other approaches, although in a few cases in a considerably different way, and accounts for a few not dealt with by other approaches. Very few types remain unaccounted for, although these are also not included in the grammars of other approaches.

LIMITATIONS ON UTTERANCE LENGTH

An inspection of the proposed approach to Stage I grammar writing reveals that the grammar allows for the generation of utterances that exceed the length of even the longest of the Stage I child's utterances. This problem is not limited to the proposed approach, of course, and it has represented one of the more perplexing methodological problems facing investigators of Stage I speech. Basically, the problem is how to justify why elements important in the underlying structure, and in fact some appearing in some utterances, do not appear in other ones. For example, Stage I children have been observed to use verbs in subject + verb and verb + object utterances, but will also be observed to use utterances such as subject + object which should, but do not, contain verbs. One means by which this occurrence is accounted for is by postulating a reduction transformation (Bloom, 1970). This transformation deletes a major element of a three-word utterance. In dealing with somewhat similar findings within the framework of transformational grammar, Bowerman (1973a) proposed a verb deletion transformation. Her contention was that the verb (not modifiers, adverbs, and the like) is the only essential element of the underlying structure whose absence in surface structure must somehow be accounted for.

Although these transformations seem to handle the problem, they are, I believe, products of the transformational grammar approach to grammar writing adopted by these investigators. However, using such an approach based on adult grammar presents other problems. If deletion rules are used to account for the limited nature of Stage I speech, they must be eliminated as children's utterances get longer. That is, the net effect of the deletion rule proposal is to suggest that a more complex stage, involving the application of deletion rules, occurs before a simple stage where no such rules are functional (Braine, 1971; Brown, 1973; Schaerlaekens, 1973).

The deletion rule proposal has been criticized on empirical grounds as well. Braine (1974) tested this proposal by comparing the length of the verb phrases in children's utterances that included subjects with those that did not. The deletion rule proposal would predict that verb phrases with subjects would be shorter than those without, since the addition of the subject in surface structure would require the deletion of some element in the verb phrase because of the length constraint. In fact, the verb phrases with subjects proved to be as long as those without. Apparently the main effect of the inclusion of manifest subjects in the children's utterances was an increase in their utterance length. The deletion rule proposal was clearly not supported.

I think a more suitable way to deal with the problem of the surface absence of underlying elements stems from another proposal by Bowerman (1973a). She suggested optionality of elements with a ceiling on the number realized in the surface structure. A few modifications are probably in order, however. It has always surprised me that investigators have been willing to postulate special rules that permit the child to delete elements from his underlying grammar in the face of the obvious evidence that no adult ever produces utterances of the length allowed for by adult grammars. This problem is typically explained away as due to performance limitations on the speaker. Few would quarrel with such an explanation. Instead of proposing some sort of deletion rule, many of the underlying elements available for surface structure realization could be viewed as optional to the speaker whose performance limits restrict full realization of elements.

I presume that this sort of optionality is not proposed for Stage I speech because some of the underlying elements not realized in the surface structure are viewed as obligatory. But isn't this an artifact of the approach to grammar writing selected? For example, an element such as verb is a required underlying element for transformational grammar with its grammatical deep structure. In the proposed approach, the underlying semantic notions are not viewed as standing in any kind of grammatical relationship to each other nor are they yet represented by morphemes. They are merely those aspects of cognitive structure the child is capable of communicating. Therefore, no *a priori* reasons exist for deeming a given element obligatory. Instead, the factors concerning which elements are realized in the surface structure in any given speaking situation are probably due to which features in the child's surroundings are most salient for communication, given his performance limitations.

It can be seen, therefore, that my preference for the "optionality of elements with a ceiling" account is qualified by the interpretation that the ceiling is dictated by performance rather than competence limitations. Viewing limitations in performance terms seems much more satisfactory when one considers that, in fact, children occasionally produce utterances longer than would be justified by a grammar containing some form of reduction transformation. The infrequent occurrence of such utterances prompted some investigators to write grammars that do not permit their entry. Such a decision is tantamount to treating these utterances as some form of accident as some clearly ill-formed utterance that does not conform to the general rules of the grammar. The difference between the two, however, is that the longer utterances will increase in frequency over time while the ill-formed utterances will not—an occurrence more consistent with a performance conception.

Braine (1974) has proposed a possible way to compute expected frequencies for utterances beyond a given length. There are some drawbacks to this method, however, as Braine himself points out. The one that I find most limiting is the assumption that the probability that two rules will be applied to the same utterance is the product of their independent probabilities of application in the child's language usage. For example, the probability of utterances of the rule subject + verb + object would be the probability of noun phrase + verb phrase multiplied by verb + noun phrase. The troublesome aspect about this is that there is little basis to assume that the child who produces an utterance such as *boy eat cookie* is performing a psychological operation equivalent to combining two rules. The psychological basis for subject + verb + object may well be based on investigators' enchantment with the two-word period of language development. The risks of this assumption are considerable, however, as it might lead to the postulation of quite faulty operations used to explain the child's acquisition process. An example of this is seen in Schlesinger's (1971a) use of combinations of relations based on word pairs to account for the more complex constructions used by the child.

THE REPRESENTATION OF SINGLE-WORD UTTERANCES

Earlier in this chapter it was noted that the proposed approach to grammar writing allows for the representation of elements in an order of emergence. One level of development included in such a representation is the single-word utterance period. The appropriateness of including single-word utterances in a Stage I grammar is a topic worthy of some discussion.

For years, investigators of child language have recognized that children's single-word utterances represent more than mere labels of entities (Preyer, 1888; Sully, 1895; Guillaume, 1925). Lewis (1951) summarizes this view quite well by noting that

> when the child first uses and responds to adult words referentially, he is referring not so much to an object—a thing within the situation—as to the situation as a whole. (p 159)

Although early investigators seemed to be aware of the holistic meanings of children's single-word utterances, the linguistic framework within which they were working did not permit a close analysis of such utterances. In particular, the distinction between a word's referential meaning and its relational meaning often became blurred (Greenfield, Smith, and Laufer, 1972). Bloch (1921) seemed to be one such investigator. Rightfully perceiving that his daughter's utterances such as *atet* ("tête" is "head"), said when she hurt her head, were not instances of naming, Bloch interpreted such utterances as evidence of the child possessing a shifting set of referential meanings for words, compared to that of the adult. Bloch did not appear to interpret the varied circumstances in which a word was used as due to its potential relational meanings.

De Laguna (1927) viewed children's single-word utterances from a grammatical perspective. She pointed out that such utterances are able to function as complete rudimentary sentences because they are produced in particular contexts and the sentence parts that are missing can be supplied by the situation. In her view, a single-word utterance serves as a predicate, a comment made by the child on the situation in which he finds himself. The accompanying nonlinguistic context represents the topic of the comment. Taken together the single-word utterance in context was thought to amount to a full sentence.

The position of de Laguna served as one of the bases of McNeill's (1970) view that children possess a concept of a sentence as a set of grammatical relations before they acquire the ability to express these relations. Ingram (1971) also seemed to view single-word utterances as sentences although he preferred representing such sentences in a deep structure that resembles Fillmore's (1968) case grammar. One of the justifications Ingram used for representing the child's single-word utterances as sentences is the gestures accompanying his utterances, which can be seen as expansions of the meanings of the words themselves.

Leopold (1949) also stressed the point that children's single-word utterances represent statements about an entire event, not simply the names of particular entities that are only incidentally involved in some event. However, he seemed to stop short of saying that such utterances represent sentences in the structural sense. According to Leopold, during the single-word period the child shows a disregard for the parts of speech in adult grammar. He uses what in the adult grammar may be a noun, adjective, or verb to express an idea and in so doing views the word used as a general carrier of meaning without any relation to sentence structure. Although operating within their own system of analysis, Werner and Kaplan (1963) seemed to arrive at similar conclusions. They recognized that precursors to identifying predications (e.g., nomination) and predications of action (e.g., agent, action, and object) could be observed during the single-word period. They were careful to note, however, that single-word utterances, particularly early in linguistic development, may refer to "total happenings" and not to "precisely delimited components such as action per se or thing per se . . ." (p 137). More recently, Greenfield, Smith, and Laufer (1972) have taken the view that while single-word utterances do not express different parts of speech of the adult grammar, such an utterance nevertheless may serve as a precise component of a proposition that, when examined in terms of its relationship with the accompanying nonlinguistic context, may express the equivalent to a sentence.

Despite the attention investigators have given to the single-word period, most formal approaches to Stage I grammar writing seem to be designed to account for the two- and three-word utterances observed. Very few single-word utterances are represented in the grammars. The work of Greenfield, Smith, and Laufer (1972) seems to be the only notable exception. One of the main reasons for the exclusion of single-word utterances in most approaches has been that, being only single words, they provide little information regarding the specific linguistic role they are playing. The only single-word utterances that are included in Stage I grammars, if any are included at all, are those occurring at a point when the child also uses utterances of greater length whose structure is more readily identifiable.

> For instance, Adam once said *ball* and then *hit ball*, and that suggests that the first utterance was an object . . . once multi-word utterances begin to occur and the ordering of words gives evidence of relational semantic intentions it seems reasonable to extend the method of "rich interpretation" to single-word utterances that occur. (Brown, 1973, p 206)

Before such single-word utterances could be incorporated into a Stage I grammar, some specific requirements had to be met. Braine (1971) suggested what some of these requirements might be by listing a set of conditions necessary for a single-word utterance to be considered part of a replacement sequence. A replacement sequence is a set of utterances such that

> (a) the utterances of the set occur during a fairly short time period during which there is no detectable change in the eliciting situation (i.e., nothing happens in the environment to indicate that utterances are not equivalent in meaning), and (b) the longer utterances of the sequence contain the lexical morphemes of the shorter utterances. (p 16)

Unfortunately, the reluctance to deal with single-word utterances *before* syntax has emerged leaves a rather discontinuous picture of early linguistic development. The exclusion of the single-word stage results in the impression that relational meaning has its birth when the child starts putting two words together. This is unfortunate for the study of the emergence of semantic notions, particularly as this emergence may relate to the child's cognitive development. Since the bulk of evidence suggests the child's cognitive development is continuous, there is little reason to permit discontinuity in the study of the semantic notions underlying the child's developing linguistic usage.

In the proposed approach to grammar writing, of course, the underlying notions do not share any grammatical relationship with one another. This allows greater freedom in the manner in which the meaning of the child's utterances can be determined. A method similar to the one used by Dore (1975) to determine the underlying meaning of single-word utterances might be quite suitable. Dore assumed that the underlying meaning of an utterance need not rest solely with the relations of underlying linguistic elements, but may also be represented in the relation between a linguistic element and a nonlinguistic, situational element. For example, in a transformational grammar approach, the meaning of *juice*, spoken by a child as he is whining and trying to reach a glass of juice, would depend upon whether or not the child's previous utterances (e.g., *want juice*) justified postulating the existence of an underlying structure permitting the interpretation that *juice* was an object. For Dore, the whining and attempt to reach for the juice would serve as a means of classifying *juice* as a rudimentary referring expression, or in the terminology of the proposed approach, *juice* would be represented by the underlying notion, designated. Since the notions in the proposed approach possess no inherent structural characteristics, such an utterance can represent the child's intention with respect to a notion without having a propositional structure (Dore, 1975). The cognitive distinction between single- and multi-word utterances made by Morehead and Morehead (1974) need not be violated since the very means by which the meaning of single-words are interpreted, through their relationship with nonlinguistic situations, is action-dependent.

The continuity provided in the proposed approach permits an inspection of how general underlying elements at the single-word stage, such as designated, become less action-dependent and begin to take on greater specificity by forming relationships with other, new elements. One hypothesis to test in this regard is the "lexical insertion" hypothesis of Braine (1974). According to this hypothesis, the child lacking command of elementary syntactic rules for precisely expressing certain relationships, attempts to express such a relationship by seizing on some salient feature of the relationship for which he has a word readily available.

> Looking at the matter formally, one might define holophrastic lexical insertion as the insertion of a word into a higher node of the rule system than that into which it would normally be inserted in the adult language . . . . As the rule system is progressively mastered, holophrastic lexical insertion becomes restricted to increasingly lower nodes in the rules. That is to say, the type of lexical insertion found in one-word utterances does not disappear with the advent of combinations; it merely becomes restricted more and more in its locus of appearance. (Braine, 1974, p 455)

According to the lexical insertion hypothesis, then, the child's use of a single-word utterance might be taken to represent an entire event. While this manner of representing such utterances in a grammar seems to constitute a new proposal, this general view of the nature of the child's single-word utterances is not. For example, Jones (1970) has noted that what the child attempts to convey by an utterance such as *Daddy* may be considerably more versatile than that conveyed by the use of the word "Daddy" in an utterance produced by an adult.

The lexical insertion hypothesis appears to be quite consistent with the proposed approach to grammar writing. As applied to the proposed approach, the use of "lexical" as a descriptive term for Braine's insertion hypothesis may seem misleading, since the deep structure I propose is unlexicalized as well as nonsyntactic in nature. But it does possess hierarchical organization. At the single-word stage, the child's grammar might be organized quite simply as

At this stage of development, designated lacks the specificity of the underlying semantic notions of subsequent periods of Stage I speech. In Braine's terms, a child's single-word utterances might be assigned to a higher node, designated, until he acquires the rules to express relationships in a more precise manner. In the proposed grammar, of course, underlying nodes are represented only when there is justification for them in the child's speech. But since designated at the single-word stage serves only a general function it can be viewed as analogous to a higher node. Evidence of this can be seen when one examines what happens to designated early in the two-word period.

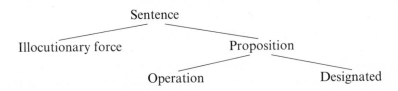

In this later period, designated is represented as a lower node.

It is not clear to me that the downward direction of insertion with continued development is due strictly to a change in the specificity that a lexical item may acquire. Rather, it may be a result of the greater specificity with which a semantic relationship may be expressed. For example, during the single-word period, designated represents the named entity toward which the child's activity or attention is directed. During the early two-word period, the underlying semantic notions subsumed under proposition are represented by operation + designated. Operation, of course, is rewritten as one of several semantic notions.

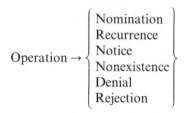

$$\text{Operation} \rightarrow \begin{cases} \text{Nomination} \\ \text{Recurrence} \\ \text{Notice} \\ \text{Nonexistence} \\ \text{Denial} \\ \text{Rejection} \end{cases}$$

But designated shows little change from this preceding period. The specificity during the two-word stage arises primarily because the activity or type of attention that the child directs toward designated is specified more precisely. That is, the relationship between designated and the event becomes more precise.

I see little reason to rewrite designated in a manner that distinguishes an element representing an entity named from an element representing an entity that recurs, or the like. Evidence from the manner in which notions such as nomination and recurrence are coded in the child's two-word utterances simply do not warrant such distinctions within designated. Since these notions seem to be acquired during the same period, the only justification for rewriting operation as several different notions is that these are associated with consistent lexical (e.g., "that" versus "more"), coding (e.g., first versus second word position), or contextual (e.g., pointing versus reaching) differences that may serve to distinguish semantic notions in the adult system. Even this condition is not met for designated; in the adult system, the underlying element reflected in "car" in utterances such as *that car* as opposed to the one reflected in "cookie" in an utterance such as *more cookie* is quite unclear. A similar argument was raised in defending why the initial appearance of utterances such as *throw ball*, usually represented by action + object is represented as action + designated in the proposed approach to grammar writing. The child during this period shows no differential treatment between objects specified and objects affected by actions and the close proximity in time between the emergence of these two types warrants the cautious manner in which I represent them. This issue is concerned only with whether the downward direction of the insertion hypothesis is related to greater specificity in a single element, such as designated, or in the relationship in which an element might be involved. Whichever proves to be the case, Braine might be correct in proposing the insertion process itself.

It should be pointed out that the above manner of characterizing single-word utterances allows for continuity between the single- and multi-word utterance periods. However, the element designated during the single-word period may not offer the kind of semantic specificity required to explore issues such as those presented in Chapters 1 and 2, pertaining to the emergence of specific semantic notions and their interaction with the linguistic code used to express them. The proposed approach to grammar writing has seemingly done its part; what is needed is a means of determining whether or not under certain conditions single-word utterances may be credited with the semantic specificity seen in multi-word utterances. Such a search for the proper conditions is considered in the next chapter, where the treatment of single-word utterance data is discussed.

4
Description of the Study

This chapter is a description of an investigation that was conducted with the aim of further examining the emergence of semantic notions and their interaction with the linguistic code. The data are not sufficiently extensive to yield conclusive results; rather they serve to both clarify and raise issues central to the study of relational meanings during Stage I speech. In Chapter 3, an approach to grammar writing that might better reflect the semantic notions underlying Stage I speech was suggested. The approach also provided a look at the sequence in which these notions are acquired. However, a number of other provisions also need to be made. If the notions underlying the child's early language usage are to be examined in terms of an order of emergence that may be related to the child's cognitive development, the origins of these notions also will require close examination. An inspection of single-word usage therefore would be most useful. With the inclusion of single-word data comes the difficulty of reliably capturing the underlying elements of single-word utterances. I have used videotape recordings in the hope of providing more valid data.

This investigation also attempts to examine the interaction between underlying semantic notions and the learning of the linguistic code used to express these notions. The resolution of this issue should provide greater insight into the degree to which linguistic development, as measured by utterance length and the use of grammatical morphemes, relates to underlying semantic notions. To make an adequate assessment of this interaction, a reasonable amount of control over the child's linguistic and nonlinguistic experience must be achieved. In this investigation, an attempt is made to provide some control through an experimental design nested within the general sampling format adopted.

DESIGN AND DATA COLLECTION

Acquiring the Language Samples

Eight children served as the source of this study's longitudinal data. The children, four males and four females, were all from middle class homes. Language samples were obtained through home visits beginning after the children acquired single-word usage. Three of the children had not yet produced any two-word utterances by the first visit; however, two others had already reached a mean utterance length of 1.26 morphemes. Each child's usage was subsequently sampled through visits averaging approximately eight weeks apart, until the child's language usage reached at least a mean of 2.30 morphemes in length. It was felt that the language span sampled more than adequately encompassed Stage I speech as it has been defined in the literature (Brown, Cazden, and Bellugi, 1969; Bowerman, 1973a; Brown, 1973). Additional identifying information is presented in Table 4–1. For each child, the samples are numbered consecutively with Roman numerals. The numbering of the samples is individual, so samples from different children that are designated by "I," for example, do not represent samples taken at the same point in linguistic development. The span of the data collection period is presented for each child in Table 4–2, in a format permitting a closer inspection of the representation of samples at each period of mean utterance length.

As can be seen from Table 4–2, a number of different levels of linguistic development, defined in terms of mean utterance length, were represented in the study. The apparently unsystematic rate at which each child progressed through the various levels of Stage I may in part be an artifact of variations in the time span between home visits. However, it may also reflect the sporadic rate of development that has previously been noted in child language (Brown, 1973).

The data of interest were the spontaneous utterances produced by the child during the home visits. The data were videotaped, using a portable AKAI VT-100 videotape recorder and VC-100 camera. To allow the child to become less leery of the recording equipment, the actual recording did not begin until the child's utterances and nonlinguistic activity no longer centered on either inspecting, or in a few cases, avoiding the equipment. Although the equipment was quite compact, the

Table 4–1

A Description of Subjects and Samples Utilized in the Study

Child	Sex	Age	Sample	Number of Spontaneous Utterances	Mean Utterance Length
Leslie	F	22;0	I	74	1.26
		23;1	II	128	1.65
		24;3	III	143	2.48
Alec	M	18;0	I	31	1.00
		19;3	II	69	1.44
		22;2	III	225	1.88
		24;0	IV	94	2.54
Kristen	F	15;1	I	27	1.06
		16;3	II	16	1.20
		23;0	III	31	1.27
		25;2	IV	43	1.44
		26;3	V	56	1.78
		27;3	VI	118	1.77
		29;2	VII	110	2.45
Lynn	F	22;2	I	23	1.26
		23;2	II	23	1.58
		25;1	III	46	1.85
		26;3	IV	115	2.38
Colin	M	19;0	I	11	1.00
		20;1	II	32	1.04
		24;1	III	25	1.04
		26;2	IV	73	1.34
		28;3	V	69	1.23
		30;1	VI	123	1.45
		32;0	VII	142	1.91
		33;3	VIII	137	2.32
Morton	M	22;0	I	18	1.12
		24;1	II	70	1.78
		25;3	III	139	1.79
		27;2	IV	167	2.56
Jennings	M	19;1	I	22	1.00
		24;1	II	37	1.60
		26;2	III	80	2.42
		28;0	IV	185	2.52
Greer	F	17;2	I	18	1.05
		22;0	II	61	1.90
		23;0	III	81	1.62
		24;2	IV	133	2.51

Table 4–2
The Span of Data Collection in the Longitudinal Study

Mean Utterance Length in Morphemes

Child	1.0	1.1	1.2	1.3	1.4	1.5	1.6	1.7	1.8	1.9	2.0	2.1	2.2	2.3	2.4	2.5	2.6	2.7
Leslie																		
Alec																		
Greer																		
Jennings																		
Kristen																		
Lynn																		
Morton																		
Colin																		

child could always see it and, perhaps quite naturally, some of the data do include utterances and actions directed toward the equipment.

During the sampling, I transcribed the child's utterances and made notations concerning the nonlinguistic contexts in which they occurred. Utterances and/or contexts were sometimes missed and these were filled in subsequently through a study of the videotape for that sample. Live transcriptions made the simultaneous video recording somewhat of a problem. Frequently I was accompanied by a research assistant who handled the video recordings. However, there were samples where I not only transcribed the child's utterances, but had the responsibility of glancing at the monitor and turning the camera (usually on a tripod in these circumstances) in order to get the child and the objects with which he was playing into the picture. Though the use of videotapes provided information that enabled me to gain information considerably more rich in detail than studies employing audio tapes, the amateur camera work (usually mine) did have its cost. Occasionally one sees in a few of the tapes close-up shots of blank walls or vacated chairs, taken while the child performed in classic fashion in some other spot in the room.

The child was always allowed the same free access to the areas of the house he was allowed to enter under ordinary circumstances. The video recording equipment was portable; however, recording was generally limited to two or three adjacent rooms. The video recorder was generally situated in the room in which the child was said to have spent most of his time. From this point, the camera could be moved to doorways in order to record the child's activities in an adjacent room. Most frequently the recorder was in the living room or den, although the kitchen was the site of some activity that could usually be recorded by moving the camera to a doorway. When the child entered a room that would require the video recorder as well as the camera to be moved, recording ceased until the child reentered a room that was more accessible to recording. Fortunately, such excursions on the part of the child were short-lived.

No doubt my presence affected the child's general behavior as well. Although the child was usually at ease with my presence by the time the video recording commenced during each visit, I was the target of a considerable number of the child's verbal and nonverbal antics that seemed to be designed for entertainment purposes. With the exceptions noted below, I did not usually request verbal responses from the child, but I often responded to his requests and questions. It would be a mistake to view me as a passive observer. My research assistant and I were frequently the only persons in the child's presence during recording. The mother was sometimes present, and her presence was more frequent during the first one or two home visits. More utterances directed at the mother may therefore have been represented in the data in the earlier samples.

An Experimental Inquiry

An experimental procedure was employed within the sampling format in order to gain greater insight into the contribution of experience to the semantic notions reflected in the child's speech. Four toys whose names the children did not know, according to parental reports and observational evidence, were introduced during each of the sampling periods. The four toys were (1) an animal composed of unidentifiable, detachable body parts with a giraffe head but short neck; (2) a camel with wheels for feet and masking tape around its midsection; (3) a pink cash register; and (4) a spinner from a board game. The names given these four toys were "zoo animal," "camel," "cash register," and "spinner," respectively. These four names will be referred to as the experimental words.

Whenever I discussed one of the toys in the child's presence, the corresponding experimental word was expressed in one of eight manners.

1. In subject position reflecting the object named, hereafter termed nomination for convenience (e.g., *A camel is what that is*)
2. In predicate position reflecting nomination (e.g., *That's a camel*)
3. In subject position reflecting instrument (e.g., *The camel's gonna get you*)
4. In predicate position reflecting instrument (e.g., *You're gonna get eaten by the camel*)
5. In subject position reflecting object (e.g., *The camel is getting hit*)
6. In predicate position reflecting object (e.g., *I'm gonna kick the camel*)
7. In subject position reflecting the object located, hereafter termed place for convenience (e.g., *The camel is under the table*)
8. In predicate position reflecting place (e.g., *Under the table is the camel*)

The four semantic notions represented one from each of the three distinguishable groups involved in the proposed sequence of acquisition (in order: nomination, object, place) and a fourth, which is usually acquired after Stage I (instrument). The utterances reflecting these notions always accompanied an activity with one of the toys that represented the nonlinguistic equivalent to that utterance. For example, if I said *That's a camel*, I was pointing to it, if the utterance was *The camel is getting hit*, I was knocking the camel over.

Table 4–3
The Experimental Words for Each Child and Experimental Condition

Child	Nomination		Instrument		Object		Place	
	Subject	Predicate	Subject	Predicate	Subject	Predicate	Subject	Predicate
Leslie		zoo animal	camel			cash register	spinner	
Alec		camel	zoo animal			spinner	cash register	
Kristen		spinner	cash register			zoo animal	camel	
Lynn		cash register	spinner			camel	zoo animal	
Colin	zoo animal			cash register	camel			spinner
Morton	camel			spinner	zoo animal			cash register
Jennings	spinner			zoo animal	cash register			camel
Greer	cash register			camel	spinner			zoo animal

Each child was exposed to all four words; one of the four semantic notion conditions per word. Four of the children were exposed to the words in the subject position condition and four were exposed to them in the predicate position condition. In order to reduce specific word effects, the sentence position and semantic notion condition in which a word appeared was different for each of the eight children, enabling each word to be presented in each of the eight sentence position/semantic notion permutations. All of the toys were exposed to the child at the same time and throughout the experimental segment all toys were equally available to the child. The order in which I expressed the utterances with the different sentence positions and semantic notions (along with presentation of accompanying activity) was random. My utterances were declarative in nature; no requirement was made that the child should respond. In some instances, however, some utterance or behavior on the part of the child prompted me to probe further by asking a direct question, but these were not frequent. My utterances were arranged to permit each experimental word to be exposed to the child three times during each visit. There were some deviations, due primarily to my repeating an utterance when doubtful that the child had heard it. The experimental condition to which each child was randomly assigned can be seen in Table 4–3.

ANALYSIS OF THE SAMPLES

I viewed the videotapes on the same day of each home visit, filling in any spontaneous utterances or nonlinguistic contextual descriptions that I missed in the live situation. The audio quality of the videotape recordings was not always high and unfortunately some of the utterances missed in the live situation were condemned to columns marked "unintelligible" after viewing the videotapes. Unquestionably some of these were not words, particularly during the single-word stage when much jargon was noted during live observation. It was those unintelligible utterances containing a recognizable word or two that proved most frustrating; particularly since these utterances, paired with nonlinguistic events, contained enough information to suggest an interpretation that, due to the presence of unintelligible elements, was not safe to report.

For reliability purposes, another transcriber was present during several home visits, in addition to the research assistant handling the camerawork. This individual made independent transcriptions. Substantial agreement between the two transcriptions was seen. Reliability was assessed by agreement on both the utterances transcribed and on "unintelligible" utterances; 84 percent of utterance transcriptions were identical. Another 8 percent differed in some detail, usually the perceived presence versus absence of /ə/, although occasionally the difference was on a major morpheme of the utterance, and 3 percent of my transcriptions had been deemed unintelligible by the other transcriber. The final 5 percent of my transcriptions had not been noted by the other transcriber; the utterances missed were heard but were contained in streams of speech produced too rapidly in succession for the other, less experienced, transcriber. The vast majority of utterances that I deemed unintelligible were classified in the same manner by the other transcriber (92 percent), 2 percent of my "unintelligible" entries were transcribed as a particular identifiable utterance by the other transcriber, and 6 percent of the utterances that I regarded as unintelligible were not present in the other transcriber's notes. All of my utterance transcriptions that were deemed unintelligible or were transcribed differently by the other transcriber were deleted from the data. Those utterances simply missed by the other transcriber were included.

All of the videotapes were viewed by a research assistant in my absence. In a few of the earlier tapes she was joined by another individual. The purpose of this viewing was to add a further check to my transcriptions and to fill in imitative utterances (although not examined in the present study), along with the contexts in which they were produced. This viewing activity could not be properly regarded as yielding further reliability data, since my transcriptions and notations of nonlinguistic contexts were made available to the research assistant. Due to the audio quality and less-than-expert camerawork, certain observations made in the live situation were unavailable to the research assistant viewing the video recordings. Instead, I could hope only for a further, rough check on the accuracy of my transcriptions. At the time of her viewing, the research assistant was unfamiliar with the hypotheses of the study and the approach to grammar writing to be employed on the data. Any of my transcriptions that were transcribed differently or classified as unintelligible by the research assistant were deleted from the data.

In order to be fairly confident that the data reflected semantic notions operative for the child, spontaneous utterances were used as the data for this study. The criterion for judging an utterance as spontaneous was any utterance that was neither imitative (repeating all or part of a model utterance) nor restricted in form because of its serving as a response to a direct question. After deleting utterances whose transcriptions were not agreed upon by all concerned in the transcribing and viewing processes, as well as deleting all nonspontaneous utterances, the final number of utterances for each sample was considerably reduced (see Table 4–1). For each sample, a grammar was written following the approach proposed in the previous chapter. It is important to point out that the construction of these grammars did not utilize utterances containing any of the experimental words. I deviated from Bloom (1970) and others in what I regarded as suitable for inclusion in the grammar. Provided that it related to some available nonlinguistic context and was not highly stereotypical, virtually every spontaneous utterance represented in the data was a candidate for inclusion in the grammar. Since factors such as productivity of word combining rules and the like are not relevant to the manner in which semantic notions are represented in the proposed grammar, apparent deviations from syntactic rules in the adult grammar did not have to be excluded as "exceptions" to some rule.

THE TREATMENT OF SINGLE-WORD DATA

In Chapter 3 a representation of the single-word period was included in the proposed approach to grammar writing in order to provide the continuity necessary for any characterization of the child's language development. It was not clear at that time, however, whether this representation would provide the semantic specificity necessary to include single-word utterances in the exploration of the issues central to this volume. In this section I conclude that the desired degree of specificity is not obtainable, through no fault of the proposed approach to grammar writing, and that single-word utterances must be excluded from the data under consideration. This decision warrants a thorough discussion, since in some specific circumstances it might be thought that single-word utterances do offer sufficient semantic specificity for their inclusion in this study. While these circumstances make it more feasible to include single-word utterance data, a careful inspection will render them insufficiently analyzable, given the current state of our sampling methodology.

Bloom (1973), among others, has noted instances where the child, instead of producing a word representing the entity toward which the child's attention or action is directed, produces a word representing the type of attention or action itself (e.g., Allison Bloom's use of *more* when pointing to a second shoe). In many instances, the child may also produce the word for the entity in these or similar circumstances (e.g., Allison's use of *shoe* when pointing to the first shoe). It is not clear how utterances such as *more* are to be represented. In these special circumstances it is worthwhile to consider the appropriateness of crediting the child with a notion such as recurrence. Brown (1973) seems to be proposing something quite similar in suggesting that in circumstances where the child alternates

Table 4–4
The Grammars for the Three Samples with Mean Utterance
Lengths of 1.00 Morphemes if Children were Credited with
Notions in Addition to Designated

	Alec I	Colin I	Jennings I
Sentence	Illocutionary force + Proposition	Illocutionary force + Proposition	Illocutionary force + Proposition
Illocutionary force	{ Declare / Request }	Declare	{ Declare / Request }
Proposition	{ Designated / Ergative }	{ Designated / Operation }	{ Designated / Operation }
Operation		Nomination	{ Nomination / Notice }
Ergative	Action		

between the name of a present object (e.g., *hat*) and the name of its possessor (e.g., *Daddy*) one might credit the child with the semantic notion of possession. If appropriate, this type of representation would be most useful since it might enable certain single-word utterances to be included as data in the present study.

I observed these types of utterances in my own data. Two examples are

1. (Jennings [I] holds up a toy train car to Larry, then
    puts it down)   this/
2. (Jennings holds up the toy train car again)   car/
1. (Alec [I], in a highchair, takes a green bean from his
    plate and puts it in his mouth)   eat/eat/
2. (Alec, still in the highchair, chews on some green
    beans and looks at Larry)   beans/

In these instances the words for the entities serving as designated were produced in circumstances highly similar to the ones in which the children produced the words for the type of attention or action directed toward the entities. How are utterances such as *this* and *eat* to be represented? One possibility is to credit the child with notions such as nomination and action, respectively. If this solution were adopted, the grammars for the three samples whose mean utterance lengths were 1.00 morphemes would look like those presented in Table 4–4.

It should be pointed out, of course, that the grammars in this table assume that a word reflecting designated alternated with one taken to reflect action, nomination, or notice in similar circumstances. If this were not the case, one would be even less certain that utterances such as *eat* or *this* referred to a specific aspect of a situation rather than to the situation as an undifferentiated whole. Greenfield, Smith, and Laufer (1972) are the only investigators of which I am aware who would be willing to accept such words as reflecting specific notions without evidence of alternating words referring to some other aspect of the situation.

Even with this qualification, the grammars in Table 4–4 do not rest well with me. One important reason is that although none of the children produced any two-word utterances, an underlying representation of their speech that attempts to portray the distinctions made between notions such as nomination and designated would allow for such utterances. For example, an underlying representation for the first samples from both Colin and Jennings would be

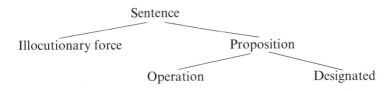

Such a representation should represent a flow chart of options that are possible within these children's semantic system. Yet a price is paid when an attempt is made to represent a distinction between operation and designated. For example, although Colin produced "that" and "TV" only in single-words, the above representation would permit *that TV*, which, of course, was not produced. Similarly, this representation would permit the utterance *this car* for Jennings, even though he only produced these words singly.

No doubt other investigators would agree that the above grammars credit the child with too much. I am not sure that they would do so for the same reason, however. The skepticism that some investigators have shown in representing such single-word utterances in their grammars often appears to rest in their approach to grammar writing. One good example is Bloom (1973) who at least in part adopted the transformational grammar approach in her work. The interpretation of an utterance in the transformational grammar approach rests in the relationship among the elements in the utterance. These elements are linguistically specified in that they have grammatical structure. Thus, in order to be interpreted, the utterance must contain at least two elements in some grammatical relation-ship in the underlying structure. Since each element is necessarily depen-dent on another before a grammatical deep structure can be postulated, it is perhaps understandable that two-word evidence is necessary before a transformational grammar will open its doors to single-word utterances.

Since Bloom operated within the transformational grammar approach that postulates the existence of a deep structure with certain obligatory elements representing the basic sentence structure, she could have tried to account for single-word utterances by proposing some form of reduction transformation that would delete all but one obligatory element from surface structure realization. She did not do this for the single-word period, fortunately, and this decision enabled her to avoid the messy issue of justifying how a child at the single-word stage can possess a rule, albeit a rule for deletion of elements, that a later stage of language development does not possess.

This decision also suggests that Bloom may have some questions about some of the assumptions behind transformational grammar, however. Most notable in this regard is her reluctance to grant any kind of grammatical status to single-word utterances. This contrasts with the more radical viewpoint of McNeill (1970). He contended that virtually every new acquisition during language development, including the child's single-word utterances, depends on prior knowledge of the basic aspects of sentence structure. This position gets one into the difficulty of having to defend an aspect of linguistic competence on the basis of no supporting evidence in the way of linguistic performance.

In other respects, the influence of the transformational grammar approach on Bloom's thinking is notable. The best example of this influence can be seen in her view of syntax, that utterances can only be given sentence status when they possess syntactic structure. This, of course, is why she stresses the point that single-word utterances are not sentences. To her, syntactic structure during Stage I speech is the use of word order to code semantic relationships between words. Word order alone is not a sufficient condition to credit the child with syntactic structure. As can be recalled from Chapter 2, Allison Bloom produced utterances with "widə" that clearly conformed to an ordering rule. Since "widə" shared no particular relationship with the words with which it was combined, utterances such as *Mimi widə* and the like were not considered syntactic. It might also be mentioned that evidence from the child's utterances that indicate that the child is aware of certain relationships among aspects of the situation may not always meet Bloom's criterion for sentences. Allison was observed to produce successive single-word utterances that were clearly identifying different related aspects of a situation. Since the relationships the child seems to recognize in these circumstances are not coded according to a word order rule, however, Bloom does not regard these utterances as sentences.

She seems to have a good point in not viewing such successive single-word utterances as sentences. In Chapter 1 it was pointed out that the distinctions between the single-word and two-word utterance periods may rest in the child's ability at the latter period to mentally represent a complete action scheme, rather than being able to represent only one successive aspect of the scheme at a time. Nevertheless, Bloom's requirement for sentencehood has some drawbacks. Her criterion that an utterance must involve the use of word order to code a semantic relationship blurs the distinction between underlying semantic notions and the way these notions are coded in the child's utterances. The lack of this distinction can be seen quite well in her frequent reference to "semantic-syntactic relations." It is difficult to see how a requirement for sentencehood involving word order rules as well as semantic relationships between words can handle the early period of two-word utterances during which Braine (1976) noted groping patterns. These patterns, it may be recalled from Chapter 3, represented instances in which the two words in the utterance share a relationship, but word order rules are not yet acquired; hence, Andrew was observed producing utterances such as *all gone juice* as well as *airplane all gone*. Since Bloom does not seem to recognize the existence of semantic relationships without the presence of syntactic structure, such utterances are probably beyond the analysis potential of the transformational grammar approach she adopted.

Since the underlying nature of the proposed grammar is not in the form of a deep structure with ordered elements, it can accommodate such groping patterns. In addition, since it contains no obligatory elements in the deep structure, it does not have to rely on any type of reduction rules in order to represent single-word utterances. Instead, the underlying nature assigned to single-word utterances need only be based on information available from the utterances themselves and the contexts in which they are produced. In most single-word utterances the word used represents the entity toward which the child's attention or action is directed. Such utterances are represented in designated in the proposed grammar. It is true that other utterances, such as *this* or *eat*, represent something other than the entity. Generally, they represent the type of attention or action directed toward the entity. In Table 4–4 grammars were presented that handled these occurrences not only by rules that allowed notions in addition to designated to be represented (e.g., nomination, action), but also that contained a deep structure richer than any single-word utterance produced. While this kind of treatment of the single-word data is possible with the proposed approach to grammar writing, I think such grammars would be incorrect for the following reasons.

In Chapter 3 it was pointed out that the proposed approach, as other approaches, allows for a grammar that permits the generation of utterances that exceed the length of even the longest of the Stage I child's utterances. In the proposed approach to grammar writing, this was justified by proposing optionality of elements with a ceiling on the number of elements realized in the surface structure; a ceiling dictated by performance rather than competence limitations. The underlying notions of the proposed approach are those elements of cognitive structure that the child is capable of communicating. They do not stand in any kind of grammatical relationship to each other, nor are they yet represented by morphemes. The particular elements that are realized in surface structure are dictated by the features in the child's immediate situation that are most useful to communicate, given his performance limitations.

Ordinarily, the proposed approach would account for single-word utterances that vary from the name of an entity (e.g., *shoe*) to the name of the type of attention (e.g., *more*) or action (e.g., *get*) directed toward it, with this same performance limitation explanation. For example, given an underlying system that includes both action and designated in Alec's first sample (see Table 4–4), Alec, whose speech was limited to single-word utterances, may have produced a word reflecting the notion that best communicated his message in that particular circumstance. The problem with this account does not rest with the performance limitation explanation itself. Rather, the difficulty is in determining whether or not evidence such as Alec's use of *eat* and *beans* in similar circumstances can serve as justification for proposing that his grammar should contain action as well as designated in the first place. This seems like a question of competence rather than performance, but perhaps it can best be portrayed as a problem in analyzing children's speech that is limited to single-word utterances.

I would have chosen to account for the speech of Alec, Jennings, and Colin at 1.00 morphemes by the grammars in Table 4–4 if I could have been more confident that action, for instance, was reflected in Alec's use of *eat* or that nomination was reflected in Jennings use of *this*. Instead, such utterances may have pertained to the situation as a whole. Thus, my reluctance to credit the child with notions such as action or nomination at 1.00 morphemes is not so much based on evidence suggesting that these notions are improper for the child's grammar, but rather on my own uncertainty as to how to interpret such utterances. Given that I had uncertainties even with videotape data that provided a close inspection of the situations in which the child produced his utterances, it should be evident that investigating the semantic notions reflected in speech during the single-word period is a difficult task.

My choice to view utterances such as *eat* as well as *beans* as utterances that pertained to the situation as a whole rather than different semantic notions, is of course consistent with Braine's (1974) lexical insertion hypothesis. It is true that Alec, Jennings, and Colin had alternate words to use in the same circumstances. When Jennings held up the toy train car, on one occasion he produced *this* and on another occasion he produced *car*. But I do not think that this is inconsistent with the lexical insertion hypothesis. Braine's position is that the child, unable to express a precise relationship, seizes on some feature of the relationship for which he has a word available. I see no reason why a child might not have more than one word available. Admittedly, this leaves open the possible interpretation that the child's use of different words in the same situations demonstrates his seizing on different aspects of the relationships he understands and choosing the word best reflecting each. One could argue that his ability to distinguish these different aspects amounts to the same thing as having more than one semantic notion in his underlying representation; this interpretation may well prove to be the case. At this point, however, I have chosen the more cautious interpretation that the child at this point may have several words available to him that may pertain to whole situations. However, their potential role in reflecting a specific aspect of that situation (e.g., action) that can be differentiated from another (e.g., agent) may not yet be clear to him. For example, Alec's use of *eat* and *beans* may have represented a synonymy in that situation. Both utterances may have referred to the entire event of eating beans rather than to the eating and the beans, respectively.

The single-word period is represented in the proposed approach to grammar writing according to the organization

However, if utterances such as *eat* and *beans* or *this* and *car* represent optional lexicalizations arising from the same node, it is clear that this node should represent something broader than designated as it was described in Chapter 3, where it represented that which is named, is not present, is acted upon etc., but not the naming, the disappearing, or the actions themselves. Designated was essentially defined as the specification of an entity; it seems preferable at this point to define designated as the specification of an entire event. Subsequently, and when the data warrant it, designated does represent the specification of an entity that is named, acted upon, and so on. This is the state of affairs during the two-word period, when the child's utterances (e.g., *more car*, *push car*) reveal that the child can represent the entity separately from the attention or action directed toward it. To put this in Braine's terms, with the appearance of two-word utterances, lower nodes in the hierarchy are reflected in the child's speech.

The major drawback to accepting the lexical insertion solution to this problem is that it is a difficult one to challenge empirically. Since the confidence one can place in interpreting that single-word utterances reflect specific semantic notions is not high, the hypothesis that such utterances reflect a node representing the whole situation the child is attending to is a reasonable one. Unfortunately, though, as long as the child's single-word utterances are words that are used in the adult system, it is difficult to challenge the hypothesis that the child's subsequent use of the word in multi-word utterances, when the semantic role played by the word is much clearer, represents a shift of the word to a lower node. I did think of one way in which the lexical insertion hypothesis could be tested; unfortunately, it relied on an assumption about the words a child might use to represent a whole situation (and thus a higher node), that may not be correct. My (quite risky) line of thinking is explained below.

The assumption was made that if the lexical insertion solution is the most appropriate way of handling alternating single-word utterances in the same or similar circumstances, the child intending to communicate about the situation as a whole rather than specific aspects of it may sometimes select available words that are inappropriate for incorporation into subsequent multi-word utterances to refer to a particular aspect of an event, such as action or nomination. On the other hand, if the use of alternating single-word utterances reflects different aspects of an event from the start, then such words should be readily incorporated in subsequent multi-word utterances that reflect these relationships. This assumption is a particularly daring one, so I attempted to gain additional information pertaining to it. First, I examined the subsequent use of words that, during the single-word period, were words potentially reflecting notions such as nomination and action (e.g., *eat*) that alternated with words reflecting designated (e.g. *beans*). I also examined the subsequent use of words potentially reflecting such notions that did not alternate with other words in similar or identical circumstances during the single-word period. For example, upon finishing his beans, Alec produced the utterance *more* (three times) but he never used the utterance *beans* in a circumstance where he wanted more beans.

In an effort to examine the possible relationship between the words used during the single-word period and those subsequently used in multi-word utterances, then, I inspected the samples from Alec, Jennings, and Colin. Since samples were obtained from each of these children when their mean utterance length was 1.00 morphemes, I could compare their

Table 4–5
Examples of Words Used in Single-Word and
Multi-Word Utterances

Child	Used Alternately with Designated	Multi-Word Example	Not Used Alternately with Designated	Multi-Word Example
Alec	eat	I eat the rabbit	come on	
			uh oh	
			bye bye	bye bye hat
			more	
Jennings	this	what's this?	hi	
			no	no Jennings name
	here	here that one		
Colin	that	that Colin	uh oh	

use of words during this sample with those of subsequent samples when the use of multi-word utterances was acquired.

A summary of the results are provided in Table 4–5, where I have provided examples of subsequent multi-word utterances containing a word potentially reflecting a semantic notion during the single-word period.

From this table, it can be seen that of the four words ("eat," "this," "here," and "that") used during the single-word period that alternated with a word reflecting designated, each was subsequently used in a multi-word utterance. In addition, the words were used in the multi-word utterances in a manner seemingly reflecting the same semantic notions (action, nomination, notice, and nomination, respectively) potentially reflected in the prior single-word use of these words. (See Chapter 3 for my treatment of words such as "this" and "that" in questions such as *what that?*) This finding, given the assumption I made, would ordinarily argue against the lexical insertion solution and for the type of grammars seen in Table 4–4.

An inspection of the single-word utterances in Table 4–5 that did not alternate with words reflecting designated, however, suggests that the lexical insertion solution should not be abandoned. Of these words, three of them ("uh oh," "hi," and the command word "come on") need not be expected to be used in subsequent multi-word utterances, since they may appear as single-word utterances in adult usage as well. But the others, "bye bye" (as it was used by Alec, to mean "take away"), "more," and "no" would be suitable words to use in subsequent multi-word utterances. In fact, two of these three words were used in subsequent multi-word utterances and, as far as I could determine, seemed to reflect the same semantic notions potentially reflected by the prior single-word utterances. Thus, if the finding that "eat," "this," "here," and "that" occurred in subsequent multi-word utterances was taken as support that during the single-word period their use did in fact reflect semantic notions such as action, notice, and nomination, then the finding that "bye bye" and "no" occurred in subsequent multi-word utterances would have to be taken as support that the use of these words reflected notions such as action and denial. Since action would have been represented in Alec's grammar at 1.00 morphemes regardless, because of his utterance *eat*, this would not be a problem. However, Jennings's grammar at 1.00 morphemes did not contain denial. To be consistent in the interpretation of the findings, Jennings's utterance *no* (which was produced as if admonishing himself for bumping into his mother) should require a new entry into his grammar.

$$\text{Operation} \rightarrow \begin{cases} \text{Nomination} \\ \text{Notice} \\ \text{Denial} \end{cases}$$

Such a representation, unfortunately, would be making the most daring assumption made thus far—that the use of a word during the single-word period may be taken to reflect a particular semantic notion even when there is no evidence that the child produces other words that may pertain to other aspects of the same situation.

In summary, I think that the representation of all single-word utterances as designated is the most appropriate at this time, with designated taken to represent a node reflecting an entire situation. The particular word used by the child is taken to be one of several possible words the child might have available to him that pertain to the situation as a whole. During this period, it is not assumed that the child's use of different words within the same situation can be interpreted to mean that he is capable of representing specific aspects of the situation with specific semantic notions. It is somewhat unfortunate that a more adequate test of the lexical insertion hypothesis could not be performed, however. It appears that we are in need of research that may further explicate the relationship between the single-word and multi-word utterance periods. One investigation that may have started us on this path is that of Starr (1975).

Starr's intent was to examine the relationship between the semantic character of children's single-word utterances and that of the children's subsequent two-word utterances. As her approach to analysis, Starr adopted Brown's (1973) system of categorizing semantic notions, although one of the eight categories on which she based her work, stative, was not Brown's. Quite understandably, Starr's observers could not use Brown's system to reliably categorize single-word utterances. She therefore chose to combine certain categories that could not be reliably distinguished from one another. The resulting categories were "people," "actions," "modifiers," "objects," "interjections," and "noise." The latter two represented utterances that did not refer to any of the features expressed within two-word utterances.

The categories also had to be combined for the analysis of the children's subsequent two-word utterances as well, apparently because with fairly small samples to work with, the computed frequencies for each category were unreliable. The resulting categories were titled "object modification sentences" (containing nomination, attribution, locative state, and possession), "action descriptive sentences" (containing action, locative action, agent, and object), and "statives." The latter primarily contained utterances that named an object the child desired (e.g., *want juice*).

Starr observed that the frequency of the children's two-word object modification utterances could be predicted by the frequency of the children's prior single-word utterances of the object category. Somewhat unexpectedly, a high frequency of two-word stative utterances was associated with a low frequency of single-word utterances of the object category. Starr offered a rather bold explanation of this finding. Discovering a high negative correlation between the frequency of single-word utterances in the object and interjection categories, she suggested that some children, preserving the self-orientation of their speech, may change from interjections that generally occur as single words, to features that can be incorporated into two-word stative utterances. None of the other single-word utterance categories served as predictors of the frequencies of any of the two-word utterance categories.

The results of Starr's investigation were interpreted as support for the position that "there is a functional continuity between single words and two-word sentences; children use language either to talk about themselves or to describe objects at both phases of linguistic development" (p 708). While I could dicker about the confidence one should have in Starr's interpretations of her findings, her results have provided useful information about the relationship between the words used during the single-word period and those subsequently used in the child's two-word utterances.

Starr may not have perceived her study in this light, but I view her investigation as dealing with the *lexical* relationship between the single- and two-word period. Starr's combining of categories seemed consistently influenced by the lexical characteristics of the words, not just by the manner in which these words may form semantic relationships with other words. The single-word category "object," for example, contained words whose similarity rested in their being inanimate and having a separate existence, not in the similarity between the semantic notions they may be involved in, such as nomination or object. Viewed in this light, it appears that Starr's interpretation of her results provides support for the position that the type of words seen during the child's single-word period may often be the same as those seen during the two-word period. But this does not necessarily mean that the particular words used during the single-word period are the same as those used subsequently in the child's two-word utterances—an issue that pertains to the adequacy of the hypothesis that with the appearance of two-word utterances the child's use of words reflects a lower node in their underlying representation than was true for the single-word period. Hopefully, investigators will soon discover a suitable means of approaching this issue.

Based on the current state of methodology, it must be concluded that there is not sufficient justification for assuming that the semantic nature of single-word utterances reflects the same degree of semantic specificity seen in multi-word utterances. Such a justification must be provided, in my mind, before single-word utterance data can be combined with that for multi-word utterances in the examination of issues dealing with Stage I speech. In the chapters to follow, single-word utterance data are not included. While this may prove to be a limitation, there is still too much that is not known about the semantic notions reflected in multi-word utterances and their interaction with the linguistic code for this to be a major hindrance in the exploration of the issues serving as the focus of this volume.

5

The Emergence of Semantic Notions

In Chapter 1 it was concluded that the semantic notions reflected in Stage I speech emerge in a fairly orderly sequence. This sequence seemed generally consistent with the course of the child's cognitive development. The following section of this chapter deals with how well the data obtained from the eight children studied conform to these conclusions.

THE SEQUENCE OF NOTIONS IN THE SPEECH OF THE EIGHT CHILDREN

Although the proposed approach to grammar writing deals with single-word utterances as well as more complex utterances, only multi-word utterances were utilized as data. Single-word utterances such as *box* could not be included since, as noted in Chapter 4, even with situational context they could only be categorized as designated without further specification of how this element is perceived in relation to another. Examples of the semantic notions evidenced in each of the eight children's samples are presented in Appendix A.

In order to derive a sequence in which the semantic notions were reflected in the speech of the eight children under investigation, the first sample in which each semantic notion was evidenced for each child was recorded. I wished to examine the emergence of semantic notions as independently as possible from the syntactic construction types through which they were coded. Therefore, the first nonstereotypical multi-word utterance produced in a context permitting analysis that reflected a particular semantic notion was taken as evidence that the notion had emerged. I recognize that such a criterion is contrary to the tradition of requiring a given number of utterance types to be observed before including a given feature in a child's grammar, in order to avoid the inclusion of mere memorizations. On the other hand, a criterion such as the latter, when used for features whose relative order of emergence is being examined, biases the resulting order in favor of the features that are most frequent in occurrence (Bowerman, 1975). Judging from an inspection of the literature on the semantic notions of Stage I speech, where notions such as nomination and action are quite frequent and those such as instrument are infrequent, the use of this kind of criterion would have assured finding an order of emergence of semantic notions consistent with those of Chapter 1. While frequency of occurrence factors may have been reduced by the criterion adopted, they were not eliminated as will be noted later in this chapter.

For each semantic notion the sample number representing the first sample in which the notion was evidenced in a child's speech was tabulated. For each child, the semantic notions were ranked according to these sample numbers. The ranks for each notion were averaged across all eight children. The resulting figures permitted the construction of a sequence of emergence. For example, evidence of nomination was noted in the third sample obtained from Colin. In Colin's second sample (his first containing multi-word utterances), two other semantic notions were noted. Nomination, therefore, received a rank of 3 since it represented the third notion to emerge. The semantic notions evidenced in the second sample were each assigned the rank of 1.5. When the ranks assigned to nomination for each of the eight children were averaged, the resulting figure was 4.38. This figure placed this notion immediately after notice (3.19) and before action (4.50).

The morpheme "no" was frequently used in contexts suggestive of each of the notions nonexistence, denial, and rejection. Some of the children used no morphemes that might have been considered specific to just one of these notions (e.g., "all gone," frequently taken to reflect nonexistence), and thus the three were not always distinguishable. A conservative course was therefore adopted; employing the category negation to represent all three of these notions. The same tactic was used by Bloom, Lightbown, and Hood (1975). The subtleties among these notions were unfortunately lost by this lack of distinction. It would have been desirable to determine whether the unclear order of emergence of these three notions seen in Chapter 1 could have been made more orderly.

No attempt was made to distinguish those instances when names of entities could be taken to reflect object from those in which they seemed best characterized as designated. This seemed proper, since the change from designated to object does not seem to arise from the child treating the names of entities differently, but rather in the appearance of new notions subsumed under designated. This notion, then, was termed designated/object.

Not all of the semantic notions were reflected in the speech of the children. Evidence of recurrence, for example, was not found in any of the samples from Jennings and Morton. The decision was made to treat such notions as if they had not yet emerged. In such instances, then, they were given the highest rank, representing the rank of the last notion to emerge. The resulting sequence took the following form.

Designated/Object
Notice
Nomination
Action
Place
Agent
Negation
Attribution
Possessor
Recurrence
Experience
Experiencer
Instrument

How does the observed sequence of semantic notions compare with previous findings? With the exception of the placement of negation and recurrence, the sequence compares quite well. Even though only multi-word utterances entered into the data, one would expect designated/object to receive the lowest rank, using the present method of computation. Whether or not notice or nomination first emerged in a child's speech, for example, it would be used in combination with designated. The finding that the operations of reference, notice and nomination, emerged next was quite consistent with other findings. Other consistent findings were the observations that action closely followed the operations of reference, with states such as attribution and possessor appearing next, followed by notions that are only beginning to appear at the end of Stage I, such as experience and instrument. Consistent with other studies, action preceded agent, which in turn emerged at approximately the same time as, or slightly before, states such as attribution. Clearly though, the positions of negation and recurrence in the sequence are inconsistent with other studies. In the Bloom, Lightbown, and Hood (1975) investigation, negation and recurrence (along with nomination) were noted before any of the other notions. Similarly, these semantic notions were the first to appear in Allison Bloom's speech (Bloom, 1973).

Why were these two notions so late in emerging in the present study? One explanation is that negation and recurrence are quite variable in their appearance and should not be viewed as universally early-appearing notions. However, when one inspects all of the available evidence, including the data of the present study, this explanation seems unsatisfactory. Not only did negation and recurrence emerge early in previous studies, but they were seen in the earliest samples containing multi-word utterances of a number of children in this study as well. A more satisfactory explanation is concerned with the frequency with which these notions were generally reflected in the speech of the children under investigation.* Even for those children showing evidence of negation and recurrence quite early, these notions were not frequent. Of the nine semantic notions that were evidenced in all children's speech, negation was the least frequent in occurrence. Of the four notions not evidenced in every child's speech, recurrence was more frequent than two, however, these notions, experiencer and instrument, have been described by other investigators as marginal, at best, during Stage I speech.

It appears that the less frequent the semantic notion, the greater the variability in the time of its first observation. This was tested by examining all of the notions accounted for in the proposed approach to grammar writing in terms of the standard deviations computed for the ranks assigned to each notion across all eight children. Of the four notions not evidenced in every child's speech, recurrence was associated with the highest standard deviation. Of the nine semantic notions that were evidenced in all children's speech, negation was associated with the highest standard deviation.

If the unexpectedly late appearance of negation and recurrence can be attributed in large part to the generally low frequency with which they were evidenced in the children's speech, the obtained sequence of emergence of the semantic notions agrees quite well with the sequence observed in other studies. In order to examine how these notions emerge within the framework of the proposed approach to grammar writing, however, a different view of the data must be arranged.

* In a later section of this chapter, I will be discussing the role of frequency of occurrence on the observed sequence of emergence as a whole. For now, I will contain my comments to negation and recurrence.

EMERGING NOTIONS IN
THE PROPOSED GRAMMAR

It appeared that an interesting view of how the semantic notions emerge within the framework of the proposed approach could be provided by utilizing samples at representative points in linguistic development. Ideally, these should include samples obtained in the early period of Stage I speech, late in this period, and beyond the Stage I period. This would provide not only a view of the emergence of semantic notions, but a presentation of how the child's development, within the proposed framework, begins to incorporate the features dealt with in approaches based on the adult system (e.g., Fillmore, 1968; 1971; Chafe, 1970). This was accomplished by writing grammars for three different periods in the data: (1) the combined samples within the mean utterance length range of 1.10–1.30 morphemes, (2) the combined samples within 1.70–1.90 morphemes, and (3) the combined samples within 2.30–2.50 morphemes. This arrangement enabled comparisons between periods that were equidistant in terms of mean utterance length. Each period incorporated samples from at least five different children and therefore seemed quite representative. This information is presented in Table 5–1.

The three periods can be compared in an order consistent with the hierarchical organization of the proposed grammar. The three periods revealed identical sentence rewrite rules, of the form

Sentence → Illocutionary force + Proposition

Since illocutionary force represents the first element of a child's developing language, its presence in the grammars of all three periods is no surprise. The same rewrite rule for illocutionary force was also appropriate for all three periods.

Table 5–1
The Composition of the Three Mean Utterance
Length Ranges Compared

Mean Utterance Length in Morphemes	1.10–1.30	1.70–1.90	2.30–2.50
Child and sample number	Morton I Lynn I Leslie I Kristen II, III Colin V	Morton II, III Lynn III Alec III Kristen V, VI Greer II	Jennings III Lynn IV Leslie III Kristen VII Alec IV Colin VIII

$$\text{Illocutionary force} \rightarrow \begin{cases} \text{Declare} \\ \text{Request} \\ \text{Question} \end{cases}$$

Recall from Chapter 3 that the first elements of illocutionary force to be realized in the child's speech are declare and request. Apparently, by the time the child's mean utterance length reaches 1.10 morphemes, question also may be acquired. Question was not limited to intonation in the samples of the five children in this period. Questions containing Wh words such as *what that?* were also observed.

Proposition required the same rewrite rule for all three periods.

$$\text{Proposition} \rightarrow \text{(Function|Designated)}$$

The finding that elements from function already combined with those of designated by the first period was expected, since this rule accounts for the earliest notions observed, such as nomination and notice, as well as those soon to follow, such as action and object. A look at the function rewrite rule for the first period indicates that just such utterances may have been used.

$$\text{Function} \rightarrow \begin{cases} \text{Operation} \\ \text{Ergative} \end{cases}$$

For the two later periods, the function rewrite rule was more complex.

$$\text{Function} \rightarrow \text{(Operation|Ergative)}$$

This rule was required because some of the children during each of these periods used some operation with action. For example, Kristen used the form "/n/ there" to call others' attention to the object that she was acting on or the event in which she was engaged. This form was clearly not performing a locative function. One such utterance during Kristen's fifth sample was *fall down /n/ there*, used in gaining my attention immediately prior to her performing a staged dying act on the stairs. This utterance was categorized as notice + action, requiring the preceding function rewrite rule.

For all three periods, operation followed the same rule.

$$\text{Operation} \rightarrow \begin{cases} \text{Nomination} \\ \text{Notice} \\ \text{Negation} \\ \text{Recurrence} \end{cases}$$

Since the notions subsumed under operation represent Brown's (1973) operations of reference, the finding that all of them were evidenced in the first period was unremarkable. The sequence of emergence of the semantic notions that was discussed in the previous section did portray negation and recurrence as notions appearing later in Stage I; an artifact, it was argued, of the low frequency with which utterances reflecting these notions were observed. It is a bit reassuring, then, that negation and recurrence were noted in the first period here.

The observation that the operations of reference were also found in the two subsequent periods merits comment. Obviously the semantic notions of operation do not simply represent elementary meanings that serve no other purpose than to ease the child from single-word utterances into syntax. From a structural standpoint, utterances such as *no ball* and *that kitty* may be quite elementary. They seem to combine in an additive fashion rather than in the relational manner seen in utterances such as *eat dinner* and *camel walk*. Nevertheless, utterances reflecting the notions of operation continue to be seen well after relational syntax is acquired. They continue serving a useful communicative function through adulthood, as evidenced in utterances such as *That's an escalator*, *My wallet is gone*, *Hi, Benny*, and *I won't go with you*.

The ergative rewrite rule for the first period was

$$\text{Ergative} \rightarrow (\text{Agent}) \text{ Action}$$

This rule was responsible for representing utterances reflecting agent + action. Agent was optional because a number of the children's utterances involving action in this period were action + object.

The rewrite rule for ergative for the second period took the form

$$\text{Ergative} \rightarrow (\text{Agent})\text{Process})$$

The more advanced development within ergative in this period called for the additional rewrite rule

$$\text{Process} \rightarrow \begin{Bmatrix} \text{Action} \\ \text{Experience} \end{Bmatrix}$$

In Chapter 1, it was noted that experience appeared quite late in Stage I speech, if at all. The above rewrite rule indicates evidence of this notion in the speech of some of the children whose mean utterance length was between 1.70 and 1.90 morphemes; a finding concurring with the observations in Chapter 1.

The rewrite rule for ergative for the third period was

$$\text{Ergative} \rightarrow (\text{Actor})\text{Process})$$

This development required the rewrite rule

$$\text{Actor} \rightarrow \left\{ \begin{matrix} \text{Agent} \\ \text{Instrument} \end{matrix} \right\}$$

Thus, although experience emerged by late Stage I speech, instrument had not, at least as measured in this manner.

In the previous section of this chapter it was observed that the notions of property, attribution, and possessor appeared later than notions such as nomination, object, and action. Nevertheless, they did appear by the first period, calling for the following rewrite rules for designated and property.

$$\text{Designated} \rightarrow \text{Goal (Property)}$$

$$\text{Property} \quad \rightarrow \left\{ \begin{matrix} \text{Attribution} \\ \text{Possessor} \end{matrix} \right\}$$

The rewrite rules for both designated and property took the same form for the two later periods.

In the first period, the relations between the entities and events in which they interacted were always object or place in the child's speech.

$$\text{Goal} \rightarrow \left\{ \begin{matrix} \text{Object} \\ \text{Place} \end{matrix} \right\}$$

For the later two periods, however, experiencer was also noted. In addition, more than one element of goal might be represented. For the second period the rewrite rule for goal took the form

$$\text{Goal} \rightarrow \left\{ \begin{matrix} \text{(Object\#Place)} \\ \text{Experiencer} \end{matrix} \right\}$$

Goal acquired still greater complexity in the third period.

$$\text{Goal} \rightarrow \text{(Object\#Experiencer\#Place)}$$

This rule accounted for utterances such as *I need pencil back*.

The new elements appearing in each successive period are summarized in Table 5–2. It can be noted from this table that a number of the notions attributed to Stage I were acquired by the first period. However, development did continue thereafter. From Table 5–2, it appears that a greater number of differences existed between the first and second period

Table 5–2

A Summary of Rewrite Rules Representing Development from
a Previous Period, with New Notions in Italics

Rewrite Rule for	New Rule, Not Required for First Period	New Rule, Not Required for Two Prior Periods
Sentence		
Illocutionary force		
Proposition		
Function	(Operation◊Ergative)	
Operation		
Ergative	(Agent◊Process)	(Actor◊Process)
Actor		$\left\{\begin{array}{l}\text{Agent}\\ \textit{Instrument}\end{array}\right\}$
Process	$\left\{\begin{array}{l}\text{Action}\\ \textit{Experience}\end{array}\right\}$	
Designated		
Property		
Goal	$\left\{\begin{array}{l}\text{(Object◊Place)}\\ \textit{Experiencer}\end{array}\right\}$	(Object◊Experiencer◊Place)

than between the second and third period. This development took two
forms: (1) the appearance of utterances reflecting a new combination of
existing underlying semantic notions, and (2) the appearance of utterances reflecting new underlying semantic notions. Both forms of development were also noted in the third period. It appeared useful to determine
whether, in addition, there were still later emerging notions reflected in
the children's utterances of the third period.

The semantic notions accounted for in the proposed grammar were
not sufficient to describe the notions reflected in the utterances of the
children in the third period. This is hardly surprising, of course, since the
proposed grammar was designed on the basis of Stage I speech data. The
new notions reflected during the third period resembled those described
in some of the other approaches to analysis (see Appendix B). They were
not frequent in my data, but those that occurred warrant mentioning.
Kristen's utterance *two camels* /ə/ *that*, for instance, seemed to reflect
quantity, a notion suggested by the Berkeley Cross-Linguistic Language
Development Project (BCLLDP) approach (1973). Leslie's *make soup*
reflected a good example of what Fillmore (1968) named factitive and
Edwards (1973) termed result. *I* /ənə/ *play tennis*, produced by Jennings,
appeared to reflect the notion range used by the BCLLDP approach
(1973).

In summary, the comparisons of the three periods revealed that the majority of the semantic notions attributed to Stage I were evidenced in the first period when mean utterance length was between 1.10 and 1.30 morphemes. By the second period, notions described as marginal during Stage I, such as experiencer, were noted and previously existing notions were combined in new and more complex ways. This combining of notions was observed again along with the emergence of instrument, in the third period—a period when, in addition, new notions not associated with Stage I were evidenced.

FACTORS RELATING TO THE EMERGENCE OF SEMANTIC NOTIONS

In this section some factors that may have a bearing on the emergence of semantic notions are discussed. As will be seen, some of them may have relevance to the sequence of emergence of semantic notions in the speech of the eight children studied.

Phonology of the Adult System

The first factor is the phonological makeup of words in the adult system. The influence on the present results of this factor cannot be assessed because I did not begin observing any of the eight children early enough. However, its potential importance should be mentioned.

This factor is familiar to the study of lexical acquisition, due to Greenfield's (1973) paper concerning the early language development of her daughter, Lauren. Lauren produced *Dada* as her first word. Initially this production was a syllable sequence that Lauren produced spontaneously with no apparent meaning. Her parents proceeded to deliberately imitate Lauren's productions. Such imitations tended to result in a repetition of Lauren's original production. Initially, an association between Lauren's father and the word "Dada" was promoted by having the father be the sole person to imitate the word. Subsequently, an increase in the frequency with which Lauren looked at her father when either spontaneously or imitatively producing *Dada* was noted. Lauren's comprehension of this word was tested systematically. She heard several productions (e.g., *dada mama, bubu*), differing from *Dada* in varying degrees. Initially, all sound entities containing the /a/ of *Dada* evoked an orienting response toward her father. Subsequently the phonetic category representing father narrowed, finally to include only *Dada*. Such findings prompted Greenfield to tentatively conclude that meaning is first imposed on sound from the outside and that spontaneous utterances only gradually take on meaning.

Carter (1975b) has suggested some ways in which the phonological makeup of adult words may influence the child's acquisition of other features of language, among them semantic notions. Carter studied the development of "more" and "my" (and its variant "mine") in the speech of a young child named David. At age 13 months, David typically requested objects with an open reach accompanied by the production of a monosyllabic utterance free-varying in vowel and intonation but consistently initiated by /m/. By age 17 months, David's /m/-initial requests were limited primarily to /mou/, the presumed phonetic antecedent of "more," and /mɔɪ/, the presumed phonetic antecedent of "my." Despite the use of two different forms, no evidence was seen that David intended these forms to be different in meaning. It was noted, however, that David's mother frequently interpreted David's productions as "more" and frequently produced *more* herself during these circumstances.

It is interesting to note in this regard that an examination of the data for David at this period indicates that in 7 of 8 instances in which he used /mou/, he was requesting an object after having previously requested it. In 12 of 12 instances in which David used /mɔɪ/ he was requesting an object after having previously requested it. By this point in development, David had begun acquiring the use of object names. When such usage is analyzed in the same manner, it can be seen that in only 4 of 10 instances in which he used such names, was David requesting the object for a second time; in the remaining 6 instances David was requesting the object for the first time. This suggests that David's use of both /mou/ and /mɔɪ/ may have reflected a type of recurrence.

By age 19 months, the use of /mou/ (solely) reflected a type of recurrence (the request for either more of a substance or an additional object), while the use of /mɔɪ/ reflected a type of possession (the request for noninterference with a toy). Further, these productions alternated with the more adult-like productions /mɔr/ and /maɪ/, respectively. Unfortunately, Carter did not present (or perhaps there were not) any examples of the use of "my" by David's mother during instances when David produced /mɔɪ/ or /maɪ/.

The disappearance of all /m/-initial utterances, except /mou/ and /mɔɪ/, and the use of these two forms in the absence of a distinction in their meaning led Carter to propose that the dimension of sound may have greater control over the child's early language than previously suspected. This certainly seems true, but the role that the caretaker may play in reacting to, repeating, and thereby molding the child's early productions must not be minimized. Just as the caretaker in Greenfield's study seemed to have influenced Lauren's acquisition of the lexical item *Dada*, so too may the caretaker in Carter's study have influenced David's acquisition of a type of recurrence, as reflected by his use of "more." (It would not be prudent, given the available information, to speculate the same type of origin for possessor).

In the discussion of lexically-based rules in Chapter 2 it was noted that a few semantic notions (including recurrence) may become associated with a particular word, notably when that word (e.g., "more") is one of only a few appropriate words in the language to reflect that semantic notion. Putting aside for a moment the issue of whether or not a single-word utterance can really be taken to reflect a specific semantic notion, such lexical considerations may have important implications. If a child's prelinguistic utterance (resembling a word frequently tied to a particular semantic notion) is reacted to and shaped by a caretaker, the result might be interpreted to mean that the phonological nature of the child's prelinguistic utterances determines (with environmental assistance) which semantic notions emerge first in the child's linguistic system. If this were a complete and accurate interpretation of things, the fairly orderly sequence in which semantic notions have been found to emerge would have to be attributed to regularity in both the phonological nature of different children's prelinguistic utterances, and the particular utterances which different caretakers single out and respond to.

Even if this interpretation were accurate for Carter's specific findings, it would not suffice as an explanation for the sequence of emergence of semantic notions in general. First, this sequence is quite similar across different languages (Slobin, 1973) and the phonological makeup of the words used to reflect the semantic notions changes in distribution from language to language. Thus far, it does not appear that there is a characteristic sequence of emergence of semantic notions for English separate from a characteristic sequence for Russian, and so on. There is another reason why this interpretation is not acceptable as a general explanation. Most of the semantic notions evidenced during Stage I speech are not integrally tied to particular lexical items. Carter's findings for recurrence may be the exception rather than the rule.

Carter's hypothesis that the dimension of sound may have greater control over the child's early language than previously assumed is not a proposal that sound takes precedence over the child's cognitive development. Clearly David must have attained the cognitive parallel to recurrence prior to his use of "more" to reflect this semantic notion. It also seemed that at the beginning of Carter's study, David was in the process of acquiring a general semantic notion serving as a precursor of recurrence.

In order for the caretaker to shape David's /m/-initial utterances into "more" David had to (1) produce some, albeit prelinguistic, utterance directed at the caretaker indicating an attempt at communication and (2) produce this utterance in a context that further specified the nature of this communication. The caretaker's success, then, rested in large part not only on David's knowledge of the nonlinguistic event, but also on his knowledge that it could be communicated as well. It would be quite doubtful that the caretaker could influence a child's language with the result being the child's use of a word reflecting a semantic notion that was not highly consistent with his prior knowledge of the nonlinguistic events during which he used its prelinguistic predecessor.

I think that these considerations suggest that there are some limits to the extent that the phonological nature of words can influence the order in which semantic notions emerge. There are some unanswered questions pertaining to Carter's findings, however. For example, why did all of the /m/-initial utterances disappear from David's repertoire at age 17 months except for the antecedents of "more" and "my," before these two forms were themselves semantically distinguishable? No doubt more will be heard about the influence exercised by the dimension of sound on other aspects of the child's linguistic development. It seems, though, that other factors may play a more major role in the the order in which semantic notions emerge.

The Course of Cognitive Development

The sequence in which the semantic notions emerged in the speech of the eight children studied in this volume appeared generally consistent with the course followed by cognitive development. Notions such as nomination and notice represent general non-core relations showing some parallel to attainments during the third stage of sensorimotor intelligence. Notions such as agent and action may be viewed as specific non-core relations resembling attainments of the fifth stage of sensorimotor intelligence. Semantic notions such as attribution and possessor might be taken to represent the child's developing ability to view relationships independently of relevant action. Experience and experiencer would be expected to emerge later because they do not deal with overt activity, the source of information for the child during the period of sensorimotor intelligence.

These kinds of observations make it most tempting to conclude that the sequence of emergence of semantic notions mirrors, and perhaps is even dictated by, the child's cognitive development—an issue discussed at length in Chapter 1. However, another possible influence on this sequence seems to exist—that of the frequency with which the semantic notions were reflected in the children's speech.

Frequency of Occurrence

It was previously mentioned that the unexpectedly late appearance of negation and recurrence in the speech of the eight children I studied may have been related to their low frequency of occurrence. It is also plausible that the position of each of the other semantic notions in the sequence may have been related to their respective frequencies.

If it were the case that all of the semantic notions reflected in Stage I speech in fact emerged at the same time, it can be seen that the most frequent of the notions would have a greater likelihood of being evidenced earlier than the less frequent notions. If frequency of occurrence pertained in some way to the order in which the notions emerged, the observed order and the frequency of occurrence of each semantic notion would have to be highly correlated. And correlated they were; a rank order correlation between the order in which the semantic notions emerged in the speech of the eight children and their respective total frequencies of occurrence was .96.

Such a correlation leaves open the possibility that the observed sequence of notions was not one that had any relevance to the children's development, but was simply an artifact of the different frequencies with which the notions occurred. It could also be argued, however, that the order in which the semantic notions emerged was valid; since the notions that emerged earlier had the opportunity to be evidenced in speech before other notions had emerged, they would be expected to have a higher frequency of occurrence. Such an explanation could account for the same findings. One way to test this explanation was to examine the frequency of occurrence of each of the semantic notions during the period when most or all of the notions had been acquired. According to this explanation, one would not necessarily expect to find a correlation between the observed sequence of notions and the frequency of these notions during this period, since by this period most of the notions had emerged.

I examined the frequency of occurrence of each semantic notion during the last sample obtained from each child. The mean utterance length of each sample exceeded 2.30 morphemes, ensuring that most of the Stage I notions had emerged in the children's speech. The rank order correlation between the order in which the notions emerged and their respective frequencies of occurrence in the children's last sample was .87. Thus, although the relationship between frequency of occurrence and the order in which the notions emerged was lower when only samples obtained during Stage II were utilized, this relationship was still quite strong.

The finding that a relationship exists between the order in which a notion emerges and its frequency of occurrence does not constitute a statement of cause and effect. Another plausible explanation for this relationship, for example, is that the semantic notions that emerge quite early may be the most important notions for communication throughout development, and hence the most frequent in occurrence. Whether or not frequency of occurrence and order of emergence relate in this way could be put to the test by examining the effects of sample size. If frequency of occurrence reflects only the relative importance to communication of some of the earliest semantic notions to emerge, one would not expect that a large sample obtained from a child at any *particular* point in time would result in the observation of semantic notions presumed to be later achievements. If this were the case, however, it would appear that a number of semantic notions could emerge at approximately the same point in development, but be reflected in a child's speech with varying frequencies.

This type of analysis could not be handled well with the data from the eight children because successive samples from each of the children happened also to be increasingly greater in size. Thus, it could not be determined whether the increasing numbers of semantic notions reflected in a child's speech were related to the increasing likelihood of evidencing a notion with greater sample size, or whether they were related to the child's development. This very difficulty in choosing which of these two accounts is correct suggests that caution should be exercised in interpreting the observed sequence in which the semantic notions emerged in the speech of the eight children. The only means by which I could use the present data to examine this question was to look at the total number of utterances used by each of the children and relate this to the number of different semantic notions reflected in their speech. This could be done since four of the notions were not evidenced in the speech of all children. With so few notions not used by all children, this type of analysis was not one that could yield conclusive results. Nevertheless, some interesting, although tentative observations could be made. Although the children with the fewest total utterances, Lynn and Greer, did not show evidence of all of the semantic notions, two children with a relatively large number of total utterances, Kristen and Morton, also did not show evidence of all of the notions. This observation suggests some possibility that the order in which a notion emerges is not related simply to sample size.

With the possible role that frequency of occurrence may play in the order in which specific semantic notions emerge, it may be possible to discuss the sequence in which notions appear with confidence only when such a sequence deals with groupings of notions rather than specific notions. In the proposed approach to grammar writing it is possible to form four groups of semantic notions that can be ordered quite generally. The four groups are the operations of reference such as nomination, notice, negation, and recurrence (Group A), the notions action, agent, and object, with object pertaining to the notion occurring with action or agent and representing a lower node than designated (Group B), the notions attribution, place, and possessor (Group C), and the notions quite marginal at Stage I, instrument, experience, and experiencer (Group D). While it was seen that two of the Group A notions, negation and recurrence, emerged at a later point in the sequence of emergence than expected, their early emergence in the samples from some of the children, their reported early emergence in the literature, and the possible influence of frequency effects on their point of emergence seemed to justify their placement in this group. The relative order of these groups of notions did not relate to their respective total frequencies of occurrence. A rank order correlation yielded a nonsignificant coefficient of .40. Although this grouping prevents an inspection of specific semantic notions, it will have useful advantages in addressing some of the issues posed in the next chapter.

6

Semantic Notions and the Linguistic Code

One purpose of this volume is to examine the manner in which underlying semantic notions interact with the linguistic code. In Chapter 2 some issues pertaining to this interaction were presented. In this chapter these issues are pursued, as they relate to the eight children studied.

THE ROLE OF LINGUISTIC EXPERIENCE

During the discussion in Chapter 2 it was noted that the role of experience in contributing to differences among children's linguistic styles during Stage I was quite unclear. Although the semantic notions reflected in a child's utterances generally emerge in a sequence that parallels the course of his cognitive development, Bloom (1973) has suggested that differences in the child's experiences can result in different styles. I do not believe Bloom meant that the child's exposure to certain relationships in his environment will enable him to gain a conceptual grasp of these relationships regardless of the order in which such cognitive attainments are ordinarily acquired. However, I do feel that she is suggesting that given a number of conceptual relationships the child does understand, the exposure to these relationships and the ways in which these relationships are coded in the language can influence his linguistic style.

This seemed like a useful issue to test empirically and represented the motivation for introducing the four toys and corresponding experimental words during the sampling situation. Before it could be determined

127

Table 6–1
Children's Use of the Experimental Words

Child	Experimental Word				Total
	zoo animal	camel	spinner	cash register	
Leslie	–	–	–	+	1
Alec	+	+	+	–	3
Kristen	+	+	+	+	4
Lynn	+	+	–	+	3
Colin	–	+	+	+	3
Morton	+	+	+	+	4
Jennings	+	+	+	–	3
Greer	+	+	+	–	3
Total	6	7	6	5	24

if the eight children used the experimental words in a manner consistent with the semantic notion and sentence position in which they were presented, the children's use of the experimental words in general needed to be assessed. The use of the experimental words by the eight children appears in Table 6–1. Instances in which the word was used are designated by "+" and instances when the word was not used are indicated by "–".

From this table it can be seen that of 32 total possible uses of the experimental words, the children showed evidence of using the word in 24 instances. All of the children used at least 1 of the experimental words in their spontaneous speech. No obvious word preferences were noted; all experimental words were used by at least 5 children. It appears, then, that the method established to examine the effects of experience resulted in sufficient use of the experimental words.

One relevant question is whether or not the experimental words used by the children were used in utterances reflecting the same semantic notions that were reflected in the utterances to which I exposed them. Since the experimental words were unfamiliar to the children prior to my visits, it seemed particularly interesting to examine the semantic notions reflected in the utterances representing the children's first use of each experimental word. This information is presented in Table 6–2. The symbol "–" indicates, as in Table 6–1, that the experimental word was not used. The entries "yes" and "no" indicate whether or not the experimental word was first used in utterances reflecting the same semantic notions reflected in the utterances to which I exposed the children.

From Table 6–2 it can be seen that fewer than one-half of the utterances marking the first use of an experimental word by the child reflected

Table 6–2

First Use of Experimental Words in Relation to
Semantic Notion Condition

Child	Experimental Word	Presented Semantic Notion	Observed Semantic Notion	Agreement between Presented and Observed Notion
Leslie	zoo animal	Nomination	—	—
	camel	Instrument	—	—
	spinner	Place	—	—
	cash register	Object	Object	Yes
Alec	zoo animal	Instrument	Object	No
	camel	Nomination	Nomination	Yes
	spinner	Object	Object	Yes
	cash register	Place	—	—
Kristen	zoo animal	Object	Notice	No
	camel	Place	Instrument	No
	spinner	Nomination	Nomination	Yes
	cash register	Instrument	Notice	No
Lynn	zoo animal	Place	Nomination	No
	camel	Object	Nomination	No
	spinner	Instrument	—	—
	cash register	Nomination	Nomination	Yes
Colin	zoo animal	Nomination	—	—
	camel	Object	Notice	No
	spinner	Place	Notice	No
	cash register	Instrument	Object	No
Morton	zoo animal	Object	Nomination	No
	camel	Nomination	Object	No
	spinner	Instrument	Nomination	No
	cash register	Place	Nomination	No
Jennings	zoo animal	Instrument	Object	No
	camel	Place	Nomination	No
	spinner	Nomination	Nomination	Yes
	cash register	Object	—	—
Greer	zoo animal	Place	Object	No
	camel	Instrument	Object	No
	spinner	Object	Notice	No
	cash register	Nomination	—	—

the same semantic notion reflected in my stimulus utterances. This finding certainly does not augur well the position that the child's first use of new words mirrors the most recent use of these words heard in the speech of others, at least as this pertains to underlying semantic notions.

The effects of the sentence position in which the experimental words were presented may have been stronger, however. The children's first use of the experimental words, plotted according to whether or not the words were used in the same sentence position in which they were exposed, appears in Table 6–3.

Over one-half of the experimental words were used initially in the same sentence position in which they were exposed. It should be borne in mind, however, that there were only two sentence positions in which the experimental words were presented; those classified in subject sentence position (e.g., *The camel is on the table*) and those in predicate sentence position (e.g., *I'm gonna hit the camel*). Since the majority of the children's utterances were two words in length, the subject versus predicate position distinction seemed to be an appropriate one to make in analyzing their use of experimental words as well. This results in a probability approaching .50 that a child's use of an experimental word will appear in the same sentence position as the one in which the word was exposed to him. In this light, the sentence position data are not very convincing.

Thus far, it has been seen that, although the children showed a substantial amount of experimental word usage, such usage did not closely correspond to the semantic notions reflected in the stimulus utterances in which the words were used. Further, the children's use of the experimental words may not have been related to the sentence positions of the words in the stimulus utterances. To what, then, can the manner in which the children used the experimental words be attributed? One likely candidate seemed to be the semantic notions reflected in each child's general usage.

Presented in Table 6–4 is the children's first use of the experimental words, categorized according to whether or not such usage was accounted for in the grammar written for the sample in which each of the experimental words was first noted. As noted in Chapter 4, the construction of these grammars did not utilize utterances containing any of the experimental words. Also included in this table is information as to whether or not the semantic notions reflected in my stimulus utterances were evidenced in the children's grammars. Corresponding information pertaining to sentence position is not provided since the proposed approach to grammar writing does not deal directly with it.

The observation that in 22 of 24 instances the first use of an experimental word could be accounted for by the respective child's grammar,

Table 6–3
First Use of Experimental Words in Relation to
Sentence Position Condition

Child	Experimental Word	Position Presented	Position Observed	Agreement between Presented and Observed
Leslie	zoo animal	Predicate	—	—
	camel	Subject	—	—
	spinner	Subject	—	—
	cash register	Predicate	Predicate	Yes
Alec	zoo animal	Subject	Predicate	No
	camel	Predicate	Predicate	Yes
	spinner	Predicate	Predicate	Yes
	cash register	Subject	—	—
Kristen	zoo animal	Predicate	Subject	No
	camel	Subject	Subject	Yes
	spinner	Predicate	Predicate	Yes
	cash register	Subject	Predicate	No
Lynn	zoo animal	Subject	Predicate	No
	camel	Predicate	Predicate	Yes
	spinner	Subject	—	—
	cash register	Predicate	Predicate	Yes
Colin	zoo animal	Subject	—	—
	camel	Subject	Predicate	No
	spinner	Predicate	Predicate	Yes
	cash register	Predicate	Predicate	Yes
Morton	zoo animal	Subject	Predicate	No
	camel	Subject	Predicate	No
	spinner	Predicate	Predicate	Yes
	cash register	Predicate	Predicate	Yes
Jennings	zoo animal	Predicate	Predicate	Yes
	camel	Predicate	Predicate	Yes
	spinner	Subject	Predicate	No
	cash register	Subject	—	—
Greer	zoo animal	Predicate	Predicate	Yes
	camel	Predicate	Predicate	Yes
	spinner	Subject	Subject	Yes
	cash register	Subject	—	—

is notable. This seems to give the impression that, although the child may
be capable of acquiring new words through his exposure to utterances
reflecting notions that are not part of his own system of semantic notions,
his *use* of these new words will be subject to this system. There are two
exceptions to this. Kristen first used "camel" in an utterance reflecting
instrument, which was not then part of her grammar. Morton first used

Table 6–4

Presentation and Use of Experimental Words in Relation to
Children's Grammars

Child	Experimental Word	Presented Notion	Observed Notion	Presented Notion Present in Grammar[a]	Notion Evidenced Present in Grammar
Leslie	zoo animal	Nomination	—	Yes	—
	camel	Instrument	—	No	—
	spinner	Place	—	Yes	—
	cash register	Object	Object	Yes	Yes
Alec	zoo animal	Instrument	Object	No	Yes
	camel	Nomination	Nomination	Yes	Yes
	spinner	Object	Object	Yes	Yes
	cash register	Place	—	No	—
Kristen	zoo animal	Object	Notice	Yes	Yes
	camel	Place	Instrument	Yes	No
	spinner	Nomination	Nomination	Yes	Yes
	cash register	Instrument	Notice	No	Yes
Lynn	zoo animal	Place	Nomination	No	Yes
	camel	Object	Nomination	Yes	Yes
	spinner	Instrument	—	No	—
	cash register	Nomination	Nomination	Yes	Yes
Colin	zoo animal	Nomination	—	Yes	—
	camel	Object	Notice	No	Yes
	spinner	Place	Notice	No	Yes
	cash register	Instrument	Object	No	Yes
Morton	zoo animal	Object	Nomination	Yes	Yes
	camel	Nomination	Object	Yes	No
	spinner	Instrument	Nomination	No	Yes
	cash register	Place	Nomination	Yes	Yes
Jennings	zoo animal	Instrument	Object	No	Yes
	camel	Place	Nomination	Yes	Yes
	spinner	Nomination	Nomination	Yes	Yes
	cash register	Object	—	Yes	—
Greer	zoo animal	Place	Object	Yes	Yes
	camel	Instrument	Object	No	Yes
	spinner	Object	Notice	Yes	Yes
	cash register	Nomination	—	Yes	—

[a] If the experimental word was not used, the entry in this column refers to whether or not the presented semantic notion was evidenced in any of the child's samples. If the experimental word was used, the entry refers to whether or not the presented semantic notion was evidenced in the same sample in which the word was used.

"camel" in an utterance reflecting object, and this notion was not part of his grammar at the time. But these instances were not observed frequently enough to offset the above impression.

The findings reported in Table 6–4 suggest that the emergence of semantic notions may be tied more to general developmental processes, that is, less sensitive to environmental influences, than the acquisition of lexical items. Considering the parallel between the sequence in which semantic notions emerge and the course of cognitive development noted in Chapter 1, this seems quite plausible.

From Table 6–4 it can be seen that in 9 of the 12 instances in which my stimulus utterances reflected a semantic notion not present in the child's grammar, the child nevertheless used the experimental word, although in an utterance reflecting a semantic notion consistent with his grammar. One might have expected that a child's ability to extract a lexical item from a stimulus utterance would be dependent upon his grasp of the semantic notion reflected by the use of the lexical item in the stimulus utterance. This did not seem to be the case. For example, at a time when no evidence of assigning instrument to their grammars existed, Alec and Kristen produced experimental words that were presented to them via stimulus utterances reflecting instrument, such as *The zoo animal's gonna tickle you.* Even if the child's use of the experimental words is consistent with his own system of underlying semantic notions, should not the ability to extract a lexical item from a stimulus utterance reflecting a new semantic notion be sufficient to assign this notion to the child's grammar?

I suspect that the answer to this question should be negative. Alec's ability to extract "zoo animal" from stimulus utterances such as *The zoo animal's gonna tickle you* could have been attributed to his ability to perceive that the unfamiliar lexical item in my utterance referred to the unfamiliar object toward which my attention was directed, or, perhaps, the object directed toward Alec. Such an ability would not seem to depend upon Alec's grasp of the semantic notion instrument. His perception that the unfamiliar object was the thing referred to seemed to be all that was necessary to acquire the new lexical item. I see no reason to assume that Alec needed to understand the specific relation in which the lexical item was involved.

A similar account might be suitable in explaining how the children could acquire new lexical items that were presented to them in utterances reflecting a semantic notion that was part of their own system, but in a sentence position not utilized by them to code the same notion. For example, Colin, Morton, Jennings, and Greer acquired the use of experimental words presented in utterances reflecting place, with such words in the predicate sentence position (e.g., *On the table is the camel*). Since these children did not produce utterances that contained prolocatives (e.g., *there ball*), the predicate position for the lexical item reflecting the object located should have been relatively unfamiliar to these children. Although the lexical item first appeared in predicate position in the speech of all children, in each instance a notion other than place was reflected in such usage. Apparently, the fact that I called the children's attention to the unfamiliar object along with providing an unfamiliar lexical item in an accompanying utterance, was sufficient for them to acquire the use of the lexical item. This is the reason that in discussing the results presented in Tables 6–2 and 6–3, I did not single out certain semantic notion/sentence position presentation conditions (e.g., nomination with experimental word in predicate position) that led to the child's use of the experimental word in the same sentence position, reflecting the same semantic notion. The children used the experimental word in the same manner because this was already part of their linguistic system. However, they may have been able to extract the experimental words from the stimulus utterances simply because they were unfamiliar words spoken in utterances that accompanied my calling attention to certain unfamiliar objects.

There is little doubt that semantic notions should be distinguished from cognitive structures since the former represent what the child intends to communicate and thus may be linguistic in nature. Bloom (1973) noted that such notions are exclusively linguistic inductions to the degree that they do not reflect the child's cognitive organization. If such inductions are not highly constrained by a child's cognitive organization, one would have expected that the children's exposure to the stimulus utterances and accompanying activities would have had more of an effect on their language. It is possible that the specific amount of exposure necessary to influence the children's language may not have been provided, preserving Bloom's proposal at least until additional investigations are undertaken. However, an alternative position can be taken.

Because this exposure did not appreciably influence the semantic notions reflected in the children's utterances, such notions may have reflected the children's cognitive organization to some degree. Such organization, it seems, would be at least as insensitive to external influences as linguistic inductions. The acceptance of this position must await substantiation in the form of data indicating that the children's cognitive organization was 1) compatible with the semantic notions reflected in the stimulus utterances that were also reflected in the children's utterances, yet 2) incompatible with other semantic notions reflected in the stimulus utterances that were not evidenced in the children's usage. For the present, the more cautious position should be taken—that a child's cognitive development

cannot be ruled out as having an influence on the specific semantic notions underlying his speech.

Three other studies of which I am aware have examined children's
acquisition of experimentally presented linguistic material, and it would
be of interest to note how the results of these studies compare with the
present results. Braine (1971) reported his attempts to introduce his
daughter Naomi to two nonsense words, "niss" and "seb" during the
Stage I period. The first of the nonsense words was presented in a manner reflecting nomination; upon pointing to a particular kitchen utensil
that Naomi was allowed to play with, Braine would name the object,
"niss." The nonsense word "seb" was presented in a manner reflecting
action. Braine used this nonsense word when making his fingers walk.

Naomi acquired the use of both nonsense words, and in a manner
consistent with the manner in which they were presented to her. Such
utterances as *more niss* (produced when Naomi was asking for the kitchen
utensil) and *this niss* (produced when seemingly identifying the utensil)
suggest that Naomi was perceiving "niss" as the name of an object. She
produced "seb" primarily in utterances that suggested that she viewed
this nonsense word as a type of action. For example, in seemingly requesting her father to walk his fingers toward her (an event that usually
terminated in her being tickled), Naomi produced *seb Naomi.* An utterance suggesting a similar function was *Daddy seb Teddy.* Braine noted
that in two other utterances, Naomi produced "seb" in a manner consistent with its treatment as the name of an object—*more seb* and *bit
more seb.*

Quite clearly Naomi readily acquired the new lexical items. This task
was made easy for her since Braine apparently produced the two nonsense words in isolation (e.g., pointing to the utensil and saying *niss*).
Naomi would therefore not have to select out the unfamiliar word from
a multi-word utterance. The relationship between the unfamiliar word
and the unfamiliar object to which her attention was directed would presumably be clearer. Judging from Braine's use of "niss" and "seb," it
does not appear that Naomi was being exposed to the unfamiliar words
in utterances reflecting new semantic notions. The two unfamiliar words
seemed to be used in utterances reflecting nomination and action, respectively. Both emerge early in Stage I speech. Although Braine did not
provide a description of the semantic notions reflected in her utterances
during this period, Naomi was producing two- and three-word utterances.
If Naomi's linguistic development was comparable to that of other
children, these notions would have been reflected in her speech.

How did Naomi's use of the new lexical items agree with the manner in which they were presented? Her use of "niss" and "seb" seemed

to conform to the adult classes of noun and verb, respectively. Utterances such as *this niss* and *seb Naomi* exemplify this impression. Naomi did use both "niss" and "seb" in two-word utterances containing "more" (*more niss, more seb*). The use of "more" with "seb," however, is not in clear agreement with adult usage; an utterance such as *seb again* would be expected. Nevertheless, children certainly produce utterances such as *more up*, so Naomi's usage is not peculiar. Presumably children say such things because "more" serves as a suitable general marker for recurrence. Since it appears to be an appropriate lexical item for noting the reappearance of objects, children may use it to note the reenactment of an event as well.

It must be stressed that although Naomi's use of the new lexical items appeared to conform to adult impressions of the role they played in Braine's stimulus utterances, all of the utterances in which she used them reflected relatively early Stage I semantic notions. These included nomination, recurrence, and action. It would be surprising if evidence of such notions could not be found in Naomi's other utterances during this period. My own interpretation of Braine's probe is that Naomi acquired two new lexical items from Braine, but simply used these in utterances reflecting already-existing semantic notions.

Another study that examined children's acquisition of new linguistic material was performed by Nelson and Bonvillian (1973). The intent of these investigators was to explore children's acquisition of names of objects. Since the method in which the new words were presented relates to a particular semantic notion, however, this study is a useful one to consider; 10 children, approximately aged 18 months, were each exposed to 16 experimental objects. None of the objects nor their names were familiar to the children. Nonsense words were not employed, but when one inspects the names of the objects one does not get the impression that they represent everyday household words—"barrel," "bobber," "caboose," "canteen," "compass," "eyebolt," "handcuffs," "hedgehog," "nozzle," "oiler," "pulley," "sifter," "silo," "sinker," "snorkel," and "whetstone." The children's mothers were instructed to draw their children's attention to the objects and teach them the appropriate words for the experimental objects. The mothers were asked to provide no corrective feedback.

Judging from Nelson and Bonvillian's descriptions of the mothers' naming activities, the contexts in which the children were exposed to the experimental words seemed highly suggestive of nomination. If this were the case, a correspondence between the manner in which the children used the new words and the manner in which they were presented should be found; nomination should have already been a component of the children's linguistic system by age 18 months. Although Nelson and Bonvillian described the children's use of the new words in general terms, this seemed to be the case. The children's uses of the new words (which, after 5 weeks, averaged 12 of the 16 experimental words) were described in terms of labeling "concept examples with appropriate words" (p 440). From this terminology, at least, it appears that the children used the new lexical items in utterances reflecting the early notion of nomination.

I also conducted a study that examined children's acquisition of new linguistic material (Leonard, 1975b). Through a modeling procedure similar to the one proposed by Bandura and Harris (1966), the 18 young children in this study were exposed to two-word subject + verb utterances such as *Larry sit*. Such utterances were not previously noted in the speech of these children. Each child was seen individually and a third participant, an adult serving as a model, joined in the activity. The child was told to listen and pay close attention to the model, for the model was going to talk about some events in a "special way." I then enacted some event and requested the model to talk about what was happening. Generally the model talked about the events by using the subject + verb form (e.g., *you jump*), which I indicated was correct. In order to assist the child in identifying the characteristics shared by all "correct" utterances, the model intentionally failed to use the appropriate form in approximately 20 percent of her utterances. I called attention to these errors.

After observing the model produce 10 utterances, the child was encouraged to talk about enactments in the same manner used by the model. At this point, the model and child alternated producing appropriate utterances to describe the enacted events. After the child produced 3 consecutive appropriate utterances about the same enacted events previously presented to the model, the child was required to produce utterances of the subject + verb form in response to novel enacted events requiring unmodeled subject + verb utterances.

In this study, I was also interested in examining how underlying semantic notions might interact with the children's acquisition of the subject + verb form. The children were randomly assigned to 1 of 3 conditions. In one of these conditions, children were exposed to events which, if described, would require utterances reflecting agent (e.g., *Larry jump*). In another condition 4 different types of events were randomly exposed: those which linguistically would reflect agent, instrument (e.g., *hammer hit*), experiencer (e.g., *Larry sneeze*), and object (e.g., *ball roll*). In the remaining condition, children were exposed only to clues to events which if described would require utterances reflecting agent, instrument, experiencer, and object. For example, I stood in the middle of the room pointing alternately to myself and a chair next to me and requested the child to "make up what's happening here." A subject + verb utterance such as *Larry sit* was required in such a circumstance. The actual event that the utterance described was never carried out.

After the experimental phase of the study, the children's use of subject + verb utterances reflecting the 4 semantic notions was assessed. Results indicated that, provided the children were exposed to events rather than clues to events, they could use subject + verb utterances reflecting notions that were not involved in their experimental sessions. The children exposed only to events that could be described by utterances reflecting agent subsequently produced subject + verb utterances reflecting agent, instrument, experiencer, and object to the same degree as the children exposed to events that would be described by utterances reflecting each of the 4 semantic notions.

It would be tempting to interpret the study's results as supporting the contention that through the manipulation of environmental events and linguistic exposure the child can acquire new semantic notions. This may not have been the case. The study had as its purpose the question as to whether or not through appropriate experiences the child could acquire a particular syntactic rule and apply this rule to utterances reflecting semantic notions other than the one reflected by the modeled utterances used to exemplify the syntactic rule.

This experimental question seemed to have been answered affirmatively. But there was no evidence that the children did not possess all of the semantic notions simply because they were not reflected in subject + verb utterances prior to the experimental sessions. In fact, this syntactic form is not a typical one for notions such as object and instrument. In selecting children for the study, I was attending primarily to their use or non-use of subject + verb utterances, but of the children's initial utterances (composed necessarily of constructions other than subject + verb) that I did transcribe, evidence of object was seen frequently, with some children producing utterances reflecting experiencer and instrument. Therefore it appears that most of the semantic notions may have been present from the start; they were simply coded by different syntactic rules. If the children did acquire a new semantic notion through linguistic exposure paired with appropriate environmental events, the obvious candidate would be agent. This semantic notion is typically coded in a manner consistent with the subject + verb form. Since this form was not used initially and it was not very likely that agent was coded by some other form in the children's speech, it is very possible that the experimental procedure enabled the children to acquire this notion. Of course, if this notion was acquired as a result of this procedure, it was not through exposure alone; responses were required of the children and feedback was provided. Thus, such acquisition took place under solicited and enforced conditions. To sum up, my study seemed to demonstrate that syntactic forms can be altered by experience, but the evidence that the semantic notions underlying children's language are subject to the same influence was not as strong.

SEMANTIC NOTIONS AND
GRAMMATICAL MORPHEMES

In the previous section it was observed that semantic notions seem to represent a component of language that is less sensitive to environmental influences than are components of language such as syntax and the lexicon. The degree to which semantic notions are bound to the child's cognitive development is not firmly established, of course, but their apparent inflexibility raises a rather interesting question: Can the semantic notions underlying a child's language affect his acquisition of more superficial language features?

The rationale behind this question is that because some semantic notions emerge earlier than others, the psychological processing requirements involved in producing utterances that reflect these earlier notions may be reduced. This reduction, in turn, may permit the realization of new linguistic features in surface structure that would not be noted in utterances reflecting later-emerging semantic notions. Such a state of affairs calls to mind Slobin's (1970a) principle that new forms are often first expressed in utterances reflecting "old" functions. This question is also related to one raised by Brown (1973). In his discussion of case grammar applied to child language, Brown suggested that the psychological reality of underlying cases might be tested by observing whether a surface structure feature might appear first in utterances where it serves to mark one case before it is seen in utterances where it marks another. For example, the preposition "with" marks instrument (e.g., *sweep with broom*) as well as what Brown terms "comitative" (e.g., *walk with Mommy*). If these cases had psychological reality, the two uses of "with" might appear at different times.

Surface structure features that would serve quite satisfactorily in this regard are the grammatical morphemes examined in the speech of children by Brown (1973), Cazden (1968), and de Villiers and de Villiers (1973). These grammatical morphemes do not generally appear in children's speech until Stage II, which in Brown's classification scheme, begins when mean utterance length exceeds 2.00 morphemes. I collected at least one sample, from each of the eight children, that exceeded the mean utterance level of 2.30 morphemes. Therefore an inspection of these morphemes seemed appropriate. I then analyzed the language samples in terms of the grammatical morphemes, using the Brown, Cazden, and de Villiers scoring instructions kindly provided me. In particular, I was interested in examining the percentage in which each grammatical morpheme was used in obligatory contexts in utterances reflecting the various semantic notions. The specific hypothesis to test was whether or not utterances reflecting earlier-emerging semantic notions would contain these grammatical morphemes before utterances reflecting later-emerging notions.

The semantic notions under examination were categorized according to their general order of emergence. It can be recalled, however, that the notions could be ordered developmentally with any degree of confidence only by grouping some of them that seem to emerge at about the same time. The result of this tactic was four groups of semantic notions, identified at the end of Chapter 5, whose time of emergence in the child's speech appeared to be different. Thus, the types of questions I was interested in asking, for example, were: Are plural morphemes observed in utterances reflecting Group A notions before Group B, C, or D notions?

An important point should be made about the grammatical morphemes before turning to the results. Apparently these morphemes are referred to as "grammatical" because they represent function words and inflections that, during Stage II, "begin to grow up between and upon the major construction blocks" of Stage I (Brown, 1973, p 249). Although they may not carry the semantic weight of underlying semantic notions, the grammatical morphemes do possess meanings of their own. Presented in Table 6–5 are the meanings of ten grammatical morphemes during Stage I speech. In this table, I have modified some of the information in Brown (1973) by combining regular and irregular past, contractible and uncontractible copula, and contractible and uncontractible auxiliary.

Most of the meanings appearing in Table 6–5 are self-explanatory; some, however, require explanation. The copula varies in form with the number (singular or plural) of the subject of the utterance and also with tense, which during Stage II is either present or past (earlier). The third person regular might also entail number and "earlierness" because this inflection is used when these dimensions are operative—singular subjects and present tense. The auxiliary always accompanies the progressive ending and therefore might entail temporary duration. In addition, the form of the auxiliary is influenced by the number of the subject as well as by tense.

Table 6–5
Ten Grammatical Morphemes and Their
Stage II Meanings

Grammatical Morpheme and Example	Meaning
Present progressive (*baby crying*)	Temporary duration
"in" (*Daddy in ɔ there*)	Containment
"on" (*tape on truck*)	Support
Plural (*that dogs*)	Number
Past (*kitty jumped up*)	Earlierness
Possessive (*Patsy's pencil*)	Possession
Article (*I got a cup*)	Specific-nonspecific
Copula (*here's ɔ yellow one*)	Number, earlierness
Third person (*here one fits*)	Number, earlierness
Auxiliary (*Daddy's sitting there*)	Temporary duration, number, earlierness

The meanings that Brown assigns to each of the three morphemes, copula, third person singular, and auxiliary, represent two or more of the unitary meanings assigned to some of the other grammatical morphemes. It is not clear, however, that these meanings are identical. For example, the child's use of the copula form in *Chris is here* is dictated by the singular nature of "Chris" and the present nature of the event. On the other hand, the child's use of the plural form in *that dogs* or the past tense in *I jumped* seems based on the plural nature of the dogs and the past nature of the event, respectively. Thus, they are based on opposite poles on the number and tense dimensions than the child's use of "is." The true number and tense equivalents to the copula "is" would be singular and present as seen in *that dog* and *I jump*, respectively. Interestingly, the child who produces such utterances is not credited with number or tense because in these instances singular and present are not marked by any grammatical morphemes, even in adult usage.

This poses some problems for the ordering of these grammatical morphemes according to semantic complexity, as seen in the work of Brown (1973) and de Villiers and de Villiers (1973). These investigators employed the principle of cumulative complexity in constructing their orders of complexity. According to this principle, any morpheme that entails knowledge of $x + y$ is presumed to be more complex than either x or y. This principle certainly seems to be a sound one; however, in application it must be certain that the knowledge of the individual elements is indeed the same type of knowledge included in the more complex element $x + y$. In the previous discussion of the copula (which may entail singular number and present tense) as it compared to the plural form and past tense, it was seen that this may not be the case. An examination of some recent work by de Villiers (1976) reveals the following predictions of cumulative semantic complexity.

plural < copula
past < copula
plural < third person
past < third person
plural < auxiliary
past < auxiliary
progressive < auxiliary
copula < auxiliary
third person < auxiliary

I found that in order to examine the appearance of grammatical morphemes in terms of the order of emergence of the semantic notions reflected in the children's utterances, not all of the grammatical morphemes could be used. The children's use of the possessive inflection, for example, could only be used in utterances reflecting possession. Similarly, "in" or "on" were too integrally related to place. Other grammatical morphemes were simply never used (the auxiliary and regular past tense) or were used only in rote phrases. I restricted my analysis to four morphemes: the article, plural, copula, and present progressive. The first two could be used in utterances reflecting semantic notions assigned to each of the four semantic notion groups. The remaining two were more restricted in usage; the copula could be used only in utterances reflecting Group A and C notions, and the present progressive was appropriate only for Group B and D notions.

As stated earlier, the hypothesis that was tested was that each grammatical morpheme would first appear in utterances reflecting Group A notions, then the notions of Group B, and so on. The results of the analysis of the children's use of articles are presented in Table 6–6.

The results presented in Table 6–6 suggest that there was a clear trend of the first appearance of articles in a child's speech to be in utterances reflecting an earlier- rather than later-emerging group of semantic notions. When one considers that 4 groups were involved, the fact that 24 of the 36 observations were in the predicted direction does not appear to be a random finding. There were 12 observations that were not in the predicted direction, however—7 of these represented instances in which the sample showing the first use of articles provided evidence of article usage in utterances reflecting an earlier- as well as a later-emerging group of semantic notions.

Table 6–6

The Number of Times Articles First Appeared in
Utterances Reflecting One Group of Semantic Notions
before or Simultaneously with Another Group

	Group A	Group B	Group C	Group D
Used before Group A		2	1	1
" " " B	5		1	0
" " " C	3	3		0
" " " D	5	5	3	
Used in same sample as Group A				
" " " " " " B	0			
" " " " " " C	1	2		
" " " " " " D	1	1	2	

The results of the analysis of the children's use of the copula appear in Table 6–7. It can be seen from this table that 5 of the 7 observations were in the predicted direction, with the remaining 2 observations representing instances in which the sample showing the first use of the copula provides evidence of such usage in utterances reflecting both Group A and C notions.

Instances in which obligatory contexts for the present progressive occurred in utterances reflecting both Group B and D notions were relatively few. From Table 6–8, it can be seen that 3 of the 4 observations were in the predicted direction. For the remaining observation the first use of the present progressive occurred in utterances reflecting Group D notions as well as Group B notions.

The identification of obligatory contexts for plural usage proved to be a tricky task. Upon reviewing the video tape recordings, I concluded that most utterances could not be interpreted with sufficient accuracy to determine if they served as obligatory contexts for plurals. A typical example was one where the child approaches a box containing several toy

Table 6–7

The Number of Times Copula Appeared in
Utterances Reflecting One Group of
Semantic Notions before or Simultaneously
with the Other Group

	Group A	Group C
Used before Group A		0
" " " C	5	
Used in same sample as Group A		
" ' " " " " " C	2	

Table 6–8

The Number of Times Present Progressive
Appeared in Utterances Reflecting One
Group of Semantic Notions before or
Simultaneously with the Other Group

	Group B	Group D
Used before Group B		0
" " " D	3	
Used in same sample as Group B		
" " " " " " D	1	

cars and says *there car*. I decided to treat such utterances as uninter-
pretable. As it turned out, the only utterances in which there were linguistic cues as to the appropriate use of plurals in them were utterances
containing a quantifier such as "two" or "three." Even these were infrequent. In fact, only two instances were noted where a plural was not
used in an obligatory context, and both were in the same circumstance.

(Morton [III] walks over and points to
the zoo animal and the camel)   two dog/one, two dog/

Thus, obligatory contexts for plural usage were identified only when (1)
plurals were actually used, or (2) an utterance was noted in which a
quantifier preceded the word that could be pluralized. As was illustrated
in the above example from Morton's usage, the reliance on quantifiers as
the sole means of identifying instances in which a plural was not used
in an obligatory context would severely constrain the number of semantic
notions that would be reflected by utterances showing absence of obligatory plurals. This necessitated the exclusion of plurals from this analysis.

In summary, the children's use of the article, copula, and present
progressive may have been related to the semantic notions underlying
their utterances. The first use of these grammatical morphemes was
usually in utterances reflecting earlier-emerging notions. This finding
could be interpreted as supporting the explanation that earlier notions
require less processing, permitting the child to apply a new morphological rule more readily. Some caution should be exercised in this interpretation, however, since the most frequent underlying notions were
those earliest to emerge, as pointed out in Chapter 5. Thus, the grammatical morphemes were more likely to be first used in utterances reflecting earlier notions in the first place.

Even most of the instances that were not in the predicted direction
did not render much damage to the hypothesis tested. Of the 15 instances

that were not in the predicted direction, 10 represented the simultaneous appearance of a grammatical morpheme in utterances reflecting more than one group of semantic notions (see Tables 6–6, 6–7, and 6–8). Of course, these 10 instances are consistent with the alternative hypothesis that the child's use of grammatical morphemes is unrelated to underlying semantic notions. Since there were 32 instances that were in the predicted direction, however, the evidence supporting the alternative hypothesis is not strong. It is plausible that these 10 instances were due to the duration of time between samples obtained from each of the children. All of the samples used for this analysis exceeded 2.30 morphemes in mean utterance length, while for the preceding sample, no child's mean utterance length exceeded 1.91 morphemes. Brown (1973) has noted that some grammatical morphemes may be used 90 percent of the time in obligatory contexts by early Stage II speech. It can be seen, therefore, that during the period before their Stage II sample, the children may have had an opportunity not only to acquire initial usage of some of the grammatical morphemes, but to become relatively proficient in their use of these grammatical morphemes in utterances reflecting some of the later emerging semantic notions as well. This raises the possibility that, had I obtained samples from some of the children at a point somewhat prior to a mean utterance length of 2.30 morphemes, a greater number of instances in the predicted direction may have been noted. Quite clearly, this issue should be examined further in future research.

SEMANTIC NOTIONS AND UTTERANCE LENGTH

The possibility that the child's use of grammatical morphemes may be an influence of the semantic notions underlying his utterances leads to another important issue. If earlier-emerging semantic notions require less psychological processing that permits surface structure realization of grammatical morphemes, should a child's mean utterance length be viewed as a measure of general linguistic development? The appearance of grammatical morphemes, of course, has an effect of increasing mean utterance length. But if they appear in association with underlying semantic notions that are firmly established in the child's linguistic system, it would seem possible that a child whose system of underlying semantic notions is in a temporary period of little change may produce utterances of equal or greater length than a child with a more rapidly developing system of semantic notions. Such a finding could occur, presumably, because the reduced processing requirements in the first child's language could permit earlier use of grammatical morphemes.

Table 6–9

A Comparison of Two Stage II Grammars for Samples of
Similar Mean Utterance Length

	Jennings IV (2.52 Morphemes)	Greer IV (2.51 Morphemes)
Sentence	Illocutionary force + Proposition	Illocutionary force + Proposition

Illocutionary force	⎰ Declare ⎱
	⎱ Request ⎰
	  Question
		⎰ Declare ⎱
		⎱ Request ⎰
		  Question

Proposition	(Function◊Designated)	(Function◊Designated)
Function	(Operation◊Ergative)	(Operation◊Ergative)
Designated	(Goal◊Property)	(Goal◊Property)
Operation	Nomination Notice Denial Nonexistence Rejection	Nomination Denial Recurrence
Ergative	(Actor◊Process)	(Agent) Action
Goal	Object Place Experiencer	Object Place
Property	Attribution Possessor	Attribution Possessor
Actor	Agent Instrument	
Process	Action Experience	

One proper way of testing this proposal would be to compare the grammars written for children's language samples that proved to be of equal mean utterance length. No two samples representing Stage II speech were found to be equal in mean utterance length. Two were found that were very close in mean utterance length, however, (2.52 and 2.51 morphemes) and I compared them according to underlying semantic notions and use of grammatical morphemes. The grammars written for these two samples, obtained from Jennings and Greer, appear in Table 6–9.

It appears that the differences in these two samples permit a prediction about the children's relative use of grammatical morphemes, following the discussion above. Jennings's grammar contains several later-developing semantic notions, experiencer, experience, and instrument, that are not noted in the grammar written for Greer. Greer's heavier reliance on earlier-developing semantic notions, then, may enable greater use of grammatical morphemes. I therefore compared the children in terms of the percentage of such usage in obligatory contexts in utterances reflecting the various semantic notions, commencing, of course, only at the point when the grammatical morpheme was first used.

An examination of the use of articles in obligatory contexts by Jennings and Greer tended to confirm predictions. Jennings produced articles in 18 percent of their obligatory contexts while Greer produced them in 86 percent. In each case where an obligatory context for article usage was noted in an utterance reflecting one of the later-developing semantic notions, Jennings did not produce the article. Since the copula would be used only in utterances reflecting semantic notions evidenced in the grammars of both children, no comparisons were made using this grammatical morpheme. No obligatory contexts for present progressive usage were noted in any of Greer's utterances, making a comparison between Jennings and Greer in the use of this grammatical morpheme impossible. Therefore, this avenue of analysis did not prove too helpful, although in the one instance in which it could be tested, the predicted direction of the differences was confirmed.

The differences in the semantic notions contained in the grammars of Table 6–9 were surprising considering that they were written for samples of very similar mean utterance length. It seemed useful to explore these differences further. Several samples from different children at Stage I were equal in mean utterance length. I therefore compared them in terms of the grammars I had written for them, with an eye on any differences in the semantic notions they contained.

Several different levels of development were represented by the samples that could be equated with one another on the basis of mean utterance length. They will be discussed in order of the level of development they represented.

The grammars of two samples with a mean utterance length of 1.26 morphemes are compared in Table 6–10. In three respects, the grammar written for Leslie appears more complex in terms of underlying semantic notions. Unlike Lynn, her grammar includes the two notions subsumed under property—attribution and possessor. Two examples of utterances reflecting these notions are

1. (Leslie [I] walks by the water bowl of
    the family dog, Morgan, and points
    to it)   bowl/Morgan bowl/

Table 6–10
A Comparison of Samples with a Computed Mean
Utterance Length of 1.26 Morphemes

	Leslie I	Lynn I
Sentence	Illocutionary force + Proposition	Illocutionary force + Proposition
Illocutionary force	{ Declare Request Question }	{ Declare Request Question }
Proposition	(Function⟩Designated)	(Operation⟩Designated)
Function	{ Operation Ergative }	
Designated	Object (Property)	
Operation	{ Notice Nonexistence }	Notice
Property	{ Attribution Possessor }	
Ergative	(Agent) Action	

2. Mother: "Tell Larry where you
    sleep."
    (Leslie looks at Larry and stretches
    her arms out)   big bed/

In addition, the rewrite rules for Leslie's grammar include agent and
action. Less important (in light of frequency of occurrence effects), Leslie's
grammar contains nonexistence, which was not the case for Lynn's
grammar.

Appearing in Table 6–11 is a comparison of two samples at a mean
utterance length level of 1.44 morphemes.

The grammar written for Kristen's sample seems to be the more
advanced of the two. Kristen's illocutionary force includes question, and
her sample contained evidence of place, which was not seen in Alec's
sample.

Two samples with a computed mean utterance length of 1.78 morphemes are compared in Table 6–12. This comparison reveals that
Morton's grammar contains nomination and agent, which was not the
case for the grammar written for Kristen.

Table 6–11

A Comparison of Samples with a Computed Mean
Utterance Length of 1.44 Morphemes

	Alec II	Kristen IV
Sentence	Illocutionary force + Proposition	Illocutionary force + Proposition
Illocutionary force	$\begin{Bmatrix} \text{Declare} \\ \text{Request} \end{Bmatrix}$	$\begin{Bmatrix} \text{Declare} \\ \text{Request} \\ \text{Question} \end{Bmatrix}$
Proposition	(Function◊Designated)	(Function◊Designated)
Function	$\begin{Bmatrix} \text{Operation} \\ \text{Ergative} \end{Bmatrix}$	$\begin{Bmatrix} \text{Operation} \\ \text{Ergative} \end{Bmatrix}$
Designated	(Object◊Property)	(Goal◊Property)
Operation	$\begin{Bmatrix} \text{Nomination} \\ \text{Notice} \end{Bmatrix}$	$\begin{Bmatrix} \text{Nomination} \\ \text{Notice} \end{Bmatrix}$
Property	Attribution	Attribution
Ergative	Action	Action
Goal		$\begin{Bmatrix} \text{Object} \\ \text{Place} \end{Bmatrix}$

Table 6–12

A Comparison of Samples with a Computed Mean
Utterance Length of 1.78 Morphemes

	Kristen V	Morton II
Sentence	Illocutionary force + Proposition	Illocutionary force + Proposition
Illocutionary force	$\begin{Bmatrix} \text{Declare} \\ \text{Request} \\ \text{Question} \end{Bmatrix}$	$\begin{Bmatrix} \text{Declare} \\ \text{Request} \\ \text{Question} \end{Bmatrix}$
Proposition	(Function◊Designated)	(Function◊Designated)
Function	(Operation◊Ergative)	(Operation◊Ergative)
Designated	(Goal◊Property)	(Goal◊Property)
Operation	Notice	$\begin{Bmatrix} \text{Nomination} \\ \text{Notice} \end{Bmatrix}$
Property	Attribution	Possessor
Ergative	Action	(Agent) Action
Goal	$\begin{Bmatrix} \text{Object} \\ \text{Place} \end{Bmatrix}$	$\begin{Bmatrix} \text{Object} \\ \text{Place} \end{Bmatrix}$

It appears evident from the comparison of grammars at the different levels of development that differences existed in grammars that were written for samples of equal mean utterance length. I think some of these differences may have been due to frequency of occurrence factors. Perhaps a more appropriate way of comparing the grammars, then, would be to look at them in terms of the groups of semantic notions that were used for analysis purposes in the previous section. Our question, then, turns to whether or not for samples matched for mean utterance length we find the same groups of semantic notions included in the respective grammars. Since these groups were formed on the basis of the general order in which semantic notions emerge, this type of comparison seemed useful.

An examination of the grammars for the samples of Leslie and Lynn at 1.26 morphemes revealed differences. Unlike Lynn's grammar, the grammar written for Leslie contained two Group B and two Group C notions. The two grammars for the samples of Alec and Kristen at 1.44 morphemes were not different when analyzed in this manner; both grammars contained Group A, B, and C notions. A similar finding was noted when the grammars of the two samples at 1.78 morphemes were compared; the grammars for both Morton and Kristen were restricted to the semantic notions of Groups A, B, and C.

It was hoped that these findings could be put to use in assessing the relative merits of two alternative explanations for the differences in the underlying semantic notions of children with equal utterance length, an issue raised in Chapter 2. One explanation, offered by Bloom (1973), was that children may differ in their strategies for learning about language. These differences in strategies are presumably due to different kinds of experience that require different mental representations. In Chapter 2, I proposed an alternative explanation—that differences in children's underlying semantic notions may represent different points on a developmental continuum. This explanation requires that the correspondence between a child's mean utterance length and the semantic notions underlying his utterances is not fixed, a requirement that seems consistent with the above findings.

Both the strategy and developmental continuum explanations allow for similarities as well as differences in the semantic notions underlying two children's samples with equivalent mean utterance length. When differences are noted, however, the developmental continuum explanation would predict that they take only one form. The notions evidenced in one but not the other sample would belong to the most advanced group of notions. The sample containing the most advanced notions would also contain all of the notions evidenced in the other sample. That is, in this explanation, earlier groups of notions would be retained when new groups appear since their original appearance would presumably be due to their communicative value, not simply to serve as stepping stones along some path leading to an adult semantic system. This is not to say, of course, that a child's early semantic notions are precisely in the form seen in the adult system. It is to say that the notions, though perhaps requiring some reshaping to be the same as those of the adult system, will continue serving a useful role.

The strategy explanation, on the other hand, does not predict differences of any particular type. There would be no requirement that a grammar containing, say, Group C notions would need to contain Group A or B notions. In fact, if two children can be described as following two different strategies, it might be expected that there would not be much overlap in the semantic notions reflected in their speech. The grammar for one child, for example, might contain semantic notions termed here as Group A or B notions, while another child's grammar may contain Group C notions.

Unfortunately, a difference in the groups of semantic notions contained in two samples of the same mean utterance length was observed in only one of the three comparisons. This difference was consistent with the developmental continuum explanation. Leslie's grammar for her sample at 1.26 morphemes contained Group A, B, and C notions. Lynn's grammar, on the other hand, contained only Group A notions. Nevertheless, this difference is not inconsistent with the strategy explanation, since this explanation allows for differences of any type. It is unfortunate that differences were not observed for the other two comparisons because an examination of their nature might allow one to choose between these two explanations.

The adequacy of the developmental continuum explanation can be tested further, it appears, by comparing two samples obtained at different periods of time from the same child. Such comparisons might be subject to the confounding effects of increased utterance length. Fortunately, though, several instances were noted where, perhaps due to transitory factors, a sample revealed a decrease rather than increase in mean utterance length from the preceding sample from the same child. The developmental continuum explanation would predict that despite the decrease in mean utterance length, the semantic notions reflected in the subsequent sample should be the same as those in the preceding sample, or should also include new, later-emerging notions not seen in the preceding sample. This explanation assumes no close correspondence between underlying semantic notions and utterance length.

The fifth sample obtained from Colin, with mean utterance length computed at 1.23 morphemes, represented a drop in mean utterance

Table 6–13
Comparison of Colin's Samples Revealing a Decrease in
Mean Utterance Length for Successive Samples

	Colin IV (1.34 Morphemes)	Colin V (1.23 Morphemes)
Sentence	Illocutionary force + Proposition	Illocutionary force + Proposition
Illocutionary force	{Declare / Request}	{Declare / Request}
Proposition	(Function∮Designated)	(Function∮Designated)
Function	Operation	{Operation / Ergative}
Operation	Notice	{Notice / Nonexistence / Recurrence}
Ergative		(Agent) Action
Designated	Goal	{Goal / Property}
Goal	(Object∮Place)	(Object∮Place)
Property		Attribution

length from the preceding sample of 1.34 morphemes. A comparison of the semantic notions contained in the grammars of these two samples is presented in Table 6–13.

It can be seen from Table 6–13 that, despite the decrease in mean utterance length, the grammar written for the fifth sample of Colin contained several new notions. No new groups of notions were evidenced in the subsequent sample, however.

The sixth sample from Kristen represented a minimal decrease in mean utterance length from the preceding sample, dropping from 1.78 to 1.77 morphemes. The grammars for these two samples appear in Table 6–14.

Both grammars contained Group A, B, and C notions; however, the grammar for Kristen VI contained two Group D notions as well. It can also be noted from this table that the grammar of the subsequent sample contained a greater number of semantic notions from each of the different groups.

Greer's third sample represented a radical decrease in mean length of utterance from the preceding sample, dropping from 1.90 to 1.62 morphemes. From the comparison of the grammars written for these two samples (Table 6–15), however, this decrease did not seem related to the

Table 6–14

Comparison of Kristen's Samples Revealing a Decrease in
Mean Utterance Length for Successive Samples

	Kristen V (1.78 Morphemes)	Kristen VI (1.77 Morphemes)
Sentence	Illocutionary force + Proposition	Illocutionary force + Proposition
Illocutionary force	Declare Request Question	Declare Request Question
Proposition	(Function⟩Designated)	(Function⟩Designated)
Function	(Operation⟩Ergative)	(Operation⟩Ergative)
Designated	(Goal⟩Property)	(Goal⟩Property)
Operation	Notice	Nomination Notice Nonexistence
Property	Attribution	Attribution Possessor
Ergative	Action	Process
Goal	Object Place	Object Experiencer Place
Process		Action Experience

groups of semantic notions underlying Greer's speech. Neither of the two grammars contained any of the Group D notions; both contained notions of each of the other three groups. As was true in the comparison of the grammars of Kristen and Colin, the grammar for the subsequent sample from Greer contained a greater number of semantic notions from each of the groups of notions.

Since the developmental continuum explanation predicts that the semantic notions reflected in a subsequent sample should be the same as those in the preceding sample or include new notions not seen in the preceding sample, this explanation was supported by the findings of each of the three grammar comparisons. In two of these comparisons, the groups of semantic notions that were represented were the same for both grammars. However, the number of semantic notions in the groups was greater for the grammar written for the subsequent sample. This finding is somewhat surprising since one might expect that whatever transitory factors were influencing the child's utterance length might be suppressing the

Table 6–15
Comparison of Greer's Samples Revealing a Decrease in
Mean Utterance Length for Successive Samples

	Greer II (1.90 Morphemes)	Greer III (1.62 Morphemes)
Sentence	Illocutionary force + Proposition	Illocutionary force + Proposition
Illocutionary force	{ Declare Request }	{ Declare Request Question }
Proposition	(Function◊Designated)	(Function◊Designated)
Function	(Operation◊Ergative)	(Operation◊Ergative)
Designated	(Object◊Property)	(Goal◊Property)
Operation	Notice	{ Nomination Nonexistence Recurrence }
Property	{ Possessor Attribution }	{ Possessor Attribution }
Ergative	(Agent) Action	(Agent) Action
Goal		{ Object Place }

semantic notions underlying his speech as well. Nevertheless, it appears that the limited number of observed differences seemed to undermine an evaluation of the relative adequacy of the developmental continuum explanation.

There are other methods of assessing the adequacy of the developmental continuum explanation. I utilized one of these in Chapter 2 when I analyzed the two-word utterances in the consecutive samples from the children studied by Ramer (1974) and Braine (1976). My reason for analyzing only the two-word utterances was the same as my reason for comparing the grammars for the above pairs of samples—to control for confounding effects due to increasing utterance length.

My analysis of the Ramer and Braine data in Chapter 2 entailed categorizing the children's two-word utterances into two groups: Group 1, which consisted of utterances reflecting semantic notions typically coded by functional relations (e.g., nomination, nonexistence), and Group 2, which consisted of utterances reflecting notions typically coded by grammatical relations (e.g., agent, action). For sake of consistency, I analyzed my own data in the same way. The results are presented in Table 6–16.

Table 6–16
Summary of Analysis of Group 1 and Group 2 Utterance Types

Child	Number of Samples with Two-Word Utterances (At Least Five Utterance Types)	Number of Sample Comparisons	Number of Comparisons Showing Decrease of Group 1 Types	Showing Increase of Group 2 Types
Leslie	3	2	2	2
Alec	3	2	1	1
Kristen	4	3	2	2
Lynn	4	3	2	2
Morton	3	2	0	2
Jennings	3	2	1	1
Greer	3	2	1	2
Colin	5	4	4	4
Total	28	20	13	16

An inspection of Table 6–16 reveals that the two-word utterances over time showed a general trend toward those utterances reflecting notions usually expressed by grammatical relations and away from those reflecting notions usually expressed by functional relations. Since the notions usually coded by functional relations seem to emerge earlier than those coded by grammatical relations, this finding might be interpreted as being consistent with the developmental continuum explanation. Some caution should be exercised in this interpretation, however, since the data are not overwhelming. The number of comparisons showing a decrease of Group 1 types is not much more than half. It appears that we must await further research before the issue of the relative merits of the developmental continuum explanation can be resolved with much certainty. In a later section of this chapter, the related issue of the use of functional and grammatical relations will be taken up more directly.

SEMANTIC NOTIONS AND THE USE OF INDETERMINATE AND EMPTY FORMS

In Chapter 2, during the discussion of differences in style among children at similar stages of linguistic development, several features of language were identified by Ramer (1974) that may have some relationship with underlying semantic notions. These features included dummy forms (usually a vowel preceding or following a word), empty forms (a "word" with no identifiable referent), reduplications (one word produced two or

more times in succession), and indeterminate forms (multi-word utterances containing recognizable words whose relationship is not clear).

There was surprisingly little use of these features in the speech of
the eight children studied. Reduplications were nonexistent, at least those
representing a repetition of a word within the same intonation contour.
Dummy forms were infrequent and were evidenced primarily at a point
well after multi-word utterances were acquired (e.g., Greer's *bug ə head*
at 1.90 morphemes). Indeterminate forms were also sufficiently infrequent
to disallow the assumption that they were part of any child's linguistic
"style," although one child, Morton, seemed to use them more frequently
than the others. Such usage never made up more than 6 percent of the
utterances in any of Morton's samples. The points at which Morton's
most frequent use of indeterminate forms occurred, however, were considerably late in the period of Stage I speech; when Morton's mean
utterance length was 1.78 and 1.79 morphemes.

Ramer noted that the children showing considerable use of indeterminate forms in her study reached the three-word period more quickly
than those who did not show such usage. She tentatively attributed such
usage to risk-taking tendencies during the acquisition process. These rapid
developers, however, apparently missed out on the opportunity to acquire
certain semantic notions evidenced in the speech of the children developing
more slowly. But Ramer's method of analysis had a syntactic emphasis,
thus making word order a variable to contend with in her data. In the
proposed approach to grammar writing, word order does not play a major
role in defining underlying semantic notions. Therefore, the risk-taking
tendencies that may enable a child to develop more rapidly, although
with a number of indeterminate productions, may also enable him to
attempt a number of utterances that, in the proposed approach to grammar writing, might be sufficient to be taken as reflecting one or more
new semantic notions.

If this were the case, it might be expected that a child with a number
of indeterminate forms in his usage might show evidence of the same
semantic notions reflected in the utterances of a child at the same level
of linguistic development who did not use many indeterminate forms.
In fact such a child might use semantic notions not evidenced in the
speech of the second child because his risk-taking behavior might lead
to the use of utterances that reflect new semantic notions even if the
coding of these notions (not of chief importance in the proposed approach
to analysis) is improper syntactically. Since the only child (Morton)
showing any appreciable use of indeterminate forms never used them in
more than 6 percent of his utterances, this question cannot be pursued
very far here. It is somewhat interesting, nevertheless, to note that a comparison between the grammar for Morton's sampled speech at a point

when his indeterminate form usage was maximal, and the grammar for Kristen's speech at the same mean utterance level (see Table 6–12) indicates that Morton's grammar contained two notions not seen in the grammar of Kristen. This issue seems worthy of further investigation, although its resolution may require a considerable amount of searching for children whose speech consists of a sufficient number of indeterminate forms.

Ramer also noted that the children she studied differed in their use of empty forms. Actually, only one of these children, discussed in Chapter 2, showed such usage. Not one of the children I studied showed this type of usage. Quite interestingly, however, two children used forms quite similar in function to that typically seen in empty form usage. Most surprising is that these children, Kristen and Colin, used the same form, "/n/ there," with both children less frequently using the variant "there." The use of "there" in Stage I speech has been reported by a number of investigators. Depending upon its apparent function, its use in utterances has been interpreted as reflecting nomination, location, and notice. I eventually concluded that the use of "/n/ there" and "there" in the utterances by Kristen and Colin represented notice, in that these forms seemed to be used to direct one's attention toward the object, state, or event specified by the other word in the utterance. For example, Kristen's use of "/n/ there" in the utterance *raining /n/ there* seemed to direct attention to the rain starting to fall outside. Similarly, Colin's use of this form in *horsie /n/ there* appeared to direct attention to his picking up the toy horse.

Even though these particular forms may be taken as true words serving an attention-directing function, they also had characteristics possessed as well by empty forms. They were used in fixed (second) word position, they eventually decreased in frequency or dropped out altogether, and the circumstances under which these forms were used in utterances were so varied as to resemble Bloom's (1973) description of empty forms—forms used for everything—and hence were so general they meant nothing. Presented below are a few examples from Kristen (V) illustrating this general usage.

zoo /n/ there
fix /n/ there
workin /n/ there
Heidi /n/ there
help me /n/ there
on /n/ there

This global manner in which "/n/ there" and "there" was used is still consistent with my treating such forms as reflecting notice. However, notice as it is used here is only intended as a very general semantic notion. One can direct attention to almost anything. To be sure, the fact that these forms coincide with words in the adult system was just as instrumental in my treating them as a type of notice as the manner in which they were used. Empty forms as seen in *Mommy widə* and *more widə* could also be taken as forms that direct attention to the objects and events specified by the words with which these forms are combined. The main reason why they are not interpreted in his manner, apparently, is that they do not resemble any words in the adult system.

Another aspect about the use of "/n/ there" and "there" was suggestive of empty form usage. Kristen and Colin used these forms most frequently during their fifth and fourth samples, respectively. The next samples obtained from these children reflected an unexpected decrease in mean utterance length. This decrease would be expected if, instead of representing true words as I regarded them, "/n/ there" and "there" were merely empty forms serving to assist the child in the process of acquiring multi-word utterances. By the next sample, when the use of these empty forms had become much less frequent, a better picture of the child's true multi-word utterance usage would be evidenced. It would be expected that such true multi-word utterances would not have been in such abundance by this point to offset the drop in mean utterance length from the preceding sample, where considerable use of (empty form) constructions only resembling multi-word utterances were in evidence.

The fact that some true multi-word utterances were produced by Kristen and Colin when their use of "/n/ there" and "there" was quite frequent does not seem to contradict the hypothesis that these forms may have functioned as empty forms. As I pointed out in an earlier paper (Leonard, 1975a), in each study reporting empty form usage by a child, the child was also observed to produce true multi-word utterances before empty form usage had disappeared from his speech (Bloom, 1973; Ramer, 1974; Leonard, 1975a). Also pointed out was the possibility that empty form constructions might be used up until the time when the child could produce a two-word utterance more precisely reflecting a particular underlying semantic notion. At such time, the empty form precursor may leave the child's repertoire or be used in juxtaposition with different words to reflect a new semantic notion.

Some predictions might be made about the semantic notions reflected in the utterances used by Kristen and Colin relative to those reflected in utterances produced by children with equivalent mean utterance length, if "/n/ there" and "there" were functioning as empty forms. Because such forms seem to prepare the child for the subsequent use of multi-word utterances reflecting new semantic notions, a child using such forms may

Table 6-17

A Comparison of the Grammar for a Sample Containing Potential Empty Form Utterances and Grammars for Samples with Similar Mean Utterance Length

	Colin IV	Leslie I	Lynn I
Sentence	Illocutionary force + Proposition	Illocutionary force + Proposition	Illocutionary force + Proposition
Illocutionary force	{ Declare, Request }	Declare, Request, Question	{ Declare, Request, Question }
Proposition	(Operation)(Designated)	(Function)(Designated)	(Operation)(Designated)
Function		{ Operation, Ergative }	
Designated	Object (Place)	Object (Property)	
Operation	Notice	{ Notice, Nonexistence }	Notice
Property		{ Attribution, Possessor }	
Ergative		(Agent) Action	

159

not have acquired a number of semantic notions already acquired by a child whose equivalent utterance length is based on true multi-word utterances. The sample of Kristen's speech that showed the most use of these forms was the fifth sample, at a mean utterance length of 1.78 morphemes. The grammar for this sample has already been compared with one written for Morton's second sample, at the same level of utterance length. This comparison, seen in Table 6–12, reveals that Morton's grammar contains nomination and agent, which was not the case for the grammar written for Kristen. No differences in terms of the groups of semantic notions represented in the two grammars were noted, however.

A somewhat different picture is obtained when Colin's grammar for the fourth sample (when the use of "/n/ there" and "there" was most frequent) is compared with grammars for two other children's samples of approximate utterance length. Colin's fourth sample, with a mean utterance length of 1.34 morphemes, could not be matched exactly with any other sample. The closest samples in mean utterance length (except Kristen's third, which showed some early use of "/n/ there" and "there") were the two samples whose grammars are compared in Table 6–10. In Table 6–17, these grammars are presented again and compared with the grammar for Colin's sample.

It can be seen from Table 6–17 that while Colin's grammar contains fewer semantic notions than Leslie's, it is comparable to the grammar written for Lynn, in terms of semantic notions. Because Colin's grammar contains place, in fact, it might even be said that it is more advanced than Lynn's.

At this point it is not clear whether the above comparisons failed to reveal any meaningful differences because empty form utterances do not represent the incomplete development of a new semantic notion or whether instead "/n/ there" and "there" in the speech of Kristen and Colin, as I have chosen to conclude, represent real words that in multi-word utterances serve a general attention-directing function appropriate to treat as a type of notice. This issue needs to be explored further before any definitive conclusions can be drawn.

SEMANTIC NOTIONS AND THE USE OF
FUNCTIONAL AND GRAMMATICAL RELATIONS

It appeared quite useful to examine the nature of the syntactic constructions used by each of the eight children to determine which children seemed to primarily make use of functional relations and which seemed to make use of grammatical relations. Once this determination was made, it could be seen whether or not any differences existed in the emergence of the semantic notions reflected in the children's speech.

The speech of four of the eight children could not properly be characterized as representing primarily functional or grammatical relations. Considering that Bloom (1973) noted that the two styles are not necessarily mutually exclusive, this was not an unexpected finding. The speech of the other four children did proceed through a phase consisting of a number of two-word utterances that seemed to primarily represent the use of either functional or grammatical relations. For three of the four children, this usage seemed to take the form of functional relations.

One of these three children was Alec, whose use of functional relations was most notable at a mean utterance length of 1.44 morphemes. The most characteristic feature of Alec's usage was the appearance of "that" in first-word position in a number of constructions.

1. (Alec points to the number "eight" in his book)   that a eight/
2. (Alec's mother takes Alec's hand off of the videotape monitor. Alec then puts his other hand on the monitor)
   Mother: "No no, you may not touch that."   that's a TV/

Functional relations in Colin's speech took a slightly different form; the word consistently combining with a number of other words occupied second-word position. This usage, exemplified below, was most prominent when Colin's mean utterance length was 1.34 morphemes. It should be recalled that Colin's use of "/n/ there," like Kristen's, was eventually deemed consistent with notice, and did not seem to be serving as empty form usage.

1. (Colin takes the toy camel from Larry and puts it in the box in which he is putting his other toys)   box /n/ there/box /n/ there/
2. (Colin tries to get Larry to disassemble the toy zoo animal, after having been unsuccessful himself)   horsie /n/ there/

Kristen, at a mean utterance length of 1.78 morphemes, used constructions of the same form used by Colin, and seemingly in a similar manner. The appearance of functional relations at so high a level of mean utterance length seems quite unusual. This level, however, appeared to be due to the fact that Kristen's two-word constructions with "/n/ there"

Table 6–18

The Sequence of Emergence of Semantic Notions in the Speech of Three Children Showing
Use of Functional Relations (Alec, Colin, and Kristen) and One Child Showing Use of
Grammatical Relations (Jennings)

Alec	Colin	Kristen	Jennings
Designated/Object, Notice, Nomination, Action, Attribution	Designated/Object, Notice Nomination	Designated/Object, Nominaton Notice	Designated/Object, Notice, Nomination, Action, Place, Agent
Recurrence, Agent, Possessor	Place Action, Recurrence, Negation, Agent,	Place, Action Attribution	Negation, Possessor, Experience, Experiencer
Negation, Experience, Experiencer	Attribution Possessor, Experience	Negation, Possessor, Experience, Experiencer	Attribution, Instrument Recurrence
Place, Instrument	Experiencer, Instrument	Recurrence, Agent Instrument	

represented the bulk of what she said. Examples are

1. (Kristen takes the spinner out of a box)   spinner /n/ there/
2. (Kristen points to the family dog, Heidi,
   who is going upstairs)   Heidi /n/ there/

Jennings was the sole child whose speech might be thought to primarily represent the use of grammatical relations. The period best illustrating this usage occurred at a mean utterance length of 1.60 morphemes. In Jennings's usage, specific words were not limited to a fixed word position serving a consistent semantic function. His use of "that" in the examples below seems to illustrate that his speech consisted of structural meanings that occurred with different words and derived from a relationship between the words.

1. (Jennings points at the videotape
   monitor)   that TV/
2. (Jennings turns the arrow of the
   spinner)   turn that/turn that/

Given that Jennings differed from the other three children in terms of the nature of his syntactic constructions, it appeared useful to determine whether or not the semantic notions reflected in his speech differed from those reflected in the speech of the other children. Presented in Table 6–18 are the sequences in which the semantic notions emerged in the speech of the four children. Since the samples were obtained at varying levels of mean utterance length, this table should not be read from left to right. What is important in this table is the comparison of the relative order in which the semantic notions emerged for the different children.

It is apparent from this table that the relative order of emergence of the semantic notions reflected in Jennings's speech, which seemed to include considerable use of grammatical relations, was generally similar to the order seen for the speech of the three children showing use of functional relations. This observation leads one to conclude that the nature or style of word-combining rules seen in a child's linguistic system does not seem to dictate the semantic notions reflected in his utterances.

The conclusion drawn in this section, coupled with the others made in this chapter, seems to paint a picture of the child's system of semantic notions representing a somewhat inflexible system tied more closely to general developmental processes than seems to be true of most other features of language. These conclusions are discussed in the Conclusion, as they pertain to the issues raised in Chapter 2.

Conclusion

This volume dealt with a number of selected issues pertaining to children's early semantic development. These issues were presented within sections devoted to the emergence of the semantic notions underlying young children's speech, and the manner in which these notions interact with the learning of the linguistic code. The major issues discussed within these sections are summarized here.

In Chapter 1, a number of investigations were reviewed that seemed to suggest that during Stage I speech semantic notions emerge in a fairly orderly sequence. This sequence appeared much more orderly when viewed independently of particular productive syntactic constructions used to code such notions. The general regularity in the order in which semantic notions emerge seemed to have some parallel in the course of children's cognitive development.

Chapter 5 contained the results of an analysis of the order in which semantic notions emerged in the language of the eight children studied in this volume. These results were in general agreement with those reviewed in Chapter 1. Not all semantic notions appeared in the order expected. One factor that seemed to be responsible for these few discrepancies, although it clearly was operating on the data as a whole, was frequency of occurrence. This factor was combated, although not eliminated altogether, by grouping semantic notions. While lacking specificity, these groupings remained consistent with the findings for the eight children as well as with those of other investigators, and showed in addition a general parallel to the course of cognitive development.

In Chapter 2, I considered the topic of observed individual differences among children in linguistic style in light of the seemingly orderly sequence of emergence of semantic notions. In the literature, these differences in style seemed to take various forms. Several types of differences had the greatest implications regarding the emergence of semantic notions. These pertained to the degree of use of presyntactic forms (e.g., empty forms as in *Mommy widə*) and indeterminate forms, and most importantly, the use of different types of word-combining rules. In one such type of rule, there are structural meanings that occur with different words and derive from a transitive relationship between the words (grammatical relations), and in another type the relational meaning between the words seems dependent upon the meaning of one of the words (functional relations).

A close inspection of the literature offered some possible reasons for the seemingly discrepant findings of a fairly orderly sequence of emergence of semantic notions on the one hand, and individual differences in linguistic style on the other. It appeared that underlying semantic notions and linguistic coding rules may be, to a degree, separable. Although a child may adopt one or another style in the manner in which semantic notions are coded in his speech, these styles do not actually determine the relative order in which these semantic notions emerge. This state of affairs seemed to suggest that underlying semantic notions and more superficial features of language, including utterance length, may not be as closely related as previously supposed. These issues were among those considered in the analysis of the longitudinal data obtained from the eight children introduced in this volume.

In Chapter 6 it was seen that the use of presyntactic and indeterminate forms by the children was insufficient to be employed in an examination of how differences in linguistic style may relate to underlying semantic notions. However, a few of the children's usage appeared to be classifiable as primarily representing either functional or grammatical relations. Regardless of which style such usage seemed to represent, however, the sequence of emergence of the semantic notions reflected in this usage did not vary appreciably.

There were also a few instances where successive samples obtained from a child revealed an unexpected decrease in mean utterance length. These instances enabled a further look into how semantic notions may interact with more superficial features of language. It was found that semantic notions did not seem affected by reductions in mean utterance length; if any change occurred at all, in fact, it was in the direction of new semantic notions being evidenced in the subsequent sample. Such a finding calls into question the uncritical application of mean utterance length as a general index of linguistic development.

The finding that underlying semantic notions do not seem especially susceptible to surface feature considerations such as syntactic style or utterance length, suggested the need to probe further to determine if other, external factors may influence the semantic notions reflected in children's speech. One particular experimental inquiry revealed that while children may acquire new words through exposure, their use of these words will reflect only semantic notions already present in their linguistic system, regardless of the semantic notions or sentence positions represented in the utterances used to expose the children to these words.

This further evidence of the relative stability of semantic notions prompted the question of whether or not semantic notions might themselves exercise an influence on more superficial features of language. Superficial features that seemed like useful gauges in this regard were grammatical morphemes such as the article and copula. Although at this point the conclusions should be considered tentative, it appeared that these grammatical morphemes may first appear in utterances reflecting semantic notions that have long been a part of the child's linguistic system. Only subsequently are the grammatical morphemes seen in utterances reflecting semantic notions representing relatively new acquisitions in the child's system. This conclusion is consistent with the view that the degree of mastery over a given semantic notion may relate to the relative degree of psychological processing available for other linguistic operations. All of the above findings taken together seem to give the impression that semantic notions are closer to more general developmental processes than appears to be the case for most other features of language.

A word should be said about the approach to Stage I grammar writing that was proposed in Chapter 3. This approach was quite useful in highlighting a number of considerations that should be accounted for in any attempt to characterize Stage I speech. Actually, the proposed approach itself did a reasonable job in handling a number of these considerations, although no doubt a number of revisions will be necessary when more is learned about the nature of the child's early relational meanings. This is particularly true regarding single-word utterances. The proposed approach possessed the means to represent such utterances in several ways. What was needed was a means of determining which of these ways captured the distinctions that were operative for the child. Since I was more interested in the semantic notions underlying Stage I speech, the proposed approach was deliberately vague on matters such as how syntactic rules are incorporated in the grammar and how the grammar expands to account for later stages of linguistic development. Further work along these lines is needed, perhaps through borrowing ideas from some of the approaches to analysis discussed in Appendix B.

The purpose of this volume was to present some important issues in the study of relational meanings during the child's early linguistic development. It was not expected that final answers would be reached to the questions raised. Instead, my intent was to sharpen the focus on a number of relevant issues and raise a few new ones that must be dealt with before anything meaningful can be concluded about the acquisition and nature of the child's early relational meanings. The number of investigations of children's linguistic development has been steadily increasing during the past decade with no sign that the growing appeal of this research topic will subside. During this period we have proceeded rapidly from a major emphasis on one interesting topic to another. It is my hope that the present volume will help ensure that important steps are not missed along this most intriguing path.

Appendices

Appendix A

Following are examples of utterances that reflect the major semantic notions. For convenience, designated/object is not given a separate example for each sample, and experience is exemplified in experiencer.

Leslie I

Notice

(Leslie turns and reaches for a box)   here box/

Nonexistence

(Leslie searches for her book)   where it/

Agent

(Leslie pulls her mother off a chair)   Mommy down/

Action

(Leslie runs to get a ball)   get it/

Attribution

Mother: "Tell Larry where you sleep."

(Leslie looks at Larry and stretches her arms

out)   big bed/

Possessor

(Leslie walks by the water bowl of the family

dog, Morgan, and points to it)   Morgan bowl/

Leslie II

Notice

(Leslie gives a zoo animal part to Larry)   here one/

Nonexistence
(Leslie closes the cash register door, thinking
she has locked the pencil inside)   no more pencil/
    Nomination
(Leslie points to a hammer)   what is this/
    Rejection
(Morgan barks, Leslie turns to Morgan)   no Morgan/
    Agent
(The camel breaks in two, Leslie picks it up)   I fix it/
    Action
(Leslie hands a pencil to Larry)   hold pencil/
    Possessor
(Leslie takes the zoo animal from the table)   here mine/

Leslie III
    Notice
(Leslie opens a book, sees a picture of Brer
Rabbit)   here Brer Rabbit/
    Nonexistence
(Leslie, looking through a book, comes upon
a blank page)
Mother: "That's an empty page."   empty page/
Larry: "Empty page."
(Leslie looks up at her mother)   no letters/
    Nomination
(Leslie holds up an alphabet card to Larry)   this is *P*/
    Denial
(Leslie tries to put the spinner in a toy stove)   no fit/
    Recurrence
(After playing with the cash register given her,
Leslie puts it back in the box and turns to
Larry)   another one please/
    Agent
(Leslie points to a picture of a rabbit eating)   Brer Rabbit eat dinner/
    Action
(The spinner falls off Larry's lap after being
put there by Leslie)   I drop it/
    Place
(Leslie bends over to pick up a box, and
looks at Larry)   take this home/
    Attribution
(Leslie points to a picture of an owl)   it big owl/

Possessor
(Leslie runs toward her book and picks it up)   my book/
   Experiencer (and Experience)
(After coming upon a blank page in a book,
Leslie points to the book, looking at her
mother)   I need letter please/

Alec I

Alec II
   Notice
(Alec's shoe gets caught in the toy box)   hey shoe/
   Nomination
(Alec points to an eight in his book)   that a eight/
   Attribution
(Alec looks at the toys brought by Larry)   that's pretty/
   Action
(Alec watches Larry turn the video tape
around)   that move/

Alec III
   Notice
(Alec picks up the zoo animal)   hi camel/
   Nomination
(Alec points to the number four on the
spinner)   that fourteen/
   Recurrence
(After putting a toy barrel on his head and
referring to it as a hat, Alec finds a different
toy barrel and puts it on his head)   that hat too/
   Agent
(Larry rolls the camel along the floor, Alec
reaches for it)   I get that/
   Action
(Alec takes the tail off of the zoo animal)   break zoo/
   Attribution
(Alec holds a toy barrel on his head)   this like hat/
   Possessor
(Alec sees a toy barrel and picks it up. He   new hat/
then puts the toy barrel on his head)   got hat/got hat/
   *Note: place not credited, coded as in
   action + object*
(Alec "walks" the zoo animal over his chest)   walk shirt/

Note: instrument not credited, coded as in
agent + action

(Alec "walks" the zoo animal over the floor)   camel walk/
                                                                camel walk/

Note: experiencer (and experience) not
credited, coded as in agent + action

(Alec sees a toy barrel on the floor)   I see hat/

Alec IV
   Notice
(Turning the pages in a book, Alec passes a
picture of an airplane)   there jet airplane/
   Nomination
(Alec points to a picture of a rooster)   that's a rooster/
   Denial
(Alec, looking at a picture of a serving of
breakfast, points to a waffle, then to a cup of   that toast hot/
cocoa)   toast . . . no cup hot/
   Agent
(Alec's father turns the page of a book for
Alec)
Father: "Oh, and here's the rabbit family's
house"   I eat the rabbit/
   Action
(Alec reaches to turn the page of the book)   turn the page/
   Attribution
(Alec sees a picture of a van with cars on it)   that big truck/
   Experiencer (and Experience)
(Alec's father joins Alec, who is looking at
the book)   I wanna read the book/

   Note: instrument not credited, coded as in
   agent + action

(Alec looks at a picture of a door that is   that's a door/open/
open)   that open/

Kristen I
   Nomination
(Kristen looks inside her family's stereo
system)   what that/

Kristen II
   Notice
(Kristen walks near Oscar, the family cat)

Mother: "Oscar"   hi Oscar/
Mother: "Hi, Oscar"

Kristen III
Action
(Larry is turning the page of a book that he
and Kristen are looking at. Kristen points out
a picture on the previous page)   look at that/
Place
(Kristen puts the camel on her mother's head)   on head/

Kristen IV
Notice
(Kristen reaches for, and gets the zoo animal
from Larry)   holding there/
Nomination
(Kristen picks up the spinner)   what that/
Action
(Larry opens up the cash register)   open it/
Attribution
(Kristen reaches for and touches one of her
shoes)   new shoes/
Place
(Kristen attaches a leg on the body of the
zoo animal)   on here/

Kristen V
Notice
(As Kristen is running, she passes Heidi, the
family dog)   Heidi /n/ there/
Action
(Kristen holds up a box to her mother)   open that/
Attribution
(Kristen points out the window; it is raining) raining /n/ there/
Place
(Kristen walks to the stairs and intentionally
falls on the first stair)   on there/

Kristen VI
Notice
(Kristen looks in the monitor, which shows
Heidi. Kristen then turns around to Heidi) Heidi there/
Nonexistence
(Kristen looking for something in the toy
box, tips the box over and continues looking) where it go/

Nomination
(As Kristen is playing with the box, she finds
some tape adhered to its side. She then looks
up at Larry)   that tape/
   Action
(Kristen picks up a toy elephant's detachable
head and brings it to Larry)   hold that/
   Attribution
(Kristen holds the camel up to Larry, pointing
to the section with the missing tail)   broken there/
   Possessor
(After playing a game of putting things on
her head as if they were hats, Kristen gets
one of her hats and puts it on the camel)   camel hat/
   Place
(Kristen places the hat on the camel again)   hat on/
   Experiencer (and Experience)
(Kristen walks over toward the monitor)   I wanna see that/

Kristen VII
   Notice
(Kristen lifts her hand with a torn fingernail
for inspection)   finger there/
   Nomination
(Kristen takes a part of the zoo animal from
the box and places it in front of her. There
are now two parts in front of her)   that two/
   Denial
(The camel is on the floor)
Larry: "The camel's on the floor."
(Kristen then puts the camel on the cash   no, the camel on
register)   that ones/
   Recurrence
(After putting the spinner down, Kristen gets
up and starts to go into her room. Earlier,
Kristen had brought in some wooden sticks   more sticks/
from her room)   more sticks/
   Agent
(Kristen looks in the drawer of the cash
register, puts her hand in the drawer, then
gets up and starts to go into the other room)   cards/play cards/
Larry: "Cards?"   play cards ə have/
                                                  I get/

Action
(As Kristen sits on a chair, the chair moves.
She then gets up and pulls it back to its
original position)   · now move it/
   Place
(Kristen lies down on the floor)   now lie down/
Larry: "Huh?"   now fall down chair/
(Kristen then goes over to a rocking chair
and sits down)   now right here in chair/
   Attribution
(Kristen holds her hair)   hair dirty/
   Possessor
(Kristen puts down the toy she was playing
with)
Larry: "What else do we have to play with?
We got your car, huh?"
(Kristen then approaches her toy car)   now my car, fix that/
   Experiencer (and Experience)
(Kristen shows Larry her finger)
Larry: "I imagine its just a little fingernail."   finger hurts/

Lynn I
   Notice
(Lynn turns the cash register over, bends
down, and looks)   see that/
   Note: nomination not credited, not
   sufficiently different in coding and context
   from notice
(Lynn looks at the video recording
equipment. Larry coaxes her to take a closer
look)
Larry: "You can look at it if you want. You
can come over and look at it. Do you see
that? Yeah, come on, take a look."
(Lynn approaches the equipment)   what's that/

Lynn II
   Notice
(Lynn takes the zoo animal apart)   see this/
   Nomination
(Lynn brings a box in to her mother)   that box/

Denial
(Lynn enters the kitchen where her mother is)
Mother: "Do you wanna go in and play
with the toys?"   no toy/
    Recurrence
(After bringing the camel to her mother,
Lynn returns to her mother with a body part
of the zoo animal)   here more Mommy/
    Action
(Lynn tries to open the cash register drawer,
looks at Larry)   open door/
    Place
(Mother returns the camel, which Lynn gave
to her)   take back/

Lynn III
    Notice
(Lynn reaches for the spinner)   see that/
    Nomination
(Lynn points to a picture of the cash
register on the box)   that cash register/
    Recurrence
(Lynn takes play money out of the cash
register and gives it to Larry)   here money/
Larry: "Thanks, any more?"   more/
(Lynn then gives Larry more play money)   here more/
    Agent (and Action)
(Lynn takes some play money out of the cash
register)
Larry: "Ooh, you got it."   I got it/
    Experiencer (and Experience)
(Lynn wanted to go upstairs to get
something, but her mother would not give her
permission. Lynn, crying, holds out her hands
to her mother)   I wanna get up/

Lynn IV
    Notice
(Lynn gets a pillow and brings it to her
mother)   here/here pillow/
    Nonexistence
(After driving a toy train on her mother's
shoulders, neck, and head, Lynn hides the
toy train behind her mother's head)   where choo choo go/

Nomination

(After touching the cash register, Lynn points to a picture of the cash register on the box)
that two there/two, look/

Rejection

(After giving her mother the toy train, Lynn approaches a ball)
no choo choo/want ball/

Denial

(Lynn's mother tries to open the cash register by banging on it. Lynn tries to get the cash register back)
no no, don't wreck/

Recurrence

(Lynn is playing a game of giving her mother the pillows from the couch. After giving her a pillow, Lynn gets another from the couch).
I want a pillow/
I want another pillow/

Agent

(Lynn puts the camel on top of the cash register)
I put it/

Action

(Lynn turns the arrow on the spinner)
turn it/

Place

(Lynn tries to put the lid on the box)
put in box/

Attribution

(Lynn points to a hole on the bottom of the cash register)
here broke/

Possessor

(After playing with the cash register, Lynn turns around to a pillow and lies on it)
my pillow/night night/

Experiencer (and Experience)

(Lynn goes over to the couch to get a pillow, turns to her mother)
Mama want pillow/

Colin I

Colin II

Notice

(The electrician, who just arrived, walks by)
hi Daddy/Daddy/

Colin III

Notice

Larry: "On the floor is the spinner."
(Colin turns and gets it)
here spinner/

Nomination

(Colin picks up and inspects the zoo animal)
'sa dog/

Colin IV
Notice
(Colin tries to get Larry to disassemble the
zoo animal)   horsie /n/ there/
Place
(Colin looks in the box)   spinner/spinner/
Larry: "What?"   spinner ə box/

Colin V
Notice
(Colin picks up the camel)   horsie /n/ there/
Nonexistence
(Colin finishes eating a banana and walks
toward his mother)   nana all gone/
Recurrence
(Colin runs into the kitchen for another
poptart)   more tart/more tart/
Agent
(Colin walks past Friday, the family dog, who
is barking)   bad dog bark/
Action
(Colin tries to put the lid on the box, which
fell off)   fix it/fix it/
Place
(Colin approaches and gets the box with the
camel in it, which is on top of a larger box)   box that on/
Attribution (see Agent)

Colin VI
Notice
(Colin tries to put the camel in the box.
Unsuccessful, he gives both to Larry)   camel there/
Nomination
(Colin sees himself in the monitor)   that Colin/that Colin/
Denial
(Colin tries to get his brother's toy trains)
Mother: "Get *your* train."
(Colin runs toward them)   no choo choo brother/
Action
(Colin runs and gets his toy trains)   get it choo choo/
Place
(Colin places, one by one, people toys into   people box/people box/
the box)   people box/people box/
Possessor (see Denial)

Colin VII
 Notice
(Colin turns, facing the window, and sees
Larry's car)   there's your car/
 Nonexistence
(The toy king figure with which Colin was
playing, falls inside his toy castle. Colin tries
to look inside to see the king)   king go/
 Nomination
(Colin points to the box)   this box/
 Recurrence
(Colin's mother walks in and Colin looks up
from his toys)   Mommy, more toys/
 Agent
(The family dog, Friday, barks)   Friday cry/
 Action
(Colin puts some toys in a box)   put the toys away/
 Place
(Colin puts the toy king figure in a box) king in the box/
 Possessor
(After allowing Larry to see it, Colin takes Momma's jewelry/
back his mother's locket)   jewelry/
 Experiencer (and Experience)
(Colin starts to connect his toy trains I wanna drive the
together)   choo choo train/

Colin VIII
 Notice
(Colin looks in the monitor and sees boxes) here's box/here's box/
             here's box/

 Nonexistence
(After having learned that the camera
controls what can be seen in the monitor,
Colin puts the lens cap on the camera and
turns to the blank monitor)   this gone/
 Nomination
(Colin points to the zoo animal's tail) that/that tail/
 Denial
(Colin looks in the monitor)   what's this/
Larry: "That's those boxes over there."
(Colin points to a door in the monitor) no, what's that/
 Agent
(Colin gives the detached zoo animal to Larry) Larry, you fix it/

Action
Colin pushes the cash register aside to make
room)   move this/
    Place
(Colin walks óver and puts the zoo animal
in its box)   I take horse box/
    Attribution
(Colin points to the broken window on the
cash register)   this broken/
    Possessor
(Colin turns and touches the box, full of
toys, brought by Larry)   these your own toys/

Morton I
    Nonexistence
(Morton, lying on the couch, looks up at
Larry)   Sherrod ə gone/
(Sherrod, Morton's sister, is at school)
    Nomination
(Larry places the cash register on Morton's
leg)   what that/

Morton II
    Notice
(Morton builds a tower by placing boxes on
top of one another)   see that/
    Nomination
(Morton points to a box with a picture of a
boy, girl, money, and cash register on it)   that a boy/
    Agent
(Morton approaches the ledge of the fireplace
and starts to sit down, gesturing toward the
spot on which he is about to sit)   I'm ə sit down there/
    Action
(After Morton stood the camel up on its
wheels, it falls over. Morton sees it and picks   uh oh camel/
it up)   camel fall down/
    Place
(Morton puts the zoo animal in a box)   in box/
    Possessor
(Morton points to the picture on a box of a
boy, girl, money, and cash register)   right there/money/
Larry: "Right there"
(Morton points again)   boy əz money/

Morton III
Notice
(Morton points to the money depicted on the
cash register box)   there money/
Larry: "Let's see."
(Morton points again)   see, money/
Nonexistence
(After putting the tail on the zoo animal,
Morton runs into the other room to show
Marlene, the housekeeper)   on/Marlene, a tail/
(Marlene was in a different room)   Marlene/gone/her
                                                       gone/

Nomination
(Morton picks up the camera lens cap)   what that/
Denial
(Morton puts some puzzle pieces in the cash
register drawer and attempts to close the
drawer)   it won't fit/
Agent
(Morton pulls the tail off of the zoo animal)   I pull on it/
Action
(Morton closes the cash register drawer)   I close it/
Place
(Morton looks at Larry, while holding the
camel)   dog/dog/dog/
Larry: "Are you saying 'dog'?"   uh huh/
Larry: "No, a camel is what this is."   a dog outside/
Possessor
(Larry puts the toy fireman's loose hat back
on its head. It was sitting on a toy firetruck
belonging to Morton)
Larry: (referring to ownership of the
firetruck)
"Is this yours?"   me hat/

Morton IV
Notice
(Morton starts to stand up, and sees the
spinner)   spinner right there/
Nonexistence
(Morton puts his hand in the empty cash
register drawer)   no money in there/
Nomination
(Morton points to the tail of the zoo animal)   that tail/

Denial
(Morton tries to put a piece of the zoo
animal into the cash register drawer)   didn't work/
   Agent
(Morton pulls the zoo animal apart)   I broke it/
   Action
(Morton pulls the head off of the zoo animal)   pull it off/
   Place
(Morton puts the tail of the zoo animal in
the cash register drawer)   put it in there/
   Attribution
(Morton tries to put the camel in the cash
register drawer)   camel too big/
   Possessor
(Morton gives an elephant head to Larry)   that your head/
(The elephant head does belong to Larry)
   Instrument
(Morton holds up the zoo animal's detached
legs)   frog/
Larry: "What?"
(Morton then points to a picture in an open
book on the floor that depicts three frogs)   frog right there/
(Morton then holds up the zoo animal's   makes a frog/
legs again)   makes a frog/
Larry: "Makes a frog."   makes a frog/
(Morton again points to the picture)   frog right there/
(Morton places the zoo animal's legs next to   frog will bite your
Larry's hand)   finger/
   Experiencer (and Experience)
(Morton hits the cash register drawer, which
opens. Morton looks inside the cash register)   I see in here/

Jennings I

Jennings II
   Notice
(The cash register opens)   here come/
   Nomination
(Jennings points at the TV)   that TV/
   Agent
(Jennings reaches for the cash register)   I /ən/ open/

Action
(Jennings turns the arrow of the spinner)   turn that/turn that/
   Place
(Jennings points to the open drawer of the
cash register)   in there money/

Jennings III
   Notice
(Jennings, looking in the monitor, sees the   there a clock/
spinner)   there a clock/
   Nonexistence
(Jennings turns toward the cash register)   where money go/
   Nomination
(Jennings points to one of his socks)   that sock/that sock/
                                                             that sock/

   Denial
(While looking in the monitor, Jennings was
asked to move. Upon doing so, he was not in
position to see the monitor. Jennings returns
to the monitor)   I can't see/
   Agent
(Jennings closes the cash register drawer)   I close it/
   Action
(Jennings holds up the camel)
Larry: "What's that?"   that camel/
(Jennings then puts the camel on the floor)
Larry: "What's he doing?"   I sit down camel/
   Place
(Jennings opens up the box that Larry brings
in and then looks up at Larry)   in there/
Larry: "Huh?"   what in there/
   Possessor
(Jennings identifies his socks)
Larry: "That's a sock. That's a sock, right."
(Jennings then leans toward the camel, looks
at it and touches his own sock)   that camel sock/
   *Experiencer (*and *Experience,* see *Denial)*
   Note: attribution not credited, coded as in
   object + place
(Jennings looks in the monitor, where he is
on camera)   Jennings/
Larry: "'Jennings', yeah, yeah, that's

Jennings, right"   that Jennings/
Larry: "Yeah, that's right."   that Jennings on TV/

Jennings IV
Notice
(Jennings walks toward some artwork   four/there four/there
hanging on the wall, which has numbers on it)   four/right there/
Nonexistence
(Jennings intentionally "hides" the camel by
putting it on a window ledge. Jennings then
turns to Larry)   where camel go/
Nomination
(Jennings picks up the head of the zoo animal)   what that/what that/
Rejection
(Jennings takes the zoo animal head from
Larry)   no have it/
Denial
(Jennings turns the arrow of the spinner   _____ /_____ /
around)   this way/this way/
Larry: "What are you doing?"   do something/hold
                                                   that clock/

Larry (correcting Jennings who had
previously called the spinner a clock): "A
spinner is what we call that."   no, four call that/
(The arrow was on the number four)
Agent
(Jennings pulls the zoo animal apart)   I did it/
Action
(Jennings walks over to one of the boxes   what that/
that Larry brought in)   open the box/
Place
(Jennings looks over at the box)   in box/what in box/
Attribution
(Jennings says something unintelligible.
Larry guesses that Jennings told Larry his
name)
Larry: "Yeah, that's your name, 'Jennings'".   I'm four/not two/
Possessor
(Jennings takes the zoo animal from Larry)   I wanna have that/
Instrument
(Jennings stands the camel on the fireplace
ledge)   camel sit/

Experiencer (and Experience)
(Jennings looks down a vent in the floor)   I can see/

Greer I

Greer II
  Notice
(Greer reaches for the spinner)   a spinner is here/
  Agent
(Greer takes the already-broken camel and
tries to push it along the floor. It breaks in
half)   I broke the camel/
  Action
(Greer drops a piece of the zoo animal)   I drop it/
  Place
(Greer's mother spots a bug on the floor
near the couch Greer is sitting in. Greer
looks down at the bug)   a buggie down there/
  Attribution
(Mother goes to throw the bug away, which   dead bug/dead bug/
was dead)   dead bug/
  Possessor
(Greer points to the camel's eye)   camel has eye/

Greer III
  Nonexistence
(Greer tries to open the cash register drawer.
She gets it open, but no money was in the   where money is/
drawer)   open/no where /I/ is/
  Nomination
(Greer points to herself in the monitor)   that me/
  Recurrence
(Greer places some toys in a box, and runs
back to the couch for more)   another one/
  Agent
(Greer tries to put the cash register on the
couch; her mother watches)   Momma put here/
  Action
(Greer tries to get some money out of the   Mommy/take it out/
cash register, and looks at her mother)   take it out/
  Place (see *Agent*)
  Attribution
(Greer puts the camel in the wrong box)

Larry: "OK, tell you what. Let's put it in
the other box."   small box/
    Possessor
(Greer holds up a piece of cardboard
packaging to her mother)   I got it/

Greer IV
    Nomination
(Greer sees her mother in the monitor)   that Mommy/
                                                        that Mommy/

    Denial
(Greer lifts the lid of the box and tries to   see/I can't open/
get the cash register out)   can't open/
    Recurrence
(Greer's mother opens the drawer for Greer,
who wants the money inside. After Greer gets   I want some more
it, she looks up)   fifty dollars/
    Agent
(Greer put some paper money in the cash
register drawer)   I put it in/I put it in/
    Action
(The cash register falls on the floor)   uh oh drop it/I drop it/
    Place
(Greer is being questioned about who she
saw the day before)
Mother: "You want to tell him who you saw?"   no/
Mother: "No?"
Mother: "Did you see Santa Claus?"   yes/
Larry: "What's he look like?"   sat on Santa Claus lap/
                                                        sat on Santa Claus lap/

    Attribution
(Larry opens the cash register)   open/open/see, its
                                                        open/open/

    Possessor
(Greer looks out the window, then looks at   where's my bike/
her mother)   where's my bike/

Appendix B

This appendix is devoted to a review and evaluation of approaches to the analysis of semantic structure. In order to provide more depth to this coverage, I deal primarily with those approaches that both enable distinctions to be made among different semantic notions and provide some details about the manner in which such notions might be organized in a grammar. Several approaches, however, have already been introduced in Chapter 1, and therefore will not be dealt with in this appendix. These are the approaches of Brown (1973), Wells (1974), and Bloom, Lightbown, and Hood (1975).

Chomsky's Transformational Grammar of 1965

One approach to grammar writing that provides for the representation of notions reflected in language usage is Chomsky's (1965) revised model of transformational grammar. It was this approach, coupled with a rich interpretation of the accompanying nonlinguistic context, that served as the method of analysis in Bloom's (1970) very important study of the different semantic roles that structurally similar child utterances may play. In the transformational grammar approach, a sentence receives two representations that are related to each other by transformational rules. The first is the surface structure that represents the sentence as it is spoken. The second is the deep structure—an abstract representation of the essential structural characteristics of the sentence. The deep structure is never directly realized in speech.

The grammar proposed by Chomsky (1965) consists of three components—syntactic, phonological, and semantic. The syntactic component, in turn, has two parts, a base component and a transformational component. The rules of the base component generate underlying structures of sentences and indicate how particular lexical items are inserted into them. The underlying structures are partially generated by phrase structure rules that specify the hierarchical organization of the elements in a sentence, in addition to such structural information as the underlying order of these elements. Familiar notations such as sentence → noun phrase + verb phrase represent phrase structure rules. Such rules serve to define sentence elements linguistically. For example, the subject is defined as the noun phrase that is directly dominated by the sentence. The predicate is defined as the verb phrase dominated by the sentence. When a noun phrase is dominated by a verb phrase, a direct object might be specified, and so on. Lexicon feature rules are also needed in the syntactic component; these provide for the insertion of lexical items into the sentence. A third type of rule in the syntactic component is the transformational rule, which specifies operations, performed on underlying strings, which describe the alteration a sentence undergoes to result in its surface structure.

The phonological component operates on the surface structures, converting them into the phonetic form they take as they are spoken. The semantic component operates on the deep structure to produce a semantic interpretation, which is performed by what are, in essence, the projection rules proposed by Katz and Fodor (1963). These add those aspects of relational meaning that are traceable to the syntactic structure, to the semantic representation of a sentence. For each rule in the grammar there is an associated projection rule, type 1 and type 2, indicating how the phrase structure or transformational rule, respectively, contributes to the sentence meaning. Rules such as these seemed to arise from increasing awareness that the formal syntactic language devices proposed in Chomsky's (1957) earlier work probably should have included explicit mechanisms for representing meaning. Rather than totally revamping the syntactic model, rules were constructed that were designed to relate the form of sentences to their meanings.

There seems to be a critical drawback in applying this kind of interpretive conception of meaning to the study of the underlying semantic notions of child language. In Chomsky's (1965) approach, the semantic component has no role in the generation of the deep structure or in the selection of transformations applied to generate the surface structure. Instead, the semantic component only serves to interpret what the syntactic component generates. As a model of a causal sequence by which an utterance is generated by a young child, it would surely be incorrect. It would suggest that the child generates an utterance and then decides what meaning he wants to convey.

Yet the transformational grammar approach was intended as a model of linguistic capacity. This problem, then, can probably be viewed more properly as a concern of developmental psycholinguists whose interest lies in determining how linguistic approaches fare as psychological models of the child's developing language. The concern in this case is certainly justified. Consider the case of attributive utterances of the adjective + noun form. In the adult model, adjectives in noun-modifying position are the result of a transformation moving the predicate adjective to the noun-modifying position. A number of children seem to express adjective + noun utterances such as *little fish* before noun + adjective (predicate adjective) utterances such as *fish little*. This finding has usually restrained investigators from granting transformational status to adjective + noun utterances (Bloom, 1970; Bowerman, 1973a).

The only means of assigning meaning to these utterances in the transformational grammar approach is via type 2 projection rules, which specify the role in meaning played by the transformational rule. Since Stage I utterances superficially resembling adult transformations cannot be given transformational status, the source of the semantic interpretation of such utterances is unclear. This problem, however, is not restricted to child language. Based on linguistic considerations, Katz and Postal (1964) detailed an account rendering type 2 projection rules unnecessary, based primarily on greater power given to the base, such as recursive properties, and further conditions being placed on transformations, such as recoverability of deleted elements.

Despite the difficulty in applying a model of linguistic capacity, such as transformational grammar, to Stage I speech, some of the first investigators making such an application seemed to think that the model fit, not only with respect to its proposed means for semantic interpretation, but to its strong emphasis on the syntactic component as well. For example, McNeill (1971) stated that

> two words—for example, one classified as a noun and the other classified as a determiner—*inevitably* comprise a particular constituent—in this case a NP if they interact meaningfully. Conversely, if two words are understood by a child as standing in a particular

grammatical relation in adult speech—for example one word modifying the other—one word is *inevitably* classified as a N and the other as Det. (p 23)

Other investigators have not found the discovery of underlying meaning from such syntactic elements (and vice versa) so simple. One of the major obstacles has been the fact that once a transformational grammar has been adopted as an approach to analysis, a base component must also be postulated that gives formal representation to grammatical relations such as "subject of," "predicate of," "direct object of," and the like. As a model of linguistic capacity, such specifications can be justified by demonstrating that such a structure is required for some grammatical rule (Chomsky, 1965). This does not always prove to be the case for Stage I speech, however. When the passive transformation, for example, is applied in the adult system, an entire noun phrase (e.g., "the pitiful animal") is moved from sentence initial to sentence final position, not just one element of the noun phrase. Such transformations, of course, are not seen in Stage I speech, and thus a constituent such as "subject" is difficult to verify as operative in the child's grammar. Slobin (1970b) and Bowerman (1973a) noted that the subjects used by children at Stage I tended initially to be restricted to the notion of agent—an observation confirmed by Wall (1974). Only subsequently do children's subjects become increasingly diverse. The postulation of "subject" rather than of "agent" as the noun that occurs in preverbal position would seem unwarranted. As Bowerman (1973a) pointed out

the structural phenomena which require the concept of subject in adult speech are evidently missing in early child speech. To credit children with an understanding of the concept is an act of faith based only on our knowledge of the adult language. (p 187)

In fact, we are not even linguistically consistent in our adoption of adult language standards. When the child produces an utterance such as *ball hit*, for example, it is often concluded that the child reversed the normal verb + object order. Quite often, these utterances are the residue of the grammar writing process, termed "indeterminate" or "unaccounted for" (Bloom, 1970; Bowerman, 1973a; Ramer, 1974). As Bowerman (1973a) stated

In summary, then, we do not even make consistent use of position to help us identify subjects in children's utterances, even though it is the only cue we have available. Instead, we simply rely on our knowledge of what the subject would be in equivalent adult utterances. (p 186)

Other problems arise in applying the hierarchical organization of transformational grammar to Stage I speech. One troublesome issue is the relationship between the verb and the other constituents in an utterance. On the basis of the high frequency of verb + object in contrast to subject + verb utterances in Stage I (McNeill, 1970), and the findings of Weir (1962) and Braine (1971; 1973) that children's replacement sequences (e.g., *donkey/fix the donkey/*) often suggested a strong verb + object relationship, proposals were made that the verb and direct object (or locative) were dominated by a verb phrase, upholding the adult relationship for Stage I. Since that time, however, Bowerman (1973a) has found several children who used subject + verb utterances more frequently than verb + object utterances, and whose replacement sequences could just as readily be interpreted as suggesting a strong subject + verb relationship. It would seem, then, that the hierarchical organization of Stage I and adult grammars may not be the same.

One particular difficulty in using transformational grammar to explore the semantic notions underlying early language usage has to do with morpheme order. The order of morphemes is specified in the deep structure proposed by Chomsky (1965), and therefore deep structure according to this approach contains language specific information. The deep structure of transformational grammar, then, contains potentially confounding information for the investigator who is interested in gaining insights into underlying and potentially universal semantic notions by examining the child's language usage.

A final troublesome issue arising from the application of transformational grammar to an analysis of Stage I speech deals with the grammar writing process. Investigators utilizing this approach have often come upon the fact that their data do not adequately fit in toto into the framework of transformational grammar. For example, Bloom's (1970) grammar for the third sample from one child, Eric, includes the following sentence rewrite rules.

$$\text{Sentence 1} \rightarrow \text{(Pivot)} \begin{pmatrix} \text{Noun phrase} \\ \text{Verb phrase} \end{pmatrix}$$

$$\text{Sentence 2} \rightarrow \text{(Noun) (Verb)}$$

While these rewrite rules might reflect those operating in the child's language usage, the resulting grammar begins to take the form of a production model for individual utterances, rather than a grammar that represents the child's linguistic system as a whole. For instance, although the child may well produce utterances of the form represented by each of the two sentence rewrite rules, surely the mechanisms responsible for the generation of each are not so unrelated as to allow for no superordinate structure that reflects a more general sentence generation mechanism. Treating sentences in this segregated manner almost invites the postulation that semantic notions underlying these sentences reflect different strategies, an issue discussed in Chapters 2 and 6.

The application of transformational grammar to Stage I speech has provided much valuable information concerning the semantic notions underlying the child's language usage, although in the interest of space, they will not be detailed here. Fortunately, many of these points have been presented by Brown (1973) and Bowerman (1973a). With the exceptions noted in this appendix, transformational grammar as an approach to Stage I speech analysis does a surprisingly good job. This is due in large measure to the fact that transformational grammar represents a fairly complete description of the linguistic system the child is starting to approximate from the outset. As noted by Brown (1973), the child's subsequent linguistic development can be captured even more fully by this approach.

Gruber

Operating within the framework of transformational grammar, Gruber (1967a; 1975a) has proposed an approach to representing early child language, that makes use of the principle of topicalization. According to his observations of the utterances produced by one child, Mackie, Gruber proposed that subject is not represented as such in surface structure in the child's speech. Gruber preferred not to assume that the noun phrase in the child's utterance, that superficially resembles subject, is actually sharing a relation to predicate, that is the same as that seen in utterances produced during a later period. Instead, the noun phrase that one would expect to be determined as subject is incorporated within the word representing predicate or at best, lexicalized as a type of prefix to it. The noun phrase only superficially resembling subject is referred to as the topic. The topic is said to be outside of the sentence that represents the child's comment, but is coreferential with some noun phrase within this sentence.

In order to represent the entire utterance as it is produced by the child, Gruber represents topic + comment utterances as possessing a copula verb structure, with the comment actually being an embedded sentence. For example, the utterance *girl go away*, in Gruber's (1975a) more recent formulation, would be represented as

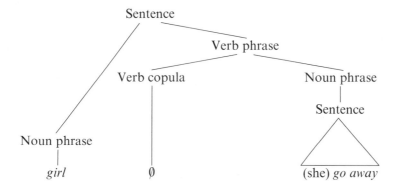

The distinction between topic and subject is not one of base structure, and therefore the above representation is one of surface structure, due, according to Gruber, to the child's manner of lexicalization.

In his more recent work, Gruber (1975b) incorporated a performative—constative distinction into his topicalization approach; the distinction is that performatives indicate something while constatives talk about something. In a constative, some entity is described by some predication. For example, in *I like malteds* and *Roberta is enormous*, one is predicating one's own feeling toward malteds, and size to Roberta, respectively. In performatives, nothing is being predicated about an entity, a state of affairs that can be seen in utterances such as *I point out to you Roberta* and *I demand of you malteds*. A performative is a direct expression of what one is in fact doing by means of the utterance. The expressed or implied subject of the performative is always the first person, the speaker, while the indirect object is always the second person, the addressee.

Based on utterances produced during a ten-week period by one child (Dory), Gruber proposed that a child's early utterances are performatives. The performative role played by the child's single-word utterances is not readily apparent since the single words produced by the child typically represent the referent, the entity talked about, or indicated. By the early two-word period this role becomes more evident.

For example, during her use of utterances such as *see book* and *see powder*, Dory was either reaching for the object named by the referent, pointing to it, or showing it to her mother. Gruber viewed the element "see" as representing the performative "I indicate to you," with "book," "powder" and the like representing simple noun phrases serving as direct object of the performative. The utterance *see book*, for example, would have the underlying representation

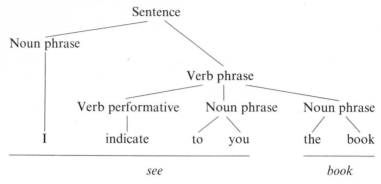

Gruber adopted the above representation from that employed by Ross (1970) to represent performative structure in an adult model of linguistic capacity. The surface forms of Dory's utterances do not reflect their underlying representation because at this stage of development she is capable of minimal "lexicalizational analyticity" (Gruber, 1975b).

In a subsequent period of development, the child acquires the capability of expressing predications of the referent. This change marks the advent of constative utterances. During this period, a number of utterances still contain a performative element; however, the constative is represented by an embedded sentence comprised of the referent and its predication. The utterances produced during this period, termed the "constative stage," are of the topic + comment form with optional surface structure realization of the performative element (Gruber, 1975a). Examples of such utterances can be seen in Dory's utterances *shoe all gone* and *see the baby looking*.

The fact that Gruber's approach is a type of adaptation of the transformational grammar approach to child language makes it vulnerable to some of the same criticisms directed at the transformational grammar approach discussed in the previous section. Because Gruber has modified this approach for application to the Stage I child's utterances, however, other comments can be made.

One difficulty with Gruber's approach is that it seems to be based on corpora of utterances that may not be representative of child language. It seems clear that Gruber would not have been so willing to make the topic–subject distinction if Mackie's samples did not contain utterances in which the topic and coreferential noun phrase were both realized in surface structure, as in the utterance *it broken, wheels*. Such utterances appear to be sufficiently infrequent in the speech of other children as to question the usefulness of the topic + comment characterization itself

(Brown, 1973). In view of this infrequency, in fact, those utterances that do take this form may be illustrating a primitive device for realizing focus rather than serving the function suggested by Gruber (Chambers, 1973).

If instances in which the topic and coreferential noun phrase appear in the same utterance are rare, the topic + comment representation for the child's utterances would have a disadvantage. For instance, compare these two representations of *shoe gone*.

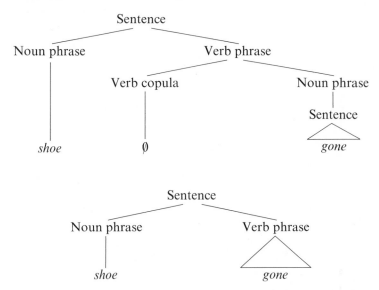

Clearly the second representation has the advantage of greater simplicity since it does not contain an embedded sentence. Gruber's own reluctance to adopt such a representation is somewhat surprising. According to Gruber, base structures are innate and do not undergo development. What the child acquires with development is the ability to analytically lexicalize the base structures. However, Gruber chooses to represent the early period of this development with a structure exceeding in complexity that of the base structures themselves. The representation of *the shoe is gone* in the adult system would not require an embedded sentence, for example. In effect then, further development by the child, according to Gruber's approach, would require a reduction in complexity as the child shows increasing capability of more faithfully representing the relations of the base structures in surface structure. This seems contrary to the expected. In addition to the appropriateness of representing children's utterances as topic + comment, this approach has been questioned in terms of its account of various structures including questions and pronominalization (Felix, 1975).

The most valuable aspect of Gruber's approach seems to be his inclusion of performatives. Many approaches to child language have virtually ignored utterances serving as performatives. The most notable are those with vocative function such as *Mommy, cookie.* Such an utterance would have the representation

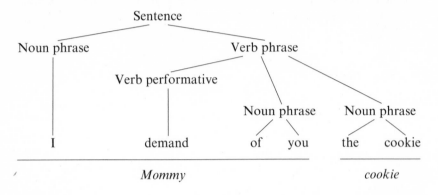

Admittedly, it is difficult to accept the complexity of the underlying performative structure. Gruber's use of Ross's (1970) account seemed to ignore the critical difference between a model of adult linguistic capacity and a description of the child's linguistic system estimated from his usage. The problems of the complexity of the underlying performative structure is made worse in the subsequent period when the referent is described by some predication. This predication requires an embedded sentence. Thus, an utterance such as *want Daddy come* requires the representation

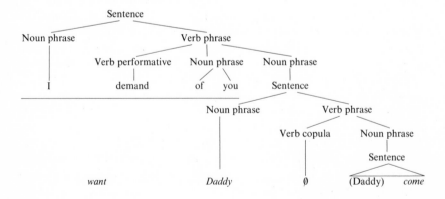

Table 1
Some of Fillmore's (1968) Case Relations

Agentive	The animate perceived as instigator of the action identified by the verb (*The dog dug the hole*)
Instrumental	The inanimate force or object causally involved in the action or state named by the verb (*He broke it with a hammer*)
Dative	The animate being affected by the action or state identified by the verb (*Ralph heard the explosion*)
Factitive	The object or being resulting from the action or state identified by the verb (*Toby made a cake*)
Locative	The location or spatial orientation of the state or action identified by the verb (*The socks are on the radiator*)
Objective	Anything represented by a noun whose role in the state or action identified by the verb depends on the meaning of the verb itself (*Reggie caught the ball*)

Such a representation seems entirely too complex to be justified by the child's actual usage. It is somewhat unfortunate that Gruber's decision to incorporate performatives in his approach in analyzing child language relied too heavily on a model of adult linguistic capacity.

Fillmore in 1968

Another approach to grammar writing that has been employed in the study of Stage I speech is the case grammar approach of Fillmore (1968). In some ways, Fillmore's case grammar is similar to transformational grammar. Syntax is viewed as central, and sentences are given both an underlying and surface representation linked by transformations. As did Chomsky (1965), Fillmore accepted the position that semantic rules would operate on the deep structure generated by the base component to derive a semantic interpretation. In many other important ways, however, case grammar differs from transformational grammar. Fillmore regarded grammatical relations such as "subject of" and "predicate of" as surface structure characteristics that may not be universal and therefore should be accounted for transformationally. Thus, the basic elements of the deep structure in case grammar are "case relations"—semantic concepts of syntactic significance. Fillmore's major case relations are presented in Table 1.

In the deep structure of a case grammar, a sentence is rewritten as a modality and a proposition. The modality contains markers for operations that act on the sentence as a whole, such as negation, tense, mood,

Table 2

Bowerman's (1973a) Comparisons of Case Grammar and
Transformational Grammar for Stage I Speech

Case Grammar	Example	Transformational Grammar
Verb + Agentive	*Ralph jump*	Subject + Verb
Verb + Objective	*kick box*	Verb + Object
	little key	Adjectival modifier + Noun
Agentive + Objective	*Daddy door*	Subject + Object
Dative + Objective	*Mommy coat*	Genitive modifier + Noun
Locative + Objective	*sweater chair*	Noun + Locative

aspect, and interrogation, in addition to certain adverbs. The proposition consists of a verb and one or more nouns associated with the verb in a particular relationship. All of the nouns have equal status with respect to the verb. Two or more nouns can be conjoined to represent a case relation, although each case relation can only occur once. One rather important feature of case grammar is that the case relations and the associated verb are considered unordered. In his 1968 formulation, Fillmore suggested that the case relations be rewritten as kasus + noun phrase. Kasus is then rewritten as the morphological marker (e.g., a preposition, affix, etc.) of the case. The noun phrase is then rewritten as noun (sentence). This appearance of (sentence) generates a number of structures derived transformationally in transformational grammar.

Bowerman (1973a) has discussed a number of advantages for a case grammar approach to Stage I speech over a transformational grammar approach. One of these is that case grammar does away with "subject," "predicate," and the like, as deep structure entities, entities whose postulation may be crediting the child with a more abstract linguistic knowledge than his behavior evidences. Another advantage is that case grammar provides for the generation of unordered deep structure elements, thereby enabling a closer approximation to a universal child grammar than is possible within the framework of transformational grammar. These advantages, coupled with the findings of Brown (1973) and Bowerman (1973a) that case grammar can account for many of the same utterances as transformational grammar, leads one to the conclusion that the application of case grammar to the analysis of Stage I speech has been fruitful. Bowerman's (1973a) comparisons of some of the Stage I utterances generated by the two accounts are presented in Table 2.

In order to make such comparisons, some alterations of Fillmore's proposals were made. Fillmore defined cases in terms of the relationships nouns may have with verbs. Bowerman (1973a) needed to extend the term "case" to include also the relationships nouns may have to other nouns. Another roughspot in the case grammar approach, seen in Table 2, is treating adjectives as verbs. While this is not new to linguistics, the postulation that adjectives may be a special type of verb has serious consequences for Stage I speech. Although attributive utterances are evidenced near or slightly after the point in development when utterances reflecting action are noted, such attributes generally refer to characteristics of other persons and objects. At the same point, the child's action utterances are usually describing his own activity. There is little Stage I evidence that suggests that the two can be coded by the same case relation.

Some of Fillmore's cases are too abstract to provide useful information regarding the semantic notions underlying Stage I speech. For example, the dative case, where the animate is affected by the state or action identified by the verb, seems too broad for Stage I, where almost all dative nouns name possessors (Bowerman, 1973a). The objective case also causes problems. Not representing a particular relation, it is used for nouns in relationships not clearly assignable to other cases. Consider the varied relations to which the objective case is assigned.

Dative + Objective	*father clock*
Objective + Locative	*chick shoe*
Verb + Objective	*drives car*
Verb + Objective	*little fish*
Objective + Verb	*tower falls down*
Essive + Objective	*that soup*

This case appears almost as general as such grammatical relations as subject or predicate.

Some of Fillmore's other cases seem to represent quite subtle relationships. It is not clear why factitive should represent a separate case, even in an adult model of competence, when a general case such as objective exists. Brown (1973), too, seems to have questions about some of the case relations. He suspects one of these, essive (as in *that soup*), to be the product of Fillmore's attempt at avoiding the violation of his own rule that a case relation can appear only once in a sentence. In this instance, the violation would be an utterance marked objective + objective.

As with the application to child language of transformational grammar, the application of case grammar sometimes forces one to account for certain children's utterances through unnecessarily complex means. With the aid of nonlinguistic context, the two utterances *Mommy has shoe* and *Mommy's shoe* may look as if they represent the same relationship from a conceptual standpoint. However, they are derived differently by a case grammar approach—the former from

Sentence → Verb + Dative + Objective

the latter from

Sentence → Verb + Dative
Dative → Kasus + Noun phrase
Noun phrase → Noun (Sentence)

In the present example, this might be represented as *shoe (shoe to Mommy)*. For surface structure realization, the repeated noun and "empty" verb are deleted and dative is reattached to the dominating noun phrase. Unless possessive utterances such as *Mommy's shoe* were only seen at a point after the appearance of utterances such as *Mommy has shoe*, there would be no justification for such an elaborate source for their generation. In fact, the whole value of Fillmore's approach in the analysis of Stage I speech is threatened when recourse is made to the kasus + noun phrase rewrite for each case; constituents such as noun phrase were already found to be too abstract for Stage I in the earlier discussion of transformational grammar.

There are a few other insufficiencies in the application of case grammar, such as the absence of a means to introduce prolocatives such as "here" and "there" into the grammar. These prolocatives are seen fairly frequently in Stage I speech. "Wh" questions of an elementary type, such as *what that?* are also seen during this stage, and Fillmore does not seem to indicate how these should be dealt with, either.

Bowerman (1973a) pointed out another difficulty—that of formulating the modality constituent of case grammars for children. Although modalities are supposed to be operations on the sentence as a whole, this does not seem true for Stage I speech. Using negatives as one of her examples, Bowerman noted that while all the children she examined produced negative constructions, the negative markers were typically combined only with simple nouns or verbs. Though utterances up to four morphemes in length were observed, these were not negated. A similar situation held true for adverbs. It did not appear, then, that the modality was external to, and operating on, the proposition as a whole.

Finally, Fillmore's position, it can be recalled, included acceptance of semantic interpretation. While questioning Chomsky's (1965) choice of a deep structure representation, he nevertheless adhered to the view that a semantic interpretation could be derived from rules operating on the deep structure. This position, as does that of transformational grammar, seems to represent a sentence generating sequence that is the exact inverse of the sequence the child uses to produce an utterance.

Table 3

The Cases Introduced in Fillmore's (1971) Revised Case Grammar

Experiencer	The animate affected by the action or event (*I'm warm*)
Source	The origin or starting point of the action or event (*He fled his native country*)
Goal	The object or endpoint of the action or event (*The plane arrived at Idlewild*)
Time	The temporal orientation of the action or event (*Laurie was here yesterday*)

Fillmore in 1971

For reasons quite independent of how well his 1968 approach handled Stage I speech, Fillmore (1971) has made a number of revisions in his case grammar approach. His new approach has eliminated modality and the marker, kasus. A sentence is viewed as a proposition consisting of a "predicator" (a verb, adjective, or noun) in construction with one or more entities. The deep structure cases identify the roles that the entities serve in the predication. Each case directly dominates its own noun phrase. The additional cases adopted by Fillmore in his more recent approach appear in Table 3. Two cases included in Fillmore's (1968) approach, dative and factitive, have been eliminated.

The deep structure of this approach is considerably more simplified than Fillmore's previous one. Although the predicator is considered central in importance, none of the elements of the deep structure are in a fixed order. With the elimination of modality, the features of negation, tense, mood, and aspect are directly adjoined to the predicator element. Case markings, previously a function of kasus, along with a number of other functions pertaining to syntax, are accomplished by a series of transformational rules.

It appears that the transformational rules proposed by Fillmore develop syntactic structures from a semantic base. Thus, Fillmore's new approach avoids the difficulties inherent in deriving a semantic interpretation from syntactic structures. Some of the new features in Fillmore's approach seem to warrant a new application of case grammar to Stage I speech.

Kernan

An approach that shares a number of characteristics with Fillmore's (1968) approach has been proposed by Kernan (1970). In this approach, semantic relationships, based on a cognitive interpretation of reality,

Table 4
Some Semantic Notions of Kernan's (1970) Approach

	Predication
Agentive	The animate perceived as instigator of the action identified by the verb (*boy run*)
Direction	The location or spatial orientation of the action identified by the verb (*sit chair*)
Objective	Anything representable by a noun, that can be identified by the semantic interpretation of the verb itself (*bring cookie*)
	Stative
Possession	The association between a person and entity or privileged access a person has with an entity (*girl ball*)
Benefit	An animate receiving or benefiting from some entity (*ball me*)
Name	The identification of an entity through the use of its name (*that can*)
Location	The spatial relationship between two entities (*ball table*)

comprise the base structures underlying a child's language. These semantic relationships represent the knowledge of the child that entities and actions in the world may enter into certain knowable and linguistically expressable relationships.

In the base structure of this approach, the semantic notions are sorted according to their general semantic functions. These functions are termed "predication" and "stative." Predication involves a notion of action while stative does not. As did Fillmore's original approach, the base structure of Kernan's approach contains modality, which operates on the sentence as a whole. Thus far, then, it can be seen that the general underlying structure of a child's utterances is

$$\text{Sentence} \rightarrow (\text{Modality}) \begin{Bmatrix} \text{Predicative} \\ \text{Stative} \end{Bmatrix}$$

Modality may be optional in Kernan's approach since during Stage I speech it contains only negation and interrogation.

Predication contains relationships involving a verb and one or more nouns. Stative contains semantic notions that involve no action. Perhaps because of this, Kernan terms these notions semantic "concepts," reserving "relationships" for the notions contained in predication. Some of the semantic relationships and concepts in this approach are presented in Table 4.

In Kernan's approach, the semantic relationships and concepts receive surface realization through lexical selection and order rules operating on the base structure.

Kernan benefited from data of a child at the Stage I level of speech when developing his approach. This proved fortunate, for it enabled him to avoid one of the difficulties that hampered Fillmore's case grammar when applied to Stage I speech. Frequently, the Stage I child's utterances contain no verb (e.g., *my candy*) and thus an approach that treats verbs as obligatory must find a way of eliminating them before surface structure realization. This observation seemed to motivate Kernan to propose the two alternative functions of predication and stative.

Another problem facing Fillmore's original case grammar was not avoided in Kernan's approach, however. Despite speaking of a base structure that represents the child's knowledge of relationships among entities and actions in the world, Kernan proceeded to formally define such relationships in terms of nouns and verbs, as in Fillmore's original approach. This decision makes the approach vulnerable to the claim that in this approach, as in transformational grammar, a semantic interpretation is derived from a syntactic base structure. It seems clear, then, that this approach could do well with a more precise specification of the nature of the semantic relationships in the base structure.

Ingram

Ingram (1971) also proposed an approach that borrows from Fillmore's (1968) case grammar and is specifically tailored for the analysis of child language. Most notable is that Ingram's approach deals with the prelinguistic and single-word stages of the child's development.

In this approach, a sentence (which in order to accommodate the prelinguistic period must be viewed quite loosely) consists of a modality and a proposition. The modality incorporates features that affect the entire proposition, such as demonstration and interrogation, along with their physical expression by gesture or intonation. Ingram's proposition differs somewhat from Fillmore's. While Ingram utilized notions such as agentive, objective, and the like, he replaced verb with the semantic category of transitivity. This alteration from Fillmore's approach converted it into a more purely semantic model that Ingram believed mirrors more closely the actual process of language acquisition by the child, that is, the child's development of semantic notions with syntactic marking occurring at a subsequent point in time.

Ingram noted that the child's early language could be represented by a proposition in the form of a stative predication, involving what is termed "semantic intransitivity." Thus, an utterance such as *that kitty*, produced while the child was pointing at a cat, might presumably be represented in this approach in the manner

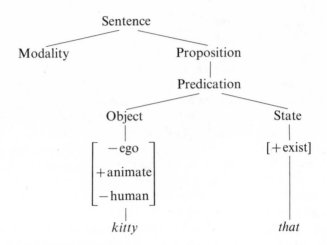

At a subsequent point in time, evidence of semantic transitivity is seen in the child's language. Semantic transitivity refers to the realization of potential activity by an agent or cause. An utterance such as *away ball*, spoken as the child throws a ball, might have the representation

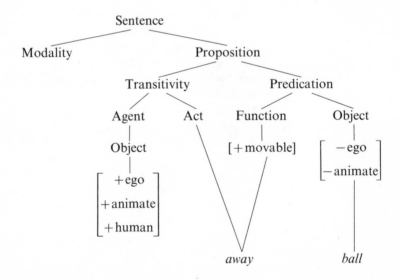

Since these are my own examples, I cannot state with certainty that Ingram would represent these utterances in exactly the same way. However, the general nature of these representations appears consistent with

his approach, including some of the aspects in the representations not seen in other approaches. One is the use of semantic features such as [+animate] and [+movable]. On first inspection it would appear that these features represent the input for conversion rules for surface structure realization. Frequently these conversion rules would be rules for lexicalization, such that act appearing with [+movable], for example, would be lexicalized as "away." Ingram also makes use of features such as [±comfort] in the prelinguistic period. Since a distinction between comfort and discomfort has a bearing on the child's output (e.g., gurgling versus crying), one might see the need to include them among the child's capabilities in some manner, but it is not at all clear that at this period the child intends to communicate them. As such, accounting for such a distinction by semantic features may be crediting the child with too much. Other examples provided by Ingram, however, suggest that such features may not really serve as input for conversion rules for surface structure realization at all. For example, he uses the features [+ego] and [+exist] in some instances, quite independently of a particular utterance, to represent the very existence of the child.

It is somewhat surprising that during the prelinguistic period, features such as [±comfort] are not part of modality, since they seem to operate on the child's entire vocalization. Instead, Ingram considers them a part of the within-proposition element, state, with modality unmarked. The features represented in modality when the child acquires his early words include [±wish] and [±question]. Since these are the equivalents of acts such as commanding and asking, which could be expressed through intonation, they appear quite appropriate. Ingram also included features within modality that may be more suspect. These features, such as [+point], pertain to gestures. While there is little doubt that gestures are communicative, I am not sure that their representation should be undifferentiated from features that have vocal realization in surface structure.

Ingram's approach was intended as a first step in representing children's early language within a semantically-based framework. As such, it seems to present some useful considerations. The deep structure in this approach contains the desirable characteristics of Fillmore's (1968) case grammar, for example, notions such as agent and object and a distinction between the proposition and the function an utterance may serve that is contained within modality. At the same time, Ingram's approach does not contain any of the remnants of syntax seen in Fillmore's case grammar, such as verb. Hopefully, this approach will undergo further development. In its present form the specific role played by the semantic features in the grammar is not clear. In addition, Ingram did not specify the nature of the possible elements of the deep structure nor the general means by which such elements are converted to surface structure. Specifications of this kind would be most useful since, according to Ingram, the meaning of utterances in this approach is not dependent on an interpretive component operating on the deep structure as seen in transformational grammar.

Greenfield, Smith, and Laufer

Another approach that shares certain similarities with Fillmore's (1968) case grammar is the one proposed by Greenfield, Smith, and Laufer (1972). As was Ingram's (1971) approach, this approach was developed with an eye toward analyzing semantic notions underlying single-word utterances.

Unlike the underlying structures of transformational grammar and case grammar, the base structure of the Greenfield, Smith, and Laufer approach is not actually linguistic in nature. Rather, it consists of a structured perception of real or imagined entities and relations. Thus it can be viewed as a perceptual-cognitive rather than linguistic base structure. It is proper to consider a level at which this structure takes a semantic form. It is assumed that what the child intends to communicate pertains to a perceived or imagined relation involving some entity. According to this approach the relations are actions or states while the entities are typically objects or persons.

Semantic structures are formed by the combination of entities and relations and these can be dichotomized into one of two divisions, depending on the role played. The two divisions are modality and event. Modality represents the speaker's relation to that which is referred to in event. By definition, then, the only entity in modality is the speaker. The relation within modality need not be expressed verbally. The entities of event can vary and presumably depend on the salient person or object involved in the relation within event about which the child is communicating. Thus an utterance such as *baby*, produced when a child sees a baby crawling, would have the representation

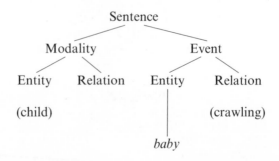

In this instance the relation within modality is unmarked. The other elements not receiving surface structure realization are considered part of the base structure but are not expressed at this point due to the child's being limited to single-word utterances. The particular elements that are realized in surface structure do vary, however. For example, if a child produced *more* when reaching for a (second) cookie, the representation would be

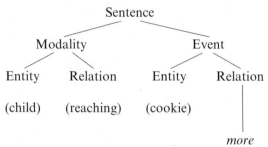

In other instances, more than one entity can be represented in the base structure. If a child produces *Mommy* when pointing to his mother's shoe, such an utterance would have the representation

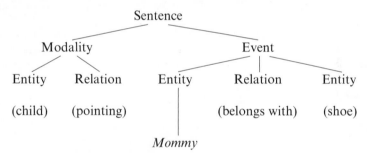

Since it is not clear that the child understands possession in the sense it is understood by adults, the information contained in the relation subsumed under event is quite speculative. Nevertheless, it can be seen that this type of relation involves more than one underlying entity.

The relatively rich base structure of the Greenfield, Smith, and Laufer approach allows the verbally encoded element to be classified according to one of a number of possible "cases." The major cases used in this approach are presented in Table 5.

With the assignment of semantic cases to single-word utterances, Greenfield, Smith, and Laufer have gone further than most investigators in recent years in what they are willing to credit the child with. At least two investigators, Bloom (1973) and Brown (1973) are somewhat skeptical of the confidence one may have in such cases during this period of language

Table 5

The Semantic Cases in the Greenfield, Smith, and Laufer
(1972) Approach

Pure performatives	Utterances considered part of a child's actions or reactions (*bye-bye*)
Naming	Utterances calling attention to objects through the use of their names (*ball*)
Vocatives	Utterances serving to call persons through the use of their names (*Mama*)
Objects of demand	Utterances requesting an object named (*milk*)
Negative or affirmative	Utterances denying or affirming some proposition, rejecting some action or object, or marking the absence of something expected (*no*)
Action performed by agent	Utterances referring to an act performed by an animate (*dance*)
Inanimate object of direct action	Utterances naming an inanimate undergoing direct action (*spoon*)
State or action of inanimate object	Utterances specifying a characteristic of an object or an activity in which it is involved (*hot*)
Possession and habitual location	Utterances referring to the relation of association or belongingness (*my*)
Location	Utterances referring to the endpoint of some action, separate from the action itself (*chair*)
Experiencer	Utterances referring to an animate affected by a state or action (*Mommy*)
Agent of action	Utterances referring to an animate performing some action (*Daddy*)
Modification of event	Utterances adding a specification that pertains to a whole event rather than a single aspect of an event (*wait*)

development. Greenfield, Smith, and Laufer would counter such sus-
picions I think by noting that this approach does not attribute more
structure of a linguistic nature to the child than he actually demonstrates
in his speech. The base structure represents perceptual-cognitive structure
and thus its richness only reflects the nonlinguistic information the child
takes into account when he produces his utterance. No assumption is made
about whether or not the child knows the linguistic correlates to this
information.

This assumption of Greenfield, Smith, and Laufer has some advantages in allowing certain obstacles facing some other approaches to be
avoided. For example, since the base structure of this approach is in
perceptual-cognitive terms, it contains no obligatory linguistic elements

that must be accounted for in instances where the child's early stage of language development does not permit full realization of all underlying elements. Since utterances are viewed in terms of salient nonlinguistic elements, the semantic nature of such utterances can be analyzed without having to sort out meaning from grammatical structure.

It is possible that the Greenfield, Smith, and Laufer approach is on relatively safe ground in terms of what it assumes to be the nature of the base structure underlying the child's language. Whether or not the child's single-word utterances can really be appropriately assigned to the semantic cases seen in their approach seems to be another matter, however. Two complications are evident. First, it appears that when an utterance is assigned to a particular case, an assumption is being made about the semantic function played by the utterance. Thus it seems that Greenfield, Smith, and Laufer renege on their original claim that they only attribute to the child the linguistic knowledge evidenced in the utterance itself. Classifying an utterance such as *Daddy* as an agent of action, for example, seems to be more than describing a relation within the situation in which the child used the utterance; it seems to represent crediting the child with the linguistic knowledge for talking about such a relation.

A second complication pertains to the potential difficulty in determining the semantic case to which a given single-word utterance should be assigned. For example, Greenfield, Smith, and Laufer assign an utterance such as *light*, produced when a child seemingly wanted a light to be turned on, to the case inanimate object of direct action. One might possibly view such an utterance as an instance of object of demand, however. While the latter case is generally reserved for utterances that involve accompanying reaching or whining it is difficult to see why a child's demanding of an object must require such accompanying behaviors. Such a requirement might serve the purpose of increasing the reliability of investigators' categorizations, but it may not be related to whether or not the distinction between these two cases is a functional one for the child. It does not appear to be sufficient, therefore, that the elements thought to underlie a child's utterances are not strictly linguistic (assuming this is the Greenfield, Smith, and Laufer position). There is the additional requirement that these elements can be assumed to play a part in determining the semantic cases of the child's utterances.

Chafe

Another approach to characterizing language is the one offered by Chafe (1970). To my knowledge, no one has applied all aspects of Chafe's approach to Stage I speech, although Nelson (1975) utilized Chafe's subclassifications of nouns (see Table 7) in her longitudinal study, and the categories of multiterm relations that Brown (1973) employed in his cross-sectional analysis of Stage I speech also seemed influenced by it.

Chafe's approach begins with the assumption that language serves to symbolize concepts as sounds that can be transmitted for purposes of communication. The sentence generation process commences with a "formation" process where configurations of meaning are assembled, representing the semantic structure. These semantic configurations are then subject to "postsemantic processes" that yield a series of differing representations, the last of which Chafe views as the surface structure. A process of "symbolization" follows, by which units of the surface structure are converted into underlying phonological configurations.

Chafe's approach does not seem to contain the interpretive components seen in transformational grammar or early case grammar. Rather than containing a semantic component by which a semantic interpretation can be derived from a syntactically-based deep structure, for example, Chafe's approach calls for an underlying semantic structure that represents an assembly of configurations of meaning. Similarly, Chafe's symbolization process seems to be a less-interpretive parallel to the phonological component of transformational grammar.

The postsemantic process of Chafe's approach deserves attention since it is responsible for functions handled quite differently in other approaches. The postsemantic process has the responsibility of converting the underlying semantic structure to a form consistent with the eventual phonetic output. In an utterance such as *John's ideas are out in left field*, for example, the underlying semantic structure of "out in left field" certainly bears little resemblance to its phonetic output. A phrase such as "highly unfeasible" might bear a closer resemblance. This relationship can be seen below (bearing in mind that the examples are not in any kind of surface form).

Semantic structure → Postsemantic structure
[highly unfeasible]   [out in left field]

The arrow in this relationship represents a postsemantic process.

Chafe dichotomizes semantic structure into two major areas: (1) the area of the verb, which embraces states (conditions and qualities) and events, and (2) the area of the noun, which embraces physical objects and reified abstractions. The verb is assumed to be central and the noun peripheral. Chafe views the relationship between the verb and the nouns in his approach to be different from the one proposed by Fillmore (1968). I consider the difference to be more one of emphasis. Chafe asserts that the nature of the verb determines what nouns will accompany it. Fillmore

Table 6

Chafe's (1970) Subclassifications of Verbs

State verb	The specification of a condition of a noun (*The shirt is stained*)
Process verb	The specification of a change in the condition of a noun (*The watch broke*)
Action verb	The specification of an activity in which a noun is involved (*The center jumped*)
Process-action verb	The specification of a change in the condition of a noun and an activity in which a noun is involved (*The man painted the fence*)
Ambient-state verb	The specification of a condition without a noun (*It's humid*)
Ambient-action verb	The specification of an activity without a noun (*It's raining*)

makes the more general assertion that a sentence will consist of one or more nouns associated with the verb in a particular relationship.

One might think that Chafe would do better in avoiding syntactic terms such as "noun" and "verb." In fact, Chafe views these as similar to what some semanticists might term "argument" and "predicate," respectively. Verbs are subclassified according to the semantic roles they play. Examples and definitions of these subclassifications appear in Table 6.

Since the verb determines the nouns that can accompany it, the nouns, too, can be subclassified into different types. These are presented in Table 7.

In Table 8, I have categorized a number of characteristic Stage I meanings according to the Chafe approach. For some of the meanings,

Table 7

Chafe's (1970) Subclassifications of Nouns

Patient	Someone or something in a given condition or undergoing a change in condition (*He opened the box*)
Agent	Someone or something that instigates an action or process (*The oaf grinned*)
Experiencer	Someone mentally disposed in some way (*Barney forgot the answer*)
Beneficiary	Someone who profits from a state or process (*He gave me the diploma*)
Instrument	Something that causes an action or process but is not the instigator (*He killed the grouper with a Hawaiian sling*)
Complement	Something that is ordinarily implied by the verb (*Tim sang a song*)
Location	The place or locus of a state, action, or process (*Butch ran onto the field*)

Table 8
Some Stage I Meanings
Categorized by the Chafe (1970)
Approach

Meanings	Examples
Action verb + Agent	*baby eat*
Action verb + Patient	*throw ball*
Action verb + Location	*sit chair*
Patient + Location	*sweater chair*
Patient + Beneficiary	*Adam shoe*
State verb + Patient	*dead bug*

at least, this seemed to be a fairly straightforward endeavor. Noticeably absent from Table 8 are the operations of reference such as nomination, nonexistence, and recurrence. These require further treatment in Chafe's approach.

Both nouns and verbs are specified in this approach in terms of selectional, lexical, and inflectional units. Selectional units are responsible for the types of nouns that must accompany certain verbs. Lexical units function by "narrowing the conceptual field" within a noun or verb until the most precise concept is arrived at. A noun or a verb may also be specified, however, in ways that are not limited to a choice of a precise concept. For example, a noun that might be specified by the selectional unit as patient and by the lexical unit as "wheel" may also be specified as plural. The latter is performed by the inflectional unit.

Nomination is treated as a noun inflectional unit that involves a "predicativizer." The predicativizer permits a semantically equivalent term for patient to be represented as state verb. For example, an utterance such as *that car* might be represented as

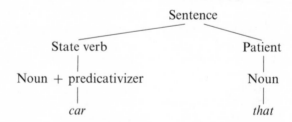

Nonexistence, rejection, and denial are treated as verb inflectional units. The presence of this verb inflectional unit results in the postsemantic conversion of the verb into a configuration of two verbs, one that contains

the main verb and the other, which is an auxiliary. An utterance such as *no break* might be represented as

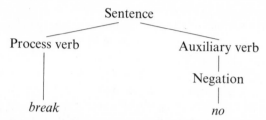

Recurrence appears to be treated as a notion requiring more than one verb. This is not unusual in Chafe's approach; it appears to be the means by which relative clauses and other complex constructions are handled. In such instances, recurrence would be treated as a state verb with a higher order element, usually patient, serving to relate the main verb to the noun it requires. During Stage I, of course, not all of these elements will be realized in surface structure. The utterance *more cookie*, for example, would be represented as

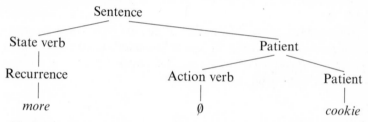

Chafe's approach was intended as a theory of the structure of language and not as an approach to the analysis of Stage I speech. In some ways this is fortunate, since it would not augur well for an approach to require some of its more elaborate operations (the use of inflectional units, the use of two or more verbs) to handle utterances reflecting the earliest semantic notions to emerge in child language.

Chafe's subclassifications of nouns are not entirely appropriate to apply to Stage I speech, although several of them would seemingly require no change (e.g., agent, location). Patient may be too broad since it can be used to represent a number of different meanings. For example, a locative state can be represented by combining patient with location (e.g., *sweater chair*), and an affected object can be represented by combining patient with action verb (e.g., *eat candy*). Not only do these two semantic relationships emerge at different times in the child's linguistic development, but patient occupies a different sentence position in the utterances used to code them. Similarly, beneficiary may be too broad. Although I can see the semantic similarities in the use of "Bozo" in the utterances *eat Bozo lunch* and *give Bozo lunch* (indicating a possessor and indirect object, respectively), the former is observed considerably earlier than the latter, in children's speech. Their assignment to the same semantic category, then, may not be ideal. Some of Chafe's categories are only marginal at best in Stage I speech, but this is hardly a flaw in his approach.

One advantage that Chafe's approach seems to possess is its directionality in the sentence generation process. All arrows, as it were, point from left to right, indicating processes that move from a semantic toward a phonetic structure. This direction characterizes language as converting meaning into sound—not the reverse. If a semantic structure follows the proper rules of semantic formation, then a well-formed phonetic output seems assured. The reverse would not be the case, particularly for utterances involving postsemantic processes. One can imagine the difficulty, for example, in trying to derive the proper semantic structure of *John's ideas are out in left field* from its phonetic output. Although proposed as a theory of the structure of language, this feature of Chafe's approach lends itself very well to an approach to the analysis of language performance.

Cook

An approach adopted from that of Chafe (1970) was suggested in a working paper by Cook (1972). Cook conceived of the structures in his approach as a matrix of case frames. The matrix consisted of 16 possible verb types, which are defined in Table 9.

Table 9
Cook's (1972) Verb Types

	Basic Verb Types
State verbs	Verbs specifying that an entity is in a certain state or condition, and that are accompanied by an object (*The car is stylish*)
Process verbs	Verbs specifying that an entity undergoes a change of state or condition, and that are accompanied by an object (*Jules is sleeping*)
Action verbs	Verbs expressing an activity, and that are accompanied by an agent (*Wanda is playing*)
Action-process verbs	Verbs that simultaneously express an action and a process, and that are accompanied by an agent and an object (*I am eating breakfast*)
	Experiential Verb Types
State experiencer verbs	Verbs that specify that an experiencer is in a certain state or condition with respect to a given object, and that are accompanied by an experiencer and an object (*Tom likes spumoni*)

Table 9
Cook's (1972) Verb Types (*cont'ed*)

Process experiencer verbs	Verbs specifying that an experiencer undergoes a change of state with respect to a given object, and that are accompanied by an experiencer and an object (*The boy heard music*)
Action experiencer verbs	Verbs expressing an activity that results in a change of mental state for someone else, and that are accompanied by an agent and an experiencer (*The stranger frightened the girl* [by sneaking up behind her, for example])
Action-process experiencer verbs	Verbs expressing an activity that places an object as a "stimulus" for someone else's mental experience, and that are accompanied by an agent, object, and experiencer (*Margaret said hello to the coach*)

Benefactive Verb Types

State benefactive verbs	Verbs that specify that a benefactor is in a certain state or condition with respect to a given object, and that are accompanied by a benefactive and an object (*I have a basketball*)
Process benefactive verbs	Verbs that specify that a benefactor undergoes a change of state or condition with respect to a given object, and that are accompanied by a benefactive and an object (*Rachel found the quarter*)
Action benefactive verbs	Verbs that specify that an agent has caused gain or loss to a benefactor with respect to a given object, and that are accompanied by an agent and a benefactive (nonexistent in English)
Action-process benefactive verbs	Verbs that specify that an agent has caused gain or loss to a benefactor with respect to a given object, and that are accompanied by an agent, benefactive, and object (*I sent Robert the letter*)

Locative Verb Types

State locative verbs	Verbs specifying that an object is in a certain location, and that are accompanied by an object and a locative (*The belt is in the closet*)
Process locative verbs	Verbs that specify that an object changes its location, and that are accompanied by an object and a locative (*The pencil fell off the table*)
Action locative verbs	Verbs expressing an activity resulting in a change of location, and that are accompanied by an agent and a locative (*The baby crawled under the table*)
Action-process locative verbs	Verbs expressing an activity involving the change of an object distinct from the agent, and that are accompanied by an agent, object, and locative (*Trixie threw Helen into the lake*)

It can be seen from Table 9 that Cook's verb types, as do Chafe's, allow not only for types that might be characteristic of Stage I, but for types seen during later periods of development as well. In a preliminary paper, Sørenson (1974) attempted to assess the appropriateness of Cook's approach for the analysis of children's utterances during Stage I. The data used by Sørenson were originally reported in papers by Lewis (1937), Braine (1963), and Albright and Albright (1956). The 5 children reported in those papers ranged in age from 13 to 26 months. Unfortunately, their mean utterance lengths were unavailable.

All of the basic verb types were evidenced in the samples obtained from the children. Utterances with process verbs (e.g., *Mommy sleep*) were noted only twice, however. This is not a surprising finding since they do not refer to overt activity, which seems to be what the Stage I child is most involved with. What was surprising was the finding that 9 of the remaining 12 verb types were evidenced.

This very finding illustrates the potential problems in applying an adult system to Stage I speech. Considerable care must be taken in saying that because a Stage I utterance could be taken as a particular verb type in the adult system, it functions in this way for the child. For example, utterances such as *want car* and *see ball* were viewed as state experiencer verbs. In fact, however, such utterances during this period are typically produced when the child is reaching for or pointing to an object, respectively. It is difficult to view the child's intent in these circumstances as communicating some presumably internal state he is experiencing.

A similar type of problem arises when utterances such as *push it* and *sit down there* are classified as different verb types (action-process locative verb and action locative verb, respectively). The distinction in the adult system rests in the former, unlike the latter, involving a change of place of an object distinct from the agent. It is quite unclear that the child is aware of this distinction.

It is possible that some of Cook's verb types will be found to be operative during Stage I, and this alone justifies the kind of application attempted by Sørenson. However, before verb types such as action-process benefactive and the like are attributed to the child, evidence should be available supporting the existence of these types in the child's system. It appears that Sørenson's data should be supplemented by data of a longitudinal nature. If it were found, for example, that a child's utterances classifiable in the adult system as containing action-process benefactive verbs were in fact acquired by the child after utterances that in the adult system could be classified as containing action benefactive verbs or process benefactive verbs, then justification for making these kinds of distinctions might be provided.

The Berkeley Cross-Linguistic Language Development Project

At the time of this writing, a group of investigators at Berkeley have been developing a semantically-based system of coding children's utterances. For convenience, the system arising from this project, the Berkeley Cross-Linguistic Language Development Project (1973) will be referred to as the BCLLDP approach. This system was not developed as an explanatory model of the notions underlying children's Stage I speech but rather as a means of coordinating and standardizing the work of investigators examining children's acquisition of various languages. However, the system contains several features worthy of comment.

Each utterance by the child is first classified as an example of a given semantic clause type. The clause types utilized represented all of the semantic configurations noted in preliminary surveys of child speech in a number of languages. Since this system is still under revision it would not be appropriate to present all of the clause types of this system here. However, in order to provide a preliminary idea of how this system might be applied to Stage I speech, several examples of clause types operative during Stage I speech appear in Table 10.

The clause types specified for each utterance are expanded to include indications of function such as the imitative nature of an utterance, modality such as the speaker's intention, and aspect such as the habitual characteristic of the described event. In addition, extra-clausal indications are made such as manner, time, and location.

Two highly positive features of the BCLLDP approach can be identified. First, it was developed with a data base of child language samples

Table 10

Some Examples of Clause Types Proposed by the BCLLDP Approach (1973) that Are Operative During Stage I Speech

Clause Type	Example
Patient + Patient	*this juice*
Patient + Physical state	*Daddy big*
Patient + Location	*sweater chair*
Possession + Patient	*Adam shoe*
Agent + Function + Patient	*eat cookie*
Change + Patient + Location	*Ernie fall down*
Agent + Cause + Change + Patient + State	*break balloon*
Agent + Cause + Change + Body part + Location	*go home*
Agent + Cause + Change + Patient + Possession	*gimme milk*

from a variety of languages. As such it does not appear to represent a forced attempt to apply a theoretical model of adult linguistic capacity to children's language usage but rather seems to have derived from the nature of children's utterances themselves, or, more probably, adult conceptions of these utterances. The second positive feature of this approach is that it is applicable to advanced as well as early stages of language development; the 1973 version of the system was developed with the benefit of samples from children as old as four years, one month. This feature reduces the likelihood that the underlying notions it postulates for Stage I speech will need to undergo massive and qualitative revisions in order to account for further development.

At the time of this writing, Stage I speech data do not play the largest role in shaping the particular categories utilized in this approach to analysis. Vocatives are omitted from analysis even though they represent utterances that appear very early in development. Some of the clause types seem too rich in semantic structure to represent the notions underlying Stage I speech. Yet these investigators cautioned that the resulting semantic configurations stemmed from adult intuitions viewed with an eye toward the end state of the child's linguistic development. An example of the questionable complexity can be seen in the utterance *I walked home*, which is analyzed as agent + cause + body part + cause + change + self + location. While it may prove true that the child conceptualizes each of these underlying components, it is debatable that they motivate the child's utterance. That is, it is not clear that these components enter into what the child intends to communicate.

Some of the categories employed in the 1973 version of this system appear too broad, however. From Table 10 it can be seen that patient can serve so many roles that it resembles a category almost as broad as noun. Another category of this system, range, seems to be quite general in meaning, serving to complete the sense of the meaning conveyed by the verb. Nevertheless, it is clear that this approach has gone far in specifying possible notions underlying language usage. If the ongoing revision of this approach makes use of additional Stage I speech data, this approach may contribute much to our knowledge of meaning in early child language.

Edwards

Another approach to analysis was developed by Edwards (1973), whose intent was to describe the relational meanings generally expressed in children's two-word utterances. The semantic approaches available to Edwards at the time of his writing were not satisfactory to him for several reasons. Semantic notions such as location, frequently cross-classified

Table 11
The Case Relations of Edward's (1973) Approach to
Semantic Analysis

Agent (A)	The animate perceived as instigator of the action identified by the verb (*The woman sipped the wine*)
Instrument (I)	The inanimate force or object causally involved in the action or state named by the verb (*He was cut by the glass*)
Object (O)	The entity whose role in the action or state named by the verb is identified by the semantic interpretation of the verb itself (*The rock hit the window*)
Experiencer (E)	The animate perceived as undergoing some kind of mental experience (*Walter believed in ghosts*)
Phenomenon (Ph)	That which is perceived, known, or reacted to by the experiencer (*The inspector heard footsteps*)
Location (L)	The static spatial position or orientation of the object (*His head was on the desk*)
Source (S)	The place from which something moves (*The family moved from Punta Gorda*)
Goal (G)	The place to which something moves (*The child ran home*)
Possessor (P)	The possessor of the object, where the possessive relation is static (*Arnold's shoe was in the wastebasket*)
Beneficiary (B)	The change in the possession of the object (*The man sold the watch to Hans*)
Result (R)	The entity coming into existence as a result of the action named by the verb (*The Greeks built the shrine*)

in syntactic terms such as noun + noun (which itself is a problem), contained no indication of any unexpressed underlying semantic elements that seemed to be essential to the interpretation of the child's utterances. Without postulating an underlying element such as "on," for instance, it seemed unclear how *block chair* could be interpreted as location. Another weakness that Edwards attributed to some of the semantic approaches was that no account was taken of how the notions reflected in a child's two-word utterances were semantically related to each other.

Edwards's approach was developed along the lines of Piaget's descriptions of sensorimotor intelligence. In some respects, the composition of his resulting semantic system resembles the categories proposed by the Fillmore (1968) and Chafe (1970) approaches. The semantic notions, or "case relations" proposed by Edwards appear in Table 11.

The similarities between Edwards's system and Fillmore's and Chafe's should be quite apparent from Table 11. Certain differences, however, can be noted. Possessor represents a relation that would be categorized as dative in Fillmore's original system. In Chafe's approach, this would be categorized as beneficiary. Edwards's beneficiary also adds greater specificity, and should be distinguished from possessor. The former specifies a change in possession. It can be recalled from the discussion of Chafe's approach that this distinction is more consistent with the findings of Stage I speech. The division of the place associated with locative action into source and goal as the place from, and to which something moves, respectively, represents a distinction seen in Fillmore's (1971) more recent approach, but not in Chafe's. Phenomenon and result are also new terms, however, result appears to be synonymous with Fillmore's (1968) factitive.

The case relations in Edwards's approach are defined according to their potentials for combining with each other. These potentials are made explicit through the introduction of verbs into the system. Verbs are subclassified according to which cases they select, and deep structure semantic clause types are formulated that consist of a single verb with its associated cases. Verbs are divided into actional verbs (e.g., "hit," "walk") and stative verbs, whose function is to describe a permanent or changing state of affairs (e.g., "own," "give"). These verb types, in turn, are subdivided. For example, stative verbs are divided into those describing locative, possessive, experiential, and attributive states, such as "enter," "buy," "like," and "break," respectively. As do Fillmore and Chafe, Edwards treats adjectives such as "broken" as a type of verb.

Edwards took the position that the resulting clause types consisting of subclassified verbs and their associated cases did not represent a sufficient description of expressable meanings. Following the proposals of Lyons (1969) and Chafe (1970), Edwards further segmented his clause types into those that expressed static, dynamic, and causative relations. Examples of some of Edwards's basic clause types are presented in Table 12.

An inspection of Table 12 reveals that Edwards's system includes a specification of the ways in which the child's utterances may be semantically related to each other. In addition, some of the particular categories that Edwards proposed seem to have developmental validity. For example, the types of relationships utilizing actional verbs are reflected in the child's utterances before those utilizing stative verbs. Similarly, an examination of children's utterances reflecting locative relations reveals that one type of relation (e.g., locative action) is evidenced before the others (e.g., locative state). Through his utilization of Piaget's descriptions of the child's sensorimotor intelligence, Edwards justifies some of these categories from the standpoint of cognitive development.

It is evident that Edwards's system includes a number of semantic notions that represent later attainments than those reflected in the utterances of children during Stage I. Edwards took the conservative view

Table 12

Some Basic Clause Types in Edwards's (1973) System of Semantic Analysis

| | Actional | | Stative | | | |
	Directed Action	Movement	Locative	Possessive	Experiential	Attributive
Static			O + V + L (*The sweater is on the chair*)	O + V + P (*The car belongs to me*)	E + V(Ph) (*Larry likes rice pudding*)	O + V (*The door is open*)
Dynamic	I + O + V (*The lamp hit the floor*)	O + V (*The ball rolled*)	O + V + {S/G} (*The letter blew off the desk*)	O + V + B (*Jill received a gift*)	E + V(Ph) (*Jeanette became interested in baseball*)	O + V (*The door opened*)
Causative	(A)I + O + V (*Winona hit Bozo with a pie*)	(A)(I)O + V (*Herman intimidated Wilbur with his growl*)	(A)(I)O + V + {S/G} (*Todd tossed the ball in the basket*)	(A)(I)O + V + B (*The stranger gave the girl a note*)	(A)(I)E + V(Ph) (*The coach interested Susan in track*)	(A)(I)O + V (*Vinnie cut the cable with a switchblade*)

that a general framework of semantic relations was satisfactory, with empirical research subsequently determining which relations might be realized in young children's speech. Nevertheless, all of the notions ordinarily reflected in Stage I speech are not included. These include nomination, notice, recurrence, nonexistence, denial, and rejection. The last three might not be expected to appear in this system, since they are assigned modality status (Fillmore, 1968), and Edwards's paper dealt only with within-proposition clause types. The absence of the other notions, however, is surprising. Not only do they seem to have cognitive precursors explainable in Piagetian terms (see Chapter 1), but the inadequacies in the manner in which other approaches had characterized the semantic notions of Stage I speech, the above operations of reference included, served as the motivation for Edwards to devise his approach in the first place.

It is possible that Edwards's adoption of complex semantic clause types in his approach is in part due to his vague demarcation between concepts and semantic notions. For example, in discussing the relational meanings of two-word utterances, Edwards stated

> Semantic interpretation demands for each of these two-term utterances the postulation of underlying, but unexpressed, semantic-relational elements that are conceptually required by the interpretation and which may actually be realized in other contextually related utterances. (1973, p 397)

Certainly those concepts (Edwards's semantic-relational elements) that are realized in the child's utterances can be granted semantic notion status in the deep structure. However, if there is no surface structure realization, it seems quite capricious to portray a child's conceptual grasp of a given relationship as a semantic notion. For instance, a child who produces *throw ball* in an appropriate context may well understand that animates can serve as agents by acting upon objects. However, if no utterances specifying animates in this role were observed in the child's speech, it could not be presumed that the child possesses the semantic notion agent. The concept of agent may not yet be one the child has the capability of communicating. The absence of a distinction between concepts and semantic notions could easily lead to the incorrect postulation of beneficiaries, instruments, and the like, as underlying elements in the child's language. The child shows the ability to give objects to others, and use objects as tools even before the period of two-word utterances. The fact that notions such as beneficiary and instrument are not reflected in the child's utterances until later, however, indicates that this distinction is a proper one.

Table 13
Semantic Relations of the Schaerlaekens (1973) Approach

Fixed allocation between two nouns	The expression of possession or destination (*chair Daddy*)
Coincidence between two nouns	The expression of place, association, or identification (*cookie table*)
Subject + Verb	The designation of an action and its subject (*Teddy walk*)
Object + Verb	The designation of an action and its object (*eat prune*)
Indirect object + Verb	The designation of an action and the place where it occurs or the person who might benefit from it (*give Maria*)
Deixis	The drawing attention to an object or attribute (*there apple*)
Negation/Affirmation	The expression of approval or disapproval of an object, action, or attribute (*no take*)
Place	The designation of the place where a noun is located by means of a qualifier (*ball in*)

Schaerlaekens

An approach that borrows some features used by Bloom (1970) was developed by Schaerlaekens (1973). Of interest to Schaerlaekens were the semantic relations evidenced in children's two-word utterances, showing some similarities in focus at least, to the approach of Edwards (1973). The semantic relation categories in the Schaerlaekens approach were based on a study of the two-word utterances of six Dutch-speaking children (two sets of triplets) during Stage I speech. These data were not longitudinal, however; categories were constructed on the basis of adult intuitions when confirmed by certain regularities in the surface structure of the child's language, notably in the form of word order. The semantic relations of this approach appear in Table 13.

This approach seems to represent a system of categorizing semantic relations. Schaerlaekens did not indicate how a grammar consistent with this approach would be organized. She did, however, suggest that each of the semantic relations would emerge from a common point where semantic relations (if they are operative at all in the child's underlying linguistic system) are not differentiated by their surface structure coding. These prior constructions were termed predicatives, since all that can be said of them is that they contain a noun about which some comment is made.

The influence of the manner of coding on the semantic relation categories of this approach can be seen from an inspection of Table 13. A number of these categories are discussed in syntactic terms such as subject and noun. This gives the impression that the manner in which two-word utterances are coded in surface structure may be more than a method of confirming whether or not certain semantic relations are operative in a child's linguistic system—it may serve to define these relations in the first place.

The use of the manner in which utterances are coded as a means of constructing semantic relation categories is not an improper enterprise. If utterances seemingly reflecting similar semantic relationships are coded by a different word order rule in the child's surface structure, for example, it seems fair to assume that the two semantic relationships may be different in his linguistic system. The problem is that there are only so many possible coding rules at the two-word stage.

This problem can be illustrated from Schaerlaekens's data. For example, one child, Joost, produced the following utterances.

auto rijdt (*car drives*)
mevrouw kuist (*lady cleans*)
tutter val (*pacifier fall*)
konijn slaapt (*rabbit sleeps*)

Schaerlaekens viewed each as an example of the relation subject + verb. From a syntactic perspective this is quite reasonable. However, in this approach this relation is supposed to be semantic in nature. In the adult linguistic system, each utterance might be taken to reflect a different semantic relation, for example, instrument, agent, object, and experiencer, respectively. Schaerlaekens's data were not longitudinal, however, and therefore she could not determine whether or not utterances such as *mevrouw kuist* emerged before those such as *konijn slaapt*. Thus, this semantic relation category was based almost entirely on coding in surface structure, therefore resembling a syntactic category. It would appear that the value of this approach might be enhanced by the incorporation of information arising from the results of longitudinal investigations of Stage I speech.

Schlesinger

The manner in which Schlesinger (1971a; 1971b) dealt with Stage I speech differs markedly from most of the treatments presented thus far. Of interest to Schlesinger were only those aspects of the underlying structure that form the basis for the actual utterances produced by the

Table 14
Schlesinger's (1971a) Position
Rules for Stage I Speech

Position Rules	Examples
Agent + Action	*baby eat*
Action + Object	*hit ball*
Agent + Object	*Daddy cookie*
Modifier + Head	*little cup*
Negation + X	*no juice*
X + Dative	*give Daddy*
Introducer + X	*there truck*
X + Locative	*sock chair*

child, that is, the child's intentions. Schlesinger used the term "input marker," or "*I* marker" for the formalized representation of the child's intentions that are expressed in the linguistic output. *I* markers do not simply represent a notational revision of deep structures in the transformational grammar sense. Unlike these deep structures, *I* markers specify semantic notions.

> In other words, the *I* marker must be assumed to contain the information that "John" is the agent of "catch," that "ball" is the direct object of "catch". . . . It is these *relations* between elements which are included in the *I* marker. (Schlesinger, 1971a, p 66)

Thus, *I* markers contain no information about grammatical categories or word order. Schlesinger therefore viewed *I* markers as less language-specific than the deep structures of the transformational grammar approach and closer to the cognitive structures that underlie early language. "Realization rules" are postulated that convert the *I* markers into utterances. In a very real sense, these can be viewed as transformational rules. Schlesinger proposed two kinds of realization rules in dealing with Stage I speech: position rules, which accord each notion in the *I* marker its position as a word in the utterance; and category rules, which determine the grammatical category that is appropriate in a given position. The particular position rules presented by Schlesinger describe most of the common two-word utterance types seen in Stage I. These position rules were postulated on the basis of the relative position of every pair of words in view of the relations between them. Schlesinger's position rules are presented in Table 14.

Schlesinger suggested that these position rules probably precede category rules. As justification for this proposal, he presented examples from the literature on Stage I speech such as *more wet*. Such utterances seemed to reflect the child's ability to express a relation by relative position, but revealed his yet undeveloped knowledge of which grammatical classes may occur in the two positions. Category rules at Stage I would be those that specified a position rule such as modifier + head as, for example, adjective + noun.

One advantageous characteristic of Schlesinger's approach is that his realization rules directly translate the underlying semantic notions into surface form by selecting words belonging to appropriate grammatical categories and assigning them the order seen in adult speech. This scheme would entirely bypass any grammatical deep structure. Since it certainly seems that the Stage I child's objectives in using language are to express meanings irrespective of adult grammatical categories, this characteristic seems most suitable. In addition, dealing with semantic notions such as agent and action seems more in keeping with Stage I than the adoption of terms such as noun phrase and verb phrase, which seem to obliterate important distinctions that may be salient for the child. Much of Schlesinger's account has been found to be consistent with the Stage I data analyzed by Braine (1976).

Not all of Schlesinger's ideas are as appropriate, however. Consider some of the varied semantic notions that could be reflected in utterances following the same position rule.

Modifier + Head	*big girl*	(Attribution)
	Mommy shoe	(Possessor)
	more milk	(Recurrence)
Negation + X	*no ball*	(Nonexistence)
	no bed	(Rejection)
	no truck	(Denial)
X + Locative	*sweater chair*	(Locative state)
	sit chair	(Action + Location)

On what basis did Schlesinger combine attribution, possessor, and recurrence under the same heading? The answer is that two-word combinations reflecting these notions are formed in much the same way, with the entity being described adopting second-word position, and the description itself taking first-word position. One cannot readily deny that utterances reflecting these three semantic notions have some characteristics in common. The most striking characteristic, though, is the word-combining rule that each usually follows. It is tempting to conclude that similarities in word-combining rules may have actually dictated the types of utterances that Schlesinger would classify as reflecting the same semantic relations. Presumably, semantic relation categories were formed on the principle of asking what the relative position of every pair of words is in view of the relations between them. An inspection of the above examples, however, suggests that such categories were formed in large part on the basis of the relative position of the word pairs. This sort of tendency leads one directly into the trap of trying to represent underlying semantic notions by categories too abstract to handle the job. For instance, the early appearance of recurrence relative to attribution or possessor in Stage I speech would be completely obscured in this approach. Other notions possibly acquired at different points in development, such as locative state and locative action, are also categorized together.

Such overinclusive categories seem to limit the scope of Schlesinger's approach to utterances of limited length, suggesting it will not fare well as a model for later linguistic development. For example, how might this account explain that a child might say *my big boat* but never *big my boat*, since "big" and "my" are both modifiers? Clearly the child would need to perceive the two as being different. Accounting for the former word order by alluding to how others around the child speak would seem inadequate since the child is still required to perceive the two types of modifiers differently in order to learn to use the appropriate order in his speech.

The limited scope of some of Schlesinger's earlier proposals seems to present difficulties in another respect as well. Although eliminating syntactic deep structures for Stage I utterances, he provided no means of handling abstract features seen at subsequent stages of linguistic development (Cromer, in Bowerman, 1974b; Stemmer, 1973). Bowerman (1974b) also raised this sort of question. If many subjects resist interpretation as agents, for example (as in *caution outweighed the need for action*), by what means will the child come to treat such abstract features as subjects in the same manner as agents? In a more recent paper, Schlesinger (1974) appears to have come up with more suitable solutions to this problem. These were discussed in the second section of Chapter 3.

There are some other minor insufficiencies in the Schlesinger approach. For example, by citing such utterances as *balloon throw* from the child language literature, Brown (1973) pointed out that the evidence does not support the hypothesis that rules of order are learned before rules of adult categorization. This same point was also made by Schaerlaekens (1973).

Simply by altering his categories, Schlesinger could improve the adequacy of his approach to Stage I speech. Before this approach could actually be viewed as an approach to grammar writing, however, another important revision would be necessary. Schlesinger's approach seems to

be a production model for the generation of single utterances. A realization rule is proposed for the generation of utterances marking location,
one is proposed for negation, and so on. The result is a situation similar
to that seen in trying to apply transformational grammar to Stage I
speech; rather than capturing the child's grammar as a whole, recourse
is made to a number of independent sentence rewrite rules.

Schlesinger apparently chose not to develop a hierarchically-
organized grammar, despite the fact that his combination of position
rules to account for individual utterances relies on it, as he himself has
noted in a later paper (Schlesinger, 1975). For example, at an early
period, *no cookie* as well as *pretty cookie* may be produced, but by different position rules; negation + x and modifier + head, respectively.
A later utterance might be *no eat cookie* (resulting from applying the two
position rules negation + x and action + object) while another might
be *eat pretty cookie*—the result of applying modifier + head and action +
object. Presumably, Schlesinger would attribute the divergent ways in
which negation + x and modifier + head combine with action + object
to the child's perception of how such combinations are formed in the
speech of those around him. But then why discuss the earlier *no cookie*
and *pretty cookie* as reflecting different position rules? I believe that the
answer rests in Schlesinger's assumption that the child intends to reject
(or deny) a whole event (e.g., eating a cookie) while he assigns attributes
to persons or objects who may or may not be involved in some event.
This implies the following hierarchy.

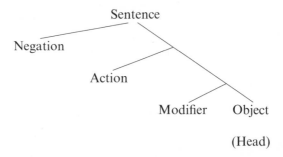

The alternative is to propose that realization rules are responsible not
only for generating the surface structure, but for specifying the meaning
of the utterance itself. Paradoxically, it was precisely Schlesinger's purpose to strip such rules of their power to specify semantic relationships,
and to assign this power to the *I* marker. Realization rules were only
responsible for how these relationships appear in the surface structure.

The type of hierarchical organization seen in the generation of individual utterances in the Schlesinger approach is also worth noting. For

Table 15
Relations in *I* Marker for *read my book*

a	Relates to	b	Notation
my	is possessor of	*book*	Modifier (a, b)
my book	is object of	*read*	Object (a, b)
∅	is agent of	*read my book*	Agent (a, b)

instance, the relations in the *I* marker for the utterance *read my book* can be seen in Table 15. These relations would yield the structure

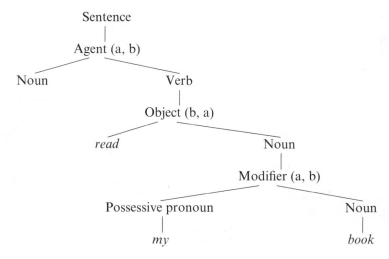

Such a structure would be represented by the three separate realization rules

1.   Modifier (a, b) → Noun (Possessive pronoun *a* + Noun *b*)
2.   Object (a, b) → Verb (Verb *b* + Noun *a*)
3.   Agent (a, b) → Sentence (Noun *a* + Verb *b*)

It is difficult to see how these realization rules reveal more information, either in underlying or surface structure form, than a more conventional grammar such as

Sentence → Agent + Object
Agent → Noun
Object → Verb + Modifier
Modifier → Possessive pronoun + Noun

Such a grammar, in fact, seems to capture the relations of the *I* marker without having to deal with all of the burdens of generating a three-word utterance from three realization rules involving a total of six words. It can also be noted that no greater level of abstraction had to be achieved in order to capture the same rules.

In summary, the Schlesinger approach seems to serve primarily as a model for the generation of single utterances. This approach would need some alteration before it could serve as a fully adequate approach for the analysis of Stage I speech. Nevertheless, this approach has made a notable contribution. Schlesinger's proposal of *I* markers that bypass any grammatical deep structure may constitute one of the most useful proposals of representing the semantic nature of Stage I speech yet offered. My own use of this proposal was seen in Chapter 3 during the presentation of the proposed approach to grammar writing, and it is clear that the idea of bypassing grammatical deep structure is being adopted in other approaches as well.

Antinucci and Parisi

Another approach to analysis that has been applied to portray underlying semantic representations in child language is that of Parisi and Antinucci (1970) and developed more fully in papers by Antinucci and Parisi (1973; 1975). According to their approach, the grammar specifies a set of well-formed semantic representations that are configurations of semantic units. Each semantic unit is formally represented as an n-place predicate, with configurations formed by combining predicates and substituting one as argument of another. In any semantic configuration of a sentence there is a particular subconfiguration that forms the sentence's predication, usually a verb. The semantic structure of the predication determines the number of noun phrases that are the complements of the predication. This semantic structure represents a cognitive structure that is constructed with the intention to communicate it (Parisi, 1974). For example, "open" is a two-place verb whose meaning can be represented by the configuration

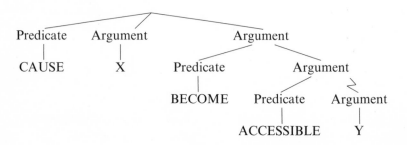

That is, two noun phrases will be substituted for x and y, corresponding presumably to agent and object, respectively.

The means to map these semantic representations onto surface strings of words is through the use of two projection mechanisms. One is the lexicon, defined as a set of entries associating subparts of semantic configurations with words. The other mechanism is syntax, a set of mapping rules that brings to the surface the structural part of the configuration.

Antinucci and Parisi suggest that this approach can be applied to Stage I speech by lexicalizing whatever number of elements in the semantic structure are appropriate to the child's "lexicalization span," be they the predicate or its noun phrases. Thus, the utterance (by Claudia, who was studied by Antinucci and Parisi), *open box*, produced when asking someone to open a box, would have the representation seen above, with only y lexicalized, such that x → ∅ and y → *box*. Antinucci and Parisi also differentiate the function of sentences, such as requesting versus describing, by proposing a performative superstructure similar to that proposed by Ross (1970).

Presented thus far are the structures involved in what Antinucci and Parisi view as representing the main configuration, consisting of a performative and a nucleus. The greater complexity seen in children's utterances with further development is subject to the operation of three optional mechanisms added to the main configuration. One operation involves the addition of an adverbial (functioning as an adverbial of place, manner, etc.) whose nucleus is treated as another argument. The other two operations involve noun modifiers and embedded sentences, and are represented as additional sentential configurations associated with the main configuration.

It is fair to say that this approach has not yet been developed to the stages of linguistic detail reached by approaches such as transformational grammar or case grammar. Nevertheless, a number of its features can be evaluated in terms of their applicability to Stage I speech. One obvious positive feature of the Antinucci and Parisi approach is that by the differentiation of the functions of utterances, the representation of vocatives is permitted. In this approach, an utterance such as Claudia's *Mommy, belly button*, spoken when showing her navel to her mother, would have the representation

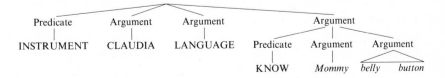

Such a representation would generally be interpreted as: the speaker (Claudia) uses language in order that the hearer (Mommy) knows x to look at Claudia's navel). As can be seen, the vocative can be perceived as the lexicalization of one of the arguments of the performative.

It would appear that the Antinucci and Parisi approach shares with case grammar and Chafe's (1970) approach an emphasis on the role of verbs in the grammar. Antinucci and Parisi avoid much of the resulting problems of many verbless utterances in Stage I speech by giving the verbs the same optionality for lexicalization as noun phrases. Unfortunately, the fact that the semantic structure of the predicate gives rise to complements in the form of noun phrases rather than, say, notions such as agent or object is a problem. As was noted earlier, the data suggest that abstract grammatical concepts such as noun phrase do not represent the most parsimonious means of capturing what the Stage I child is expressing in his language usage.

Schlesinger (1974) and Bowerman (1974c) share an objection to the large number of elements contained in the semantic structures proposed by Antinucci and Parisi. Bowerman argues quite clearly

> it is not at all necessary to postulate semantic structures containing elements like Cause, Become, Accessible, and Coincide to account for the fact that a child uses "open" and "give" in a referentially appropriate way with nouns representing entities which play different roles in the situation . . . . We as yet do not know which of the cognitive distinctions associated with this general paradigm the child at first regards as critical to the meanings of "give" and which are incidental (the extension of the hand? The use of a hand rather than a foot or a pair of tongs? The changed status of the giver? [He no longer is in contact with the object.] The changed status of the recipient? [He now is in contact with it.] The connection between the action of the giver and the status of the recipient?) Yet when a meaning such as "cause to come to coincide" is postulated for the early utterances with "give," the first three possible criteria are omitted as irrelevant and the last two are retained as criterial, in the form of Become, Coincide, and Cause. (pp 157–158)

It would appear, then, that it is one thing to base an analysis of child language on a model of linguistic capacity, and another to assume that the child's underlying notions and those proposed by the model are necessarily isomorphic. This type of problem can be illustrated by the findings of Carter (1975a) who examined the early language of one child and found that the child's meanings often differed considerably from those of the adult system. For example, the child's early use of "here" and "have," semantically unrelated in adult speech, both represented requests for transfer of an object in the child's system. Problems such as these must be dealt with satisfactorily before the Antinucci and Parisi approach can be applied with ease to the study of the notions underlying Stage I speech. Describing the complexity recognized in the proposed semantic structures as the product of a "linguistically justified model of linguistic capacity" (Parisi, 1974, p 104) will not make this approach automatically fit in the study of early child language.

In defense of their crediting such rich underlying semantic structures to the child's single-word utterances, Antinucci and Parisi point out that it is difficult to think that when a child produces an utterance such as *juice*, he does not know who is to receive it and who is to give it, along with what is to be given. I would certainly agree with this position. However, this pertains to the child's conceptual knowledge, not his semantic knowledge. If Antinucci and Parisi are to use a cognitive justification for their proposed underlying structures, the structures themselves should not be restricted to the elements (e.g., giver and hence agent, object given and hence object) that are realized in language.

In cases where the child has shown evidence of multi-word utterance usage, the rich underlying structure credited to his single-word utterances is somewhat more justified. However, given that an utterance such as *give* is represented as a predicate, with n (in this case three) obligatory arguments, then some mechanism should be proposed that attempts to explain which particular underlying arguments (if not the predicate) will be lexicalized.

Halliday

A rather different approach to analyzing Stage I speech was adopted by Halliday (1975a; 1975b). The focus of this approach was the functions that language can serve. For the adult system, Halliday (1970) postulated three functions that appeared sufficient to contain the options involved in establishing the "meaning potential" of language. The first two are considered basic functions; one is the ideational function, which entails the expression of content, and the second is the interpersonal function through which communicative and social roles are expressed. The third, the textual function, is thought to arise out of the nature of language itself and thus does not have an independent origin in the developmental process. In this function, language is used to make links with itself, thereby providing for connected discourse.

Halliday (1975a; 1975b) did not view these three functions as present in the linguistic system of the child beginning to speak—not, at least, in

Table 16

The Early Uses of Language in Halliday's (1975a; 1975b) Approach

Instrumental	The use of language to satisfy one's own material needs (*I want the ball*)
Regulatory	The use of language to exert control over others (*Close the door*)
Interactional	The use of language to establish and maintain contact with people who are important (*Hi, Daddy*)
Heuristic	The use of language to explore the objective environment (*There's a plane*)
Personal	The use of language to express one's own individuality and self-awareness (*I'm climbing the stairs*)
Imaginative	The use of language to create an environment of one's own (*I'm a bunny rabbit*)
Informative	The use of language to give information to someone who did not have the information (*Eric is sick today*)

these forms. For the early period of linguistic development, Halliday proposed seven somewhat different functions, or more precisely, uses of language. These are presented in Table 16.

The first two uses, instrumental and regulatory, can be viewed as pragmatic since they seem to require a response from the listener. The other uses are primarily "mathetic" in nature; they do not necessarily require a response. Since they operate independently of linguistic structure, these uses can serve as a means of describing the young child's earliest communicative attempts. In his longitudinal study of one child, Nigel, Halliday found evidence of the instrumental, regulatory, and interactional uses by age 9 months. The informative use, the last to emerge, was evidenced at age 21 months.

Halliday viewed the child's acquisition of single-word utterances as a period when content was added to the expression of these uses. The acquisition of two-word utterances was viewed as a period when linguistic form was interposed between content and expression. These two developments were also thought to enable the child to combine different uses in the same utterance.

In the early period of linguistic development, a child's utterance typically has only one particular use associated with it. With development an utterance may be used in different ways. This change represents a recasting of the concept of function on to a more abstract plane. Thus, function that was previously equivalent to use, becomes distinct from it.

With the development of the more abstract concept of function, the child's system begins to approximate that of the adult. Halliday has suggested that with development, the two broad types of language use, the pragmatic and the mathetic, may lead directly to the abstract functions interpersonal and ideational, respectively. Schmidt (1974), using utterances collected from a 31-month old child, Peter, as data has provided a detailed look at how the child's usage might approximate that associated with the interpersonal function of the adult system.

There is little doubt that Halliday's approach has much potential for providing useful information about a child's early language usage. By operating with an approach that does not rely on linguistic structure, Halliday seems to have developed a means of examining the nature of a child's communicative system prior to his first word. Judging from the longitudinal study of Nigel, not all of these uses emerge by this time, but it is worthy to note that even the last use to appear was evidenced only two months after the first appearance of two-word utterances. Even this use, the informative, may not have emerged so late had Halliday not defined it in such strict terms. This use was defined as giving information to a listener who presumably did not already have the information. Such a finding seems to exemplify how much information about the child's developing linguistic system is lost by concentrating only on the period when syntax is acquired—a tendency that investigators have only recently started to remedy.

What appears to be the biggest obstacle facing the adoption of this approach is the unclear degree of confidence that can be placed in assigning a child's utterance to one use or another. For example, Halliday would classify an utterance such as *two book*, produced while the child points to two books next to one another, as expressing a "blend" of the personal and heuristic uses. This classification would imply that the child expresses an awareness of something that the listener is presumably aware of, and that might be explained by the listener. Yet this same utterance in the same context might be spoken to a visiting relative or family friend and might therefore be taken to express the informative use. This problem is made even more clear in an utterance such as *Mummy('s) book*, since Halliday also classifies this as expressing a blend of the personal and heuristic uses. It seems that some method of differentiating the uses that a child's utterances may serve needs to be more clearly specified in the Halliday approach. The potential value of this approach warrants such elaboration.

Generative Semantics

With the exception of the type of semantic representation seen in the Antinucci and Parisi (1973) approach (one that was deemed too rich for the Stage I child), little from the approach utilized by generative semanticists (Lakoff, 1970; 1972; McCawley, 1968) has been applied to Stage I grammar writing.

Generative semantics represents a theory of grammar that evolved out of the transformational grammar proposed by Chomsky (1965), from which it differs in a number of respects. Unlike Chomsky, generative semanticists have proposed that language is best viewed as *starting* with a semantic interpretation, from which an utterance is generated by application of transformations. Unlike the phrase structure rules that generate deep structures specifying information such as word order in the transformational grammar approach, the underlying structures of generative semantics represent the semantic content of the sentences. In transformational grammar, lexicon feature rules subsequently operate in order to provide for the insertion of lexical items into the sentence. At this point, transformational rules operate to alter the sentence, yielding the surface structure form. In generative semantics, the terminal elements of the underlying structure are in the form of universal notions that are not yet lexicalized. To these notions, a series of transformations are applied that serve to introduce lexical items and to accomplish alterations such as reordering, adding, and deleting elements. The order of such a series is not fixed, however. Lexical items can be introduced after as well as before the other transformations are applied.

Chomsky (1971) argued that the generative semantics approach is simply a notational variant of transformational grammar, since both approaches contain many of the same mechanisms: a semantic interpretation, a deep structure, a surface structure, and a phonological representation. This view is not shared by generative semanticists, who point out that their account (1) does not contain a deep structure based on structural considerations such as subject and predicate, (2) starts with a semantic interpretation, and (3) does not require all lexicon feature rules to be applied before the application of reordering, addition, or deletion rules.

It is true that generative semanticists claim that their semantic structures are of the same formal nature as syntactic structures and can be viewed as labeled trees. It is also true that generative semanticists have sometimes made use of node labels such as sentence, noun phrase, and verb. But instead of representing syntactic categories in the sense used by Chomsky, these categories correspond more closely to terms used in logic. For example, sentence corresponds generally to proposition, noun phrase to argument, and verb to predicate. Such terms, it may be recalled, are similar to those used by Antinucci and Parisi (1973).

The underlying structure is expressed in terms of a predicate (f) that is the center of a set of relationships, and a series of arguments (x, y) that are related to the predicate. Thus, the underlying structure can be expressed by formulae such as f (x, y). For example, the underlying structure of an utterance such as *shoe all gone* would be represented as ALL GONE (shoe), with the predicate, by convention, capitalized, and with both predicate and argument considered not yet lexicalized. Such structures can also be represented as trees. The utterances *shoe all gone* and *want shoe*, for example, have the following representations.

From the above examples it can be seen that the elements listed under predicate are not restricted to those viewed as verbs. They may also be what in lexicalized form would be adjectives, predicate nouns, negatives, quantifiers, and adverbs. There may also be more than one predicate in underlying structure. Such instances are handled as embedded sentences, as seen in the underlying representation of the utterance *see little bug*.

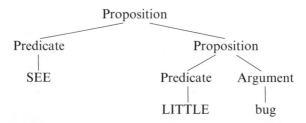

Since the underlying structure is unordered, transformations are necessary for ordering elements prior to surface structure realization. For example, an ordering transformation involved in an utterance such as *shoe all gone* might be

$$ALL\ GONE\ (shoe) \Rightarrow shoe + ALL\ GONE$$

In some instances, the transformations responsible for lexicalization might be quite straightforward, as for the above utterance.

$$ALL\ GONE \Rightarrow all\ gone$$
$$shoe \Rightarrow shoe$$

In other instances, however, much more is involved. As was illustrated in the work of Antinucci and Parisi (1973), the elements underlying certain lexical items (notably those arising from a predicate) can be quite complex. For example, "kill" involves three predicates, DIE, CAUSE, and COME ABOUT. Before a lexicalization rule operates, successive rules for predicate raising are carried out. These rules are illustrated using the underlying structure of the utterance *kill bug*.

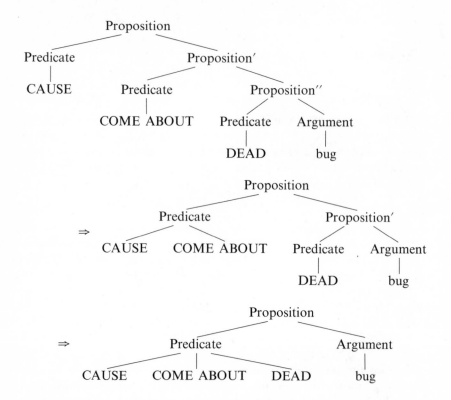

From the viewpoint of generative semantics, these structures are incomplete, for a predicate such as CAUSE-COME ABOUT-DEAD requires two arguments, not one, as seen in the example

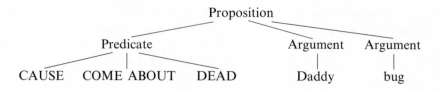

It should be evident that the complexity attributed to such utterances will pose problems for the analysis of Stage I speech. In this regard, generative semantics is open to the same criticisms directed at the related approach adopted by Antinucci and Parisi (1973).

It is possible that one might view the generative semanticists' claim that syntax and semantics are of the same formal nature (and hence inseparable), as obviating the use of generative semantics as an approach to analyzing the semantic notions underlying Stage I speech, independently of the manner in which they are coded syntactically. A closer inspection of the generative semantics position indicates that this need not be the case. The position that syntax and semantics are inseparable is a statement (directed in particular at those adopting the interpretive position of Chomsky) that the meaning of utterances cannot be accounted for without the type of semantic structures proposed by the generative semanticists. Since syntactic structure represents the organization of elements for surface structure realization it is quite difficult (or in the view of generative semanticists, impossible) to distinguish the two. This is quite different from the position that the underlying structure is syntactic in nature.

Although the generative semantics approach was proposed as a theory of grammar, many of its features may in fact be suitable for analyzing Stage I speech. The fact that a semantic interpretation is present from the outset makes this approach more feasible as a model reflecting the Stage I child's linguistic system; obviously a child intends to communicate something before any particular utterance is generated. This feature has a clear advantage over the interpretive framework of transformational grammar. The fact that the notions in the deep structure of generative semantics contain no lexical items also has application to Stage I speech. It is quite reasonable that at some point the child has some nonverbalizable conception before the specific lexical items of the utterance are generated.

The fact that the order of application of lexicon insertion rules and those that reorder, add, or delete elements is variable would also seem to have some value to writing grammars for Stage I speech. In particular, this variable order of transformation application may help explain the thorny problem of the superficial absence of constituents that are seemingly needed in the underlying structure. This problem has resulted in such proposals as a reduction transformation (Bloom, 1970) as well as a verb deletion transformation and optionality of constituents with choices limited to some maximum number (Bowerman, 1973a). The need for such reduction rules arises in the first place when an approach to grammar writing is adopted that requires obligatory structural elements (e.g., subject, verb, object) in the deep structure and lexicalization before the application of rules generating the surface structure form. As a result of adopting such an approach, investigators have found themselves with some deep structure constituents (e.g., verb) that they somehow had to "lose" before the surface structure form (e.g., subject + object) was seen. Clearly the postulation of an underlying structure containing no such structural information as in generative semantics moves toward solving the problem.

Even if the underlying structure contained elements more semantic in nature, the problem is not eliminated, if a position such as that of Chomsky's transformational grammar is accepted. At some point the elements of the underlying structure would have to be lexicalized before transformations that reorder, add, or delete elements were applied. Therefore, whether they are subsumed under higher order constituents or not, lexical items such as "boy," "hit," and "ball" would be coded in the underlying structure awaiting transformational action. Once again, then, something would need to be lost.

This problem may be solved by the nature of the transformations in the generative semantics approach. At no point do the underlying structures in this approach contain lexical items; instead they contain non-verbalizable notions (primitives, or "atomic predicates" in Lakoff's [1970] terms). Therefore, applying the series of transformations results in generating the entire sentence, excluding phonological representation. Since these notions are not analyzable into such entities as subject, verb, object, or "boy," "hit," "ball," it would be quite meaningless to propose how they meet their fate of nonoccurrence in the child's speech. Rather, the generation of an utterance such as *Mommy cookie* (subject + object) seems more a product of the application of a series of transformations (that include lexicon selection rules in variable order in the series) on an unanalyzable notion.

An explanation of why in some cases the surface structure might be *Mommy cookie* while in others it might be *Mommy eat* might include some kind of proposal of optionality. But the optionality of linguistic operations (such as the optionality of many transformations in the adult model) is of quite a different nature. Problems arise only when optionality is suggested for particular constituents thought to be required in the underlying structure for all utterances. The optionality rule: sentence → (subject) (verb) (object) would be one such kind of controversial proposal, particularly if the child were seen to use subject + verb, subject + object, and verb + object, but never subject + verb + object, although the latter can be generated by the rule. This issue of the surface structure absence of elements that may be in the underlying structure was raised in Chapter 3.

It appears that much of the generative semantics approach is highly appropriate for application to the analysis of Stage I speech. Some modifications are in order, however. For example, the derivations of most adult sentences, as in other models of linguistic capacity, are far too complex for Stage I. Although the underlying structures contain nonverbalizable notions, they are often represented as arguments and predicates of the type illustrated earlier and seen also in the work of Antinucci and Parisi (1973). These clearly would have to be altered to represent the notions safely attributable to the child's underlying knowledge. In a model of linguistic capacity, the postulation of an underlying representation such as X CAUSE Y (TO) COME ABOUT DEAD, for "kill" may be justified; however, the assumption that the Stage I child's utterances must also contain such elements would be tantamount to adopting the position that there are obligatory elements in the underlying structure. In fact, this position would nullify a number of the promising features that generative semantics may possess for application to the analysis of Stage I speech.

Speech Acts

A rather interesting view of language has been provided by Searle's (1970) study of speech acts. Although Searle's study had its origins in philosophy (Austin, 1962) and was not in a form readily translatable into a system of grammar writing, Dore (1973; 1974) offered a method of analyzing speech acts that is much more suitable to Stage I speech. In the speech act approach, the features underlying an utterance consist of propositional acts and illocutionary acts. A third underlying feature, correlated with illocutionary acts, consists of perlocutionary acts. Propositional acts contain some reference (the topic, such as "baby" in *baby fall down*) and some predication of the reference (e.g., "fall down"). Illocutionary acts refer to such acts as asserting, questioning, and commanding. They seem to be analogous to the performatives of Gruber (1975b) and Antinucci and Parisi (1973), which, according to Gruber, can also be attributed to Austin's (1962) influence. An utterance containing the same reference and predication may express different illocutionary acts, depending on the child's intended use—for example, *baby fall down* contrasted with *baby fall down?* Perlocutionary acts refer to the effects that illocutionary acts may have on others. For example, a parent's response to a child's command would represent a perlocutionary act.

Dore's work centered on whether, before he acquires sentential structures, the child acquires certain elementary illocutionary acts. Dore termed such acts "primitive speech acts," defined as containing a "rudimentary referring expression" generally expressed by single-words, and a "primitive force" generally expressed by intonation patterns (Dore, 1975). The primitive speech acts proposed for two children observed at the single-word stage of linguistic development included labeling, repeating, answering, requesting, calling, greeting, protesting, and practicing. Some of Dore's primitive speech acts (e.g., repeating, answering) seem quite related to discourse rules that might be quite difficult to incorporate into a Stage I grammar such as those devised thus far. Nevertheless, some features of this speech act approach may prove quite useful.

It appears that the underlying representation of illocutionary acts in the speech act approach may have advantages over that of the performatives of Gruber (1975b) and Antinucci and Parisi (1973), since the former, at least initially, seems to represent simple instructional markers whose surface structure realization takes the form of intonation contours. Illocutionary acts do not appear to require the kind of underlying structures seen for performatives.

In addition to handling functions similar to those seen in performative structures, illocutionary acts seem to operate much as do the elements in Fillmore's (1968) modality. When applied to Stage I speech, it was seen that the elements included in the modality constituent frequently did not meet Fillmore's own requirement that modality operate on the sentence as a whole. If modality is, in fact, to be proposed as a constituent separate from proposition, it would seem that the elements contained in it should serve considerably different functions. The functions served by some of the illocutionary acts in the speech act approach seem more in keeping with operations on the sentence as a whole. Perhaps, then, if a Stage I modality is to be proposed, it should be composed of early illocutionary acts.

To be sure, the functions served by some illocutionary acts seem quite appropriate to Stage I speech. In fact, these functions, such as asserting, questioning, and commanding may even have their origins at a point prior to the appearance of the child's first words (Ingram, 1971; Dore, 1974). According to du Preez (1974), these functions, expressed by "tone groups," communicate attitudes and emotions even before the child can articulate words. Dore (1973) related the functions of speech acts to the child's earlier cries serving as primitive performatives or actions accomplished through vocalizations. According to Dore, these vocal performatives can be evaluated according to whether or not they are effective as actions, and thus the speech act approach also seems to contribute to the view that a child's language is in some way related to his actions. A failure to incorporate these functions into a Stage I grammar, then, might mean the exclusion of the first features of language acquired by the child—features that could even serve as the very foundation on which subsequent development is based.

References

Albright R, Albright J: The phonology of a two-year old child. Word 12:382–390, 1956

Antinucci F, Parisi D: Early language acquisition: A model and some data, in Ferguson C, Slobin D (eds): Studies of Child Language Development. New York, Holt, 1973

Antinucci F, Parisi D: Early semantic development in child language, in Lenneberg E, Lenneberg E (eds): Foundations of Language Development. New York, Academic, 1975

Austin J: How to Do Things with Words. London, Oxford University Press, 1962

Bandura A, Harris M: Modification of syntactic style. J Exp Child Psychol 4:341–352, 1966

Bates E: Pragmatics and sociolinguistics in child language, in Morehead D, Morehead A (eds): Normal and Deficient Child Language. Baltimore, University Park Press, 1976

Bates E, Camaioni L, Volterra V: The acquisition of performatives prior to speech. Merrill-Palmer Q 21:205–226, 1975

Bates E, Benigni L, Bretherton I, Camaioni L, Volterra V: From gesture to the first word: On cognitive and social prerequisites, in Lewis M, Rosenblum L (eds): Origins of Behavior: Communication and Language. New York, Wiley, 1976

Berkeley Cross-Linguistic Language Development Project Coding Manual. Unpublished manuscript, Berkeley, University of California, 1973

Bloch O: Les premiers stades du langage de l'enfant. J Psychol 18:693–712, 1921

Bloom L: Language Development: Form and Function in Emerging Grammars. Cambridge, Massachusetts, M.I.T. Press, 1970

Bloom L: One Word at a Time. The Hague, Mouton, 1973

Bloom L: Language development, in Horowitz F (ed): Review of Child Develop-
    ment Research, vol. 4. Chicago, University of Chicago Press, 1975
Bloom L, Lightbown P, Hood L: Structure and variation in child language. Monogr
    Soc Res Child Dev 40:1975
Blumenthal A: Language and Psychology: Historical Aspects of Psycholinguistics.
    New York, Wiley, 1970
Bowerman M: Early Syntactic Development: A Cross-Linguistic Study with Special
    Reference to Finnish. New York, Cambridge University Press, 1973a
Bowerman M: Structural relationships in children's utterances: Syntactic or seman-
    tic?, in Moore T (ed): Cognitive Development and the Acquisition of Language.
    New York, Academic, 1973b
Bowerman M: Relationship of early cognitive development to a child's early rules
    for word combination and semantic knowledge. Paper presented to American
    Speech and Hearing Association, Las Vegas, 1974a
Bowerman M: Discussion summary: Development of concepts underlying language,
    in Schiefelbusch R, Lloyd L (eds): Language Perspectives: Acquisition, Retar-
    dation, and Intervention. Baltimore, University Park Press, 1974b
Bowerman M: Learning the structure of causative verbs: A study in the relationship
    of cognitive, semantic, and syntactic development. Papers Rep Child Lang
    Dev 8:142–178, 1974c
Bowerman M: Commentary, in Bloom L, Lightbown P, Hood L: Structure and
    variation in child language. Monogr Soc Res Child Dev 40:1975
Bowerman M: Semantic factors in the acquisition of rules for word use and sentence
    construction, in Morehead D, Morehead A (eds): Normal and Deficient
    Child Language. Baltimore, University Park Press, 1976
Braine M: The ontogeny of English phrase structure: The first phrase. Lang 39:
    1–14, 1963
Braine M: The acquisition of language in infant and child, in Reed C (ed): The
    Learning of Language. New York, Appleton-Century-Crofts, 1971
Braine M: Three suggestions regarding grammatical analyses of children's language,
    in Ferguson C, Slobin D (eds): Studies of Child Language Development. New
    York, Holt, 1973
Braine M: Length constraints, reduction rules, and holophrastic processes in chil-
    dren's word combinations. J Verb Learn Verb Behav 13:448–456, 1974
Braine M: Children's first word combinations. Monogr Soc Res Child Dev 41:1976
Brown R: A First Language: The Early Stages. Cambridge, Massachusetts, Harvard
    University Press, 1973
Brown R, Cazden C, Bellugi U: The child's grammar from I to III, in Hill J (ed):
    Minnesota Symposia on Child Development, vol. 2. Minneapolis, University
    of Minnesota Press, 1969
Bruner J: Competence in infants. Paper presented to the Society for Research in
    Child Development, Minneapolis, 1971
Bruner J: From communication to language: A psychological perspective. Cogni-
    tion 3:255–287, 1974
Bruner J: The ontogenesis of speech acts. J Child Lang 2:1–19, 1975

Burling R: Cognition and componential analysis: God's truth or hocus-pocus? Am Anthropol 66:27, 1964

Campbell R, Wales R: The study of language acquisition, in Lyons J (ed): New Horizons in Linguistics. Baltimore, Penguin, 1970

Carter A: The transformation of sensorimotor morphemes into words. Papers Rep Child Lang Dev 10:30–47, 1975a

Carter A: The transformation of sensorimotor morphemes into words: A case study of the development of "more" and "mine." J Child Lang 2:233–250, 1975b

Cazden C: The acquisition of noun and verb inflections. Child Dev 39:433–448, 1968

Chafe W: Meaning and the Structure of Language. Chicago, University of Chicago Press, 1970

Chambers J: Remarks on topicalization in child language. Found Lang 9:442–446, 1973

Chomsky N: Syntactic Structures. The Hague, Mouton, 1957

Chomsky N: Aspects of the Theory of Syntax. Cambridge, Massachusetts, M.I.T. Press, 1965

Chomsky N: Deep structure, surface structure, and semantic interpretation, in Steinberg D, Jakobovits L (eds): Semantics: An Interdisciplinary Reader in Philosophy, Linguistics, and Psychology. New York, Cambridge University Press, 1971

Clark E: What's in a word? On the child's acquisition of semantics in his first language, in Moore T (ed): Cognitive Development and the Acquisition of Language. New York, Academic, 1973

Clark E: Knowledge, context and strategy in the acquisition of meaning. Paper presented at the Georgetown University Round Table, Washington, D.C., 1975

Cook W: A case grammar matrix. Georgetown University Working Papers on Languages and Linguistics 6:15–47, 1972

Crystal D: Grammatical Analysis of Language Disability. London, Edward Arnold, 1976

Darwin C: A biographical sketch of an infant. Mind 2:285–294, 1877

de Laguna G: Speech: Its Function and Development. New Haven, Connecticut, Yale University Press, 1927

Derwing B: Transformational Grammar as a Theory of Language Acquisition. Cambridge, England, Cambridge University Press, 1973

de Villiers J: Fourteen grammatical morphemes in acquisition and aphasia, in Zurif E, Caramazza A (eds): The Acquisition and Dissolution of Language. Baltimore, Johns Hopkins Press, 1976

de Villiers J, de Villiers P: A cross-sectional study of the acquisition of grammatical morphemes in child speech. J Psycholinguis Res 2:267–278, 1973

Dore J: The development of speech acts. PhD dissertation, New York, City University of New York, 1973

Dore J: A pragmatic description of early language development. J Psycholinguis Res 3:343–350, 1974

Dore J: Holophrases, speech acts and language universals. J Child Lang 2:21–40, 1975

Dore J, Franklin M, Miller R, Ramer A: Transitional phenomena in early language acquisition. J Child Lang 3:13–28, 1976

du Preez P: Units of information in the acquisition of language. Lang Speech 17:369–376, 1974

Edwards D: Sensory-motor intelligence and semantic relations in early child grammar. Cognition 2:395–434, 1973

Felix S: Concerning "topicalization in child language." Found Lang 13:41–55, 1975

Fillmore C: The case for case, in Bach E, Harms R (eds): Universals in Linguistic Theory. New York, Holt, 1968

Fillmore C: Some problems for case grammar. Georgetown Univ Monogr Lang Linguis 24:35–56, 1971

Fodor J, Garrett M: Some reflections on competence and performance, in Lyons J, Wales R (eds): Psycholinguistics Papers. Edinburgh, Edinburgh University Press, 1966

Fodor J, Bever T, Garrett M: The Psychology of Language. New York, McGraw-Hill, 1974

Fromkin V: Speculations on performance models. J Linguis 4:47–68, 1968

Greenfield P: Who is "dada"? Unpublished paper, Syracuse University, 1967

Greenfield P: Who is "dada"? Some aspects of the semantic and phonological development of a child's first words. Lang Speech 16:34–43, 1973

Greenfield P, Smith J, Laufer B: Communication and the Beginnings of Language: The Development of One-Word Speech and Beyond. Unpublished Paper, Harvard University, 1972

Gruber J: Topicalization in child language. Found Lang 3:57–65, 1967a

Gruber J: Correlations between the syntactic constructions of the child and of the adult. Paper presented to Society for Research in Child Development, 1967b

Gruber J: Correlations between the syntactic constructions of the child and of the adult, in Ferguson C, Slobin D (eds): Studies of Child Language Development. New York, Holt, 1973

Gruber J: "Topicalization" revisited. Found Lang 13:57–72, 1975a

Gruber J: Performative—constative transition in child language development. Found Lang 12:513–527, 1975b

Guillaume P: L' Imitation chez l' Enfant. Paris, Alcan, 1925

Halliday M: Language structure and language function, in Lyons J (ed): New Horizons in Linguistics. Baltimore, Penguin, 1970

Halliday M: Learning how to mean, in Lenneberg E, Lenneberg E (eds): Foundations of Language Development. New York, Academic, 1975a

Halliday M: Learning How to Mean: Explorations in the Development of Language. London, Edward Arnold, 1975b

Howe C: The meanings of two-word utterances in the speech of young children. J Child Lang 3:29–47, 1976

Ingram D: Transitivity in child language. Lang 47:888–910, 1971

Ingram D: Language development during the sensorimotor period. Paper presented at the International Child Language Symposium, London, 1975

Ingram D: Sensorimotor intelligence and language development, in Lock A (ed): Action, Gesture, and Symbol: The Emergence of Language. New York, Academic (in press)

Ingram D, Ingram J, Neufeld W: A longitudinal study of language development during the sensorimotor period (to be published)

Jackendoff R: Semantic Interpretation in Generative Grammar. Cambridge, Massachusetts, M.I.T. Press, 1972

Jacobs R, Rosenbaum P: English Transformational Grammar. Waltham, Massachusetts, Blaisdell, 1968

Jones R: System in Child Language. Cardiff, Wales, University of Wales Press, 1970

Katz J, Fodor J: The structure of a semantic theory. Lang 34:170–210, 1963

Katz J, Postal P: An Integrated Theory of Linguistic Descriptions. Cambridge, Massachusetts, M.I.T. Press, 1964

Kernan K: The acquisition of language by Samoan children. PhD dissertation, Berkeley, University of California, 1969

Kernan K: Semantic relationships and the child's acquisition of language. Anthropol Linguis 12:171–187, 1970

Lakoff G: Irregularity in Syntax. New York, Holt, 1970

Lakoff G: Generative Semantics. New York, Holt, 1972

Lange S, Larsson K: Syntactical development of a Swedish girl Embla, between 20 and 42 months of age. Project child language syntax, no. 1, Institionem for nordiska sprak, Stockholms Universitet, 1973

Leech G: Semantics. Baltimore, Penguin, 1974

Leonard L: From reflex to remark. Acta Symbol 5:67–99, 1974

Leonard L: On differentiating syntactic and semantic features in emerging grammars: Evidence from empty form usage. J Psycholinguis Res 4:357–363, 1975a

Leonard L: The role of nonlinguistic stimuli and semantic relations in children's acquisition of grammatical utterances. J Exp Child Psychol 19:346–357, 1975b

Leopold W: Speech Development of a Bilingual Child: A Linguist's Record. Evanston, Illinois, Northwestern University Press, 1949

Lewis M: The beginning of reference to past and future in a child's speech. Br J Educ Psychol 7:39–56, 1937

Lewis M: Infant Speech: A Study of the Beginnings of Language. New York, Humanities Press, 1951

Lyons J: A note on possessive, existential, and locative sentences. Found Lang 3:390–396, 1967

Lyons J: Introduction to Theoretical Linguistics. Cambridge, England, Cambridge University Press, 1969

Macnamara J: Cognitive basis of language learning in infants. Psychol Rev 79:1–13, 1972

McCawley J: The role of semantics in grammar, in Bach E, Harms R (eds): Universals in Linguistic Theory. New York, Holt, 1968

McNeill D: A question in semantic development: What does a child mean when he says "no"?, in Zale E (ed): Conference on Language and Language Behavior. New York, Appleton-Century-Crofts, 1968

McNeill D: The Acquisition of Language. New York, Harper & Row, 1970

McNeill D: The capacity for the ontogenesis of grammar, in Slobin D (ed): The Ontogenesis of Grammar. New York, Academic, 1971

McNeill D: Semiotic extension. Paper presented at Loyola Symposium on Cognition, Chicago, 1974

Menyuk P: Sentences Children Use. Cambridge, Massachusetts, M.I.T. Press, 1969

Moerk E: Piaget's research as applied to the explanation of language development. Merrill-Palmer Q 21:151–170, 1975

Morehead D, Morehead A: From signal to sign: A Piagetian view of thought and language during the first two years, in Schiefelbusch R, Lloyd L (eds): Language Perspectives: Acquisition, Retardation, and Intervention. Baltimore, University Park Press, 1974

Nelson K: Structure and strategy in learning to talk. Monogr Soc Res Child Dev 38:1973

Nelson K: Concept, word, and sentence: Interrelations in acquisition and development. Psychol Rev 81:267–285, 1974

Nelson K: The nominal shift in semantic-syntactic development. Cog Psychol 7:461–479, 1975

Nelson K, Bonvillian J: Concepts and words in the 18-month-old: Acquiring concept names under controlled conditions. Cognition 2:435–450, 1973

Olson D: Language and thought: Aspects of a cognitive theory of semantics. Psychol Rev 77:257–273, 1970

Parisi D: What is behind child utterances? J Child Lang 1:97–106, 1974

Parisi D, Antinucci F: Lexical competence, in Flores G, Levelt W (eds): Advances in Psycholinguistics. Amsterdam, North-Holland, 1970

Piaget J: The Origins of Intelligence in Children. New York, International Universities Press, 1952

Piaget J: The Construction of Reality in the Child. New York, Basic Books, 1954

Preyer W: The Mind of the Child. New York, Appleton, 1888

Quine W: Word and Object. New York, Wiley, 1960

Ramer A: Syntactic styles and universal aspects of language emergence. PhD dissertation, New York, City University of New York, 1974

Ramer A: The merging of the communicative and categorical functions of language. Paper presented to the American Speech and Hearing Association, Washington, D.C., 1975

Ross J: On declarative sentences, in Jacobs R, Rosenbaum P (eds): Readings in English Transformational Grammar. Waltham, Massachusetts, Ginn and Company, 1970

Rydin I: A Swedish child in the beginning of syntactic development and some cross-linguistic comparisons. Unpublished paper, Harvard University, 1971

Schaerlaekens A: The Two-Word Sentence in Child Language Development. The Hague, Mouton, 1973

Schlesinger I: Production of utterances and language acquisition, in Slobin D (ed): The Ontogenesis of Grammar. New York, Academic, 1971a

Schlesinger I: Learning grammar: From pivot to realization rule, in Huxley R, Ingram E (eds): Language Acquisition: Models and Methods. New York, Academic, 1971b

Schlesinger I: Relational concepts underlying language, in Schiefelbusch R, Lloyd L (eds): Language Perspectives: Acquisition, Retardation, and Intervention. Baltimore, University Park Press, 1974

Schlesinger I: Grammatical development: The first steps, in Lenneberg E, Lenneberg E (eds): Foundations of Language Development. New York, Academic, 1975

Schmidt R: The functional development of language in a child of two-and-a-half years. Lang Speech 17:358–368, 1974

Searle J: Speech Acts: An Essay in the Philosophy of Language. New York, Cambridge University Press, 1970

Sinclair H: Developmental psycholinguistics, in Elkind D, Flavell J (eds): Studies in Cognitive Development. New York, Oxford University Press, 1969

Sinclair H: The transition from sensory motor behavior to symbolic activity. Interchange 1:119–126, 1970

Sinclair H: Sensorimotor action patterns as a condition for the acquisition of syntax, in Huxley R, Ingram E (eds): Language Acquisition: Models and Methods. New York, Academic, 1971

Sinclair H: Some remarks on the Genevan view on learning with special reference to language learning, in Hinde R, Stevenson-Hinde J (eds): Constraints on Learning. New York, Academic, 1973

Sinclair H: The role of cognitive structures in language acquisition, in Lenneberg E, Lenneberg E (eds): Foundations of Language Development. New York, Academic, 1975

Sinclair-deZwart H: Language acquisition and cognitive development, in Moore T (ed): Cognitive Development and the Acquisition of Language. New York, Academic, 1973

Slobin D: Comments on McNeill's developmental psycholinguistics, in Smith F, Miller G (eds): The Genesis of Language. Cambridge, Massachusetts, M.I.T. Press, 1966

Slobin D: Suggested universals in the ontogenesis of grammar. Working paper 32, Language-Behavior Research Laboratory, Berkeley, University of California, 1970a

Slobin D: Universals of grammatical development in children, in Flores G, Levelt W (eds): Advances in Psycholinguistics. Amsterdam, North-Holland, 1970b

Slobin D: Cognitive prerequisites for the development of grammar, in Ferguson C, Slobin D (eds): Studies of Child Language Development. New York, Holt, Rinehart, and Winston, 1973

Sørenson M: Case grammar and child language acquisition. Georgetown University Working Papers on Languages and Linguistics 8:72–98, 1974

Starr S: The relationship of single words to two-word sentences. Child Dev 46: 701–708, 1975

Stemmer N: An Empiricist Theory of Language Acquisition. The Hague, Mouton, 1973

Stern C, Stern W: Die Kindersprache. Leipzig, Barth, 1907

Sully J: Studies of Childhood. London, Logmans, 1895

Taine H: On the acquisition of language by children. Mind 2:252–259, 1877

Tiedemann D: Beobachtungen über die Entwicklung der Seelenfähigkeiten bei Kindern (1787). Reprinted in Ped Sem 34:205–230, 1927

Tolbert K: Pepe Joy: Learning to talk in Mexico. Unpublished paper, Harvard University, 1971

Tyler S: Cognitive Anthropology. New York, Holt, Rinehart, and Winston, 1969

van der Geest T: Evaluation of Theories on Child Grammars. The Hague, Mouton, 1974

Vygotsky L: Thought and Language. Cambridge, Massachusetts, M.I.T. Press, 1962

Wall C: Predication: A Study of Its Development. The Hague, Mouton, 1974

Weir R: Language in the Crib. The Hague, Mouton, 1962

Wells G: Learning to code experience through language. J Child Lang 1:243–269, 1974

Werner H, Kaplan B: Symbol Formation. New York, Wiley, 1963

Index

253